writing
home

writing home

INDIGENOUS NARRATIVES OF RESISTANCE

MICHAEL D. WILSON

Michigan State University Press • East Lansing

⊛ The paper used in this publication meets the minimum requirements
of ANSI/NISO Z39.48-1992 (R 1997) (Permanence of Paper).

 Michigan State University Press
East Lansing, Michigan 48823-5245

Printed and bound in the United States of America.

13 12 11 10 09 08 07   1 2 3 4 5 6 7 8 9 10

An earlier version of chapter 1 appeared as "Speaking of Home: The Idea
of the Center in Some Contemporary American Indian Writing," *Wicazo
Sa Review* 18, no. 1 (1997): 129–47.

An earlier version of chapter 4 appeared as "Writing a Friendship Dance:
Orality in Mourning Dove's *Cogewea*," *American Indian Culture and
Research Journal* 20, no. 1 (1996): 27–41.

LIBRARY OF CONGRESS CATALOGING-IN-PUBLICATION DATA
Wilson, Michael D., 1960–
Writing home : indigenous narratives of resistance / Michael D. Wilson.
p. cm.
Includes bibliographical references and index.
ISBN 978-0-87013-818-8 (pbk. : alk. paper)
1. American literature—Indian authors—History and criticism.
2. Indians in literature. I. Title.
PS153.I52W53 2008
810.9'897—dc22
2007038514

Cover design by Erin Kirk New
Book design by Sharp Des!gns, Lansing, MI

g **green** Michigan State University Press is a member of the Green
press Press Initiative and is committed to developing and
INITIATIVE
encouraging ecologically responsible publishing practices. For more
information about the Green Press Initiative and the use of recycled
paper in book publishing, please visit *www.greenpressinitiative.org*.

Visit Michigan State University Press on the World Wide Web at
www.msupress.msu.edu

Contents

■   v

Acknowledgments

I could not have completed this project without the generosity of time and spirit from many people. I would especially like to thank my friends, colleagues, teachers, and financial supporters at Oklahoma State University, Cornell University, and the University of Wisconsin–Milwaukee. I am profoundly grateful to those who have read and offered thoughtful, encouraging comments on chapters of this book: Ken McClane, Shirley Samuels, Kathryn W. Shanley, Greg Jay, Linda Sue Warner, and David L. Moore. I would also like to acknowledge those who have kindly offered support and guidance to me over the years: Ron LaFrance, Vine Deloria Jr., Edward Walkiewicz, David Shelley Berkeley, Kimberly Blaeser, Grayson Noley, Elizabeth Cook-Lynn, and Henry Louis Gates Jr. I would also like to offer my gratitude to the indigenous authors whose works framed this study on national narratives: Paula Gunn Allen, Taiaiake Alfred, Leslie Marmon Silko, N. Scott Momaday, Christine

Quintasket (Mourning Dove), Simon Ortiz, Gerald Vizenor, Louise Erdrich, and Ray A. Young Bear.

I want to express my appreciation to the editors and staff at the Michigan State University Press. Martha Bates has been supportive of this project from the beginning. Kristine M. Blakeslee has remained extraordinarily helpful and patient throughout the entire process. Gordon Henry has been a welcome source of encouragement and support. Bonnie Cobb has done a first-rate job of copyediting the manuscript, as have Annette Tanner and Kendra Slayton in the production of this book.

I am thankful for the love and support from my mother Leona and my father Randall Wilson; to my sisters, Margaret, Donna, Tracy, and Sandy and their families; and to our extended Choctaw families, the Impsons and Wilsons. Above all, my greatest appreciation, love, and gratitude go to my wife, Nancy and our children, Ben, Sarah, Abbie, and Katie.

Indigenous Resistance Fiction

I ndigenous peoples in the United States have a long history of voicing resistance through literature to destructive policies and attitudes of colonialism. In most cases, indigenous resistance writing uses both the conventional language and form that is acceptable to a general American readership: essays, histories, newspaper writing, sermons, autobiographies, short stories, and novels. William Apess, for instance, a Christian Pequot minister writing in the 1830s, admonishes Americans for their treatment of indigenous peoples, employing innovative and at times brilliant rhetorical strategies, yet remaining firmly within the conventional traditions of "conversion narratives," according to Barry O'Connell (1992, xiv). Similarly, indigenous writers George Copway, William Whipple Warren, and Chief Elias Johnson, among others, offer historical narratives quite different from the American vision of heroic triumph over the forces of pagan savagism, yet they write within the linear tradition of European historiography.

Other writers resisting destructive representations of indigenous peoples through conventional forms include Pauline Johnson, who offers a critique of the philosophical relationship between Americans and indigenous peoples through short fiction, and Charles Eastman, who quietly exposes the hypocrisy of a Christian nation's relationship to indigenous peoples in his autobiography. Although these writers challenge the institutions that attempt to erase indigenous peoples from the landscape of America, they do not challenge the institutional language and forms. And rightly so, for indigenous writers are not likely to gain the attention of a large audience if they experiment with conventional forms. As Roland Barthes observes, "'provocative' *thought*, insofar as it is immediate (without mediation), can only exhaust itself in the no man's land of form: the scandal is never total" (Barthes 1972, 149). Disembodied and institutional, the forms of literature such as the sermon or short story nonetheless provide a useful (but not neutral) medium of exchange for the provocative thought of resistance literatures. Indeed, these forms seem to promise a transparent (Barthes might say theological) medium through which indigenous writers can communicate reason and evidence to sway public opinion against oppression and injustice.

Although useful and even necessary, conventional forms of writing are in fact neither neutral nor transparent, for they sometimes carry within them philosophies or relationships of power that do not always reflect the interests of indigenous peoples. Sermons, for instance, provide Samson Occum and William Apess with a means to discuss colonialism in addressing their intended audiences; but at the end of the day this institutional form, by its very nature, expresses a hierarchical relationship between Christian religions and indigenous beliefs and practices. Similarly, autobiographies such as Sarah Winnemucca's *Life among the Piutes* and Luther Standing Bear's *My People, the Sioux* are useful vehicles for explaining the cultural practices of a tribal group or personalizing the destructive forces of colonialism; yet the autobiographical form itself suggests an ethos of individualism that is contrary to a vision of communal identity that is central to many indigenous groups. In short fiction and novels, perhaps the most conventional forms in contemporary fiction, the structure of conflict and resolution may appear to some readers to be a natural element of the human experience—humanity against humanity; humanity against nature; the individual against culture, against a particular ideology, or against the forces of history. Indigenous writers such as John Joseph Mathews, N. Scott Momaday, and James Welch, working within the modernist tradition of American literature, have used this thematic approach with considerable artistry to express the conflict between indigenous societies and the forces of colonialism. Within the philosophies of indigenous peoples, however, the idea of conflict as the basis of cultural expression may be antithetical to a relational, perhaps familial attitude toward the world and the people around them. Certainly, the indigenous relationship between humanity and nature is unlikely to have either the kind or the degree of conflict held by Europeans who saw the New World as an untamed wilderness or as a blank slate upon which one writes the story of triumph and conquest.

In her *The Sacred Hoop: Recovering the Feminine in American Indian Traditions*, Paula Gunn Allen observes that in many works about indigenous peoples, the form greatly determines the content, particularly in fiction by nonindigenous writers. Allen writes: "Perhaps as a result of following western literary imperatives, most writers of Indian novels create mixed-blood or half-breed protagonists, treating the theme of cultural conflict by incorporating it into the psychological and social being of the characters" (Allen 1986, 81). In such narratives of conflict, success for characters often depends on their ability to overcome psychological or social conflict and then to (re)integrate themselves into a tribal world (rarely, if ever, into the non-Indian world). William Bevis calls these representations of success "homing in" narratives, centripetal movements of the characters back to traditional centers of culture. Indeed, for Bevis, "coming home . . . is not only the primary story, it is a primary mode of knowledge and a primary good" (Bevis 1987, 582). Almost all modernist novels by indigenous writers follow this general format: for instance, McNickle's *Winds from an Enemy Sky*, Momaday's *House Made of Dawn*, and Welch's *Winter in the Blood*. In contrast, narratives of conflict result in failure when protagonists are unable to envision their identities in either indigenous or nonindigenous societies (the tragic Indian "caught between two worlds"), a result of either their own personal failings or destructive forces beyond their control. Examples include McNickle's *The Surrounded*, Welch's *The Death of Jim Loney*, and Linda Hogan's *Mean Spirit*. Indeed, Allen claims that this narrative form may even determine the racial makeup of protagonists, for "mixed blood" characters provide a visible sign of social tension to readers.

Indigenous fiction that focuses on conflict and resolution, then, may tell much less about the cultural narratives of an indigenous community than they tell about necessities of the literary form—in other words, fiction that is not "true to life" so much as it is "true to form." Indigenous people in America—and indeed nonindigenous people as well—live in culturally hybrid environments, where resolutions of cultural conflict are neither possible, given the limits of nativism (what or when is "true" indigenous or American culture?), nor always desirable, especially now that indigenous peoples appropriate world cultures for their own ends. Yet in contemporary fiction, as Kimberly Blaeser points out, "homing in" narratives demand resolutions to culturally hybrid positions, for unresolved liminality remains thematically untenable and stylistically unsatisfactory. Unless the mixed-blood characters in fiction "reach that resolution," Blaeser writes, "they exist in and are depicted in a tragic state" (1996, 158). She argues that writers such as Gerald Vizenor challenge these forms of fiction, revising the figure of the liminal mixed blood from one of unresolved tragedy into one of vitality, humor, and survival (or *survivance*, to use Vizenor's neologism: a combination of survival and resistance). In his novel *Bearheart*, for example, Vizenor offers a quite different form of mixed-blood fiction, where success in the novel is not determined by the resolution of a protagonist's mixed-blood identity, but by whether or not the characters demonstrate compassion for those around them. The narrative form of *Bearheart* follows this unconventional approach to mixed-blood identity, offering within a metafictional frame two distinct forms of narrative: an indigenous four-worlds narrative and a regressive, linear narrative recapitulating the stages of American progress. Vizenor's resistant narrative is thus an implicit critique of forms such as mixed-blood conflict or Manifest Destiny that legitimate destructive representations of indigenous peoples.

The primary focus of this book is to examine different ways in which writers such as Vizenor use indigenous oral traditions to resist the metanarratives and other forms of representation that demand the disappearance of indigenous peoples—for example, Manifest Destiny, social Darwinism, and the inevitable plight of the tragic mixed blood. Yet, when writers use oral traditions to counter the discourse of colonialism, shifting the context of indigenous traditions from orality to writing, they inevitably foreground important questions of authenticity and ethics. Indigenous writers Jana Sequoya Magdaleno and David Treuer point out that oral traditions, taken from their authentic contexts as living traditions existing for the benefit and enjoyment of indigenous communities, ironically become merely signs of authenticity for many readers when placed within the foreign context of contemporary fiction. As signs rather than systems, oral traditions become like any other repeatable sign of Indianness frequently appearing in fiction (and elsewhere): wise elders, environmentalism, exotic spirituality, fatalism, and so on. And like these signs of Indianness, oral traditions are easily adopted and reproduced by writers whose relationships to these traditions are largely textual, academic, and even imaginary—including such writers as Carlos Castaneda, Tony Hillerman, Jamake Highwater, Forrest Carter, and Lynn Andrews. Furthermore, Magdaleno argues that even in the hands of gifted indigenous writers such as N. Scott Momaday and Leslie Marmon Silko, oral traditions necessarily become part of an "alienated context" that provides only the illusion of authenticity, in fact denying the existence of vital traditions and instead producing "textual necrophilia" (Magdaleno 2000, 292). Treuer adds a similar view of Silko's use of mythological stories in *Ceremony*. He writes: "They are stage props. They are on the stage but they are not the play" (Treuer 2002, 60).

While many writers certainly use the oral tradition as a kind of prop within the context of conventional narratives, some indigenous writers have instead based the entire trajectory of their novels either on specific oral stories or on narratives derived from concepts of orality, such as the use of multiple narrators that suggest subjectivity both in points of view and in the grain or nuance of the spoken voice. While these novels do not, of course, escape questions of authenticity and ethics, especially when the novels unwisely include sacred or private tribal information, the oral stories in these novels are sometimes both the stage and the props, offering alternative, even resistant forms of narratives against generic expectations. For example, the first novel based on an indigenous oral story is Mourning Dove's *Cogewea* (1929), a narrative that foregrounds its resistance to previous representations of indigenous people in stock Western novels. Specifically, when the eponymous protagonist reads a Western novel entitled *The Brand*—an actual 1914 book by Theresa Broderick—she becomes so enraged with the actions of a subservient Indian character that she throws the book into the fire. Rather than mimic the form and thematic conventions of the stock Western, Mourning Dove conceived the book as the rewriting of a traditional Okanogan oral story about a chipmunk and Owl Woman (Mourning Dove 1990, 51–59). As an itinerant farm worker, however, who carried her typewriter from job to job, Mourning Dove had little hope of finding a publisher until she met Lucullus McWhorter, an amateur ethnologist and collector of Indian artifacts. It is both tragic and telling that McWhorter revised the novel so that it might be more appealing to an American reading public—adding footnotes, epigraphs, and sections depicting indigenous peoples as mythical, warring, and ultimately doomed. The result is a highly uneven novel that oscillates between visions of indigenous survival and destruction, but is it also a novel that starkly demonstrates how differing beliefs about representation produce much different kinds of fiction about indigenous people.

In the first chapters of this book, I consider questions of authenticity and ethics as they relate to different works of indigenous literature such as Momaday's *Way to Rainy Mountain*, Silko's *Storyteller*, and her novel *Ceremony*. In particular, I examine how traditions of the social sciences such as ethnology and anthropology, which have predominated in studies of indigenous people and continue in recent literary studies, foreground the binary opposition of purity and impurity, authenticity and inauthenticity, necessarily placing all contemporary forms of indigenous expression in a subaltern position. I also consider Magdaleno and Treuer's incisive criticism that the use of oral traditions in contemporary literature is frequently offered as a sign of authenticity, rather than an expression of indigenous sensibilities. In the second part of the book, I look at specific works of indigenous literature that do not use indigenous traditions as signs of authenticity, but instead as patterns, to use Frantz Fanon's term,[1] for narrative of resistance: Mourning Dove's *Cogewea*, Vizenor's *Bearheart*, Louise Erdrich's *Love Medicine*, and Ray Young Bear's *Black Eagle Child*. With the exception of the conflicting structure in *Cogewea*, the trajectory of the narratives in these later novels reflects aspects of orality that not only suggest indigenous forms of fiction, but also underscore areas of concern quite different from plots based on conflict and blood identity. In Erdrich's *Love Medicine*, for instance, the novel enacts some of the complexities of orality by using the form of multiple "voices," each providing different perspectives on people and events in this tribal community. This narrative form coincides with one of the central questions for the characters: namely, whether they are able to "hear," or at least accept, the changing, contradictory, and often unfathomable subjectivities of others. Young Bear's *Black Eagle Child* also draws from indigenous oral tradition by shaping the lives of the characters and the history of community in a metamorphic journey that mirrors a religious ceremony in the early chapters of the novel. In this metamorphic narrative, characters leave their homeland—physically and sometimes spiritually—and attempt to return with new perspectives about themselves and their community. The novel suggests that such journeys are important and even necessary, especially if the community is to complete its journey back to its traditional system of governance. At the same time, the journeys are also quite dangerous, for characters sometimes lose their way, return home damaged, or perhaps worst of all, return home to find that the community no longer accepts them or their new perspectives. Rather than completely reject culturally hybrid positions, then, *Black Eagle Child* uses a metamorphic approach that both complicates the "homing in" narrative, and also foregrounds the necessity of incorporating aspects of other cultures into one's own.

This book follows the trajectory of several studies that examine resistant narratives, including Phyllis Peres's *Transculturation and Resistance in Lusophone African Narrative*, Mudrooroo Narogin's *Writing from the Fringe*, and Barbara Harlow's *Resistant Literature*. These authors examine poetic and fictional works by postcolonial writers who appropriate literary forms to resist colonial representations of cultures and history that are both false and self-justifying. In her chapter "Narratives of Resistance," for example, Harlow demonstrates how authors such as Sergio Ramirez (Nicaragua), Manio Argueta (El Salvador), and Sipho Sepamla (South Africa) reconstruct historical narratives so that they expose the language of colonial control. For instance, Ramirez's *To Bury Our Fathers* contains six distinct but somewhat fragmented plots, each representing different threads of Nicaraguan history. Both the complexity of differing historical narratives and also the complexity of the psychology of speakers create, according to Harlow, "a panoramic vision of contradictions riddling Nicaraguan society in the first half of the century" (Harlow 1987, 93). Stylistically and thematically, this irreducible complexity in the novel undermines Anastasio Samoza's dictatorial attempt "to maintain systemic control over the popular chorus of oppositional elements within the society" (93–94). Harlow writes: "Formal experimentation is in fact characteristic of these 'resistant narratives'" (95). Consequently, these novels not only expose the narrative alibis for colonial power, they also reflect the complex, internal tensions within postcolonial societies through the use of innovative narrative structures.

Citing Harlow's book as a resource, Phyllis Peres similarly demonstrates how prominent Angolan writers Luandino Vieira, Uanhenga Xitu, Pepetela, and Manuel Rui appropriate colonial discourse through the process of transculturation to create an imagined, hybrid, and contentious nation-space. She writes:

> Homi Bhabha has described the liminality of the nation-space as that narration of selfhood that does merely define itself in otherness, that is, in relation to other nations. Rather the narration of nation creates a liminal signifying space that deconstructs the monolithic construct of "we, the people" so that the imagined community is that of a heterogeneous, oftentimes contentious people. (Peres 1997, 67)[2]

In her chapter on the fiction of Pepetela, for instance, Peres describes how his novel *Lueji* enacts or performs its own central tensions between historical truth (*verdade histórica*) and the truth of oral stories (*verdade estória*) by offering a narrative strategy that includes multiple levels, variations of tales, and contradictory narratives. This strategy not only reflects the contentious versions of history in Angola, it also foregrounds the importance of oral stories, "the narrative form that has become most identified with emergent Angolan national literature" (82). Likewise, in her chapter on the works of Manuel Rui, Peres once again shows how fiction performs the tensions of orality and writing in "the complex and changing narration of nation" (95) Specifically, in his short story "O Relógio," Rui describes the performance of a former guerrilla commander who tells a group of children about a watch taken from a Portuguese major and later offered in exchange for prisoners. Peres writes: "Each week, the estoría is transformed through the active role of the commander's audience—children who ask questions, change details, and thus re-tell the tale as collective authors" (94). Just as the exchange of the watch challenges linear, hegemonic concepts of the time, so too does the oral story challenge the received colonial narration of history and offer the possibility of "future imaginations of nation and possibilities of collective authorship" (95).

In similar fashion, Mudrooroo Narogin demonstrates how Aboriginal artists in Australia appropriate and revise non-Aboriginal forms of expression in poetry, fiction, drama, the visual arts, and music. Mudrooroo is responding in part to Australian critics from "Anglo-Celtic" traditions who dismiss the works of Aboriginal artists as being more protest than poetry, and he is also responding to Aboriginal poets who, in his view, rely too heavily on European forms for their works. Thus, while Mudrooroo defends the works of Aboriginal writers against these critics, he also harshly critiques their approach, even suggesting that their works should be replaced entirely.[3] He writes: "The aim is to destroy the type of poetry directed at the majority community by poets such as Jack Davis and Oodgeroo Noonucal and to replace it with the desires in the shape of language and structure which are found in the depths of Aboriginal being" (Mudrooroo 1990, 38). Mudrooroo has in mind the unconventional poetry of Lionel Fogarty, a writer whose work not only reflects an Aboriginal sensibility in both substance and form, but also a writer who enacts the very processes of Aboriginal artistic expression by finding his inspiration in dreams.[4] It is a method, Mudrooroo tells us, that corresponds to "traditional Aboriginal society," where "the dreaming of literary works such as the Ngurlu of the Kimberly region of Western Australia is the accepted form of literary creation" (Mudrooroo 1990, 37). In drama, the visual arts, and music, Mudrooroo locates similar examples of expression that resists non-Aboriginal forms and subsequently helps to resist the process of assimilation of Aboriginal people into a metropolitan Australia. Thus, for Mudrooroo, literature plays an important part in an active struggle to maintain an Aboriginal "independent identity" within the larger desire for political independence in Australia (14).

As with poetry, Mudrooroo finds few novels that employ Aboriginal forms, offering as an example only his own *Doin' Wildcat* because it "utilizes Aboriginal speech patterns throughout" (Mudrooroo 1990, 28). Mudrooroo cites two reasons for the dearth of such Aboriginal novels: the cost of producing longer works of fiction, and the editing process of the publishing industry. On the one hand, Mudrooroo sees little evidence of a growing body of Aboriginal resistance fiction. He writes: "Except for *Doin' Wildcat*, there is no sign that the Aboriginal novel will break radically from European-derived models" (28). Yet on the other hand, Mudrooroo appears to hold out for the possibility that small Aboriginal publishing houses will exert more editorial control when publishing fiction by Aboriginal writers who are "least affected by assimilation" (30). Furthermore, Mudrooroo applies Frantz Fanon's three stages of intellectual decolonization to Aboriginal literatures, perhaps in the hope of demonstrating how future novels may move toward forms of resistance. For example, to illustrate Fanon's first stage of decolonization, where writers imitate European forms because they desire acceptance or equality, Mudrooroo offers his own novel *Wildcat Falling* (1965), "with its emphasis on the outsider and laced with quotations from Samuel Beckett" (29). Mudrooroo does not give examples of Fanon's second stage, in which the colonized writer "has only exterior relations" with his own people "and is content to recall their lives" (29).[5] Fanon himself suggests that the colonized writer in this stage produces only a kind of ineffective literary ethnology; he or she has "no hesitation in using a dialect in order to show his will to be as near as possible to the people" (Fanon 1963, 223). In this second stage, Fanon observes that "old legends will be reinterpreted in the light of a borrowed estheticism and of a conception of the world which was discovered under other skies" (222). In his 1959 address "On National Culture" to the second Congress of Black Writers and Artists, Fanon emphasizes again and again that the most important goal of any colonized people is not the expression of their unique cultures, but the struggle for freedom and independence. In a famous observation, Fanon writes: "You will never make colonialism blush for shame by spreading out little-known cultural treasures under its eyes" (223).

The signal feature of his third stage, the "fighting" stage, Fanon tells us, is that the author desires to "shake the people," to become an "awakener of the people" by writing a literature that inspires a communal desire for the liberation of their nation. He writes:

> The crystallization of the national consciousness will both disrupt literary styles and themes, and also create a completely new public. While at the beginning the native intellectual used to produce his work to be read exclusively by the oppressor, whether with the intention of charming him or of denouncing him through ethnic or subjectivist means, now the native writer progressively takes on the habit of addressing his own people. (Fanon 1963, 240)

For Fanon, the crystallization of consciousness is the battleground upon which liberation depends: similar to ideology, crystallization is a particular vision of the nation that reflects, as he writes in "The Pitfalls of National Consciousness," "the innermost hopes of the whole people" (148). Yet as a kind of ideology, the hopes of a people may focus on ideas that are theoretically suspect, or that reinscribe colonialist, hierarchical relations among classes and "races." In *Black Skins, White Masks*, for instance, Fanon writes of the "black schoolboy in Antilles" who comes to believe in the racial hierarchies of black and white, savage and civilized, through "illustrated magazines for children" such as Tarzan and Mickey Mouse. He writes: "Little by little, one can observe in the young Antillean the formation and crystallization of an attitude and a way of thinking and seeing that are essentially white" (Fanon 1967, 148). In his address "On National Culture," Fanon also warns of the problems of unifying African consciousness through questionable assumptions about négritude, "race" or culture. He writes, for instance, that proponents of négritude offer an "unconditional affirmation of African culture" through essentialist and even stereotypical binary oppositions between African and European people: "old Europe to a young Africa, tiresome reasoning to lyricism, oppressive logic to high-stepping nature" (213). Likewise, solidarity based on "race" or culture elides important differences between and among groups that have far different hopes, tactics, and goals. Fanon points out that the struggle for civil rights by black Americans is much different than the Angolan fight for independence against the Portuguese. Solidarity based on culture offers similar difficulties: "There is no common destiny to be shared between the national cultures of Senegal and Guinea; but there is a common destiny between the Sengelese and Guinean nations which are both dominated by the same French colonialism" (234).

For indigenous tribal groups in America, as with the colonized peoples of Africa, the issues of "race" and culture are often more differentiating than cohesive. Although we understand that a woefully inexact science of genetics determined the "blood quantum" of individuals at the end of the nineteenth century, these fractional markers of identity remain intact and powerful for many individual and tribal groups even today. And although culture has at times become a cohesive presence for indigenous people in the history of the Americas (e.g., the Tree of Peace of the Haudenosaunee, the Ghost Dance of Wovoka, the culture of the Lakotas for the American Indian Movement), no single indigenous culture has become a crystallizing force for all indigenous peoples, not only because there are over five hundred tribal groups in the United States, with many different cultural beliefs and practices, but because many of these groups are profoundly committed to the personal, communal, spiritual, and even geographic truth of their beliefs. Despite their many differences in culture, most (if not all) tribes today crystallize their national focus on their assertions of tribal sovereignty, self-government, and self-determination—in other words, their status as "domestic dependent nations" as defined by the United States Supreme Court in 1832. It is a constant struggle, for a federal policy terminating this dependent, national status between 1954 and 1966 ended self-government for over one hundred tribal nations. While many tribes regained their status, the policy of Termination was a stark reminder not only that indigenous peoples must keep constant vigilance if they wish to maintain their semi-sovereign status, but that the United States exerts ultimate political and military power over them to determine their fates.

Resistant indigenous fiction in the Americas corresponds to this struggle, asserting the contemporary existence of indigenous peoples as cultural, political, and geographic entities. Since the first European settlers arrived in this hemisphere, almost every religious and cultural narrative that legitimated the actions of the colonists left little or no place for indigenous peoples. With the exception of the Spaniards in the American Southwest, whose social system required a peasant, farming class, these grand narratives of America envision indigenous peoples primarily as obstacles to be removed or eliminated (Wilson 1999, 194–95). Examples of such narratives include the creation of the City on the Hill, progress from savagery to civilization, divinely inspired visions of Manifest Destiny and *E Pluribus Unum*, and the natural and purported objectivity of the science of social Darwinism. Combined, this cultural ethos of America (ironically its vision of its best self) denies the possibility of tribal groups as contemporary and equal peoples, and instead requires that indigenous peoples be relegated to images of the past or of loss—for instance, the tragic mixed-blood figures in literature, sports mascots in popular culture, and place names on the landscape. Consequently, although indigenous fiction displaying images of loss, tragedy, and despair foregrounds the terrible effects of a history of colonialism, this literature does not serve to resist colonial discourse or destructive metanarratives. On the contrary, such fiction is well received because, as Fanon argues, cataloging the ills of colonized peoples in "tragic and poetic style" only "serves to reassure the occupying power" (Fanon 1963, 239). He writes: "The colonists have in former times encouraged these modes of expression and made their existence possible. Stinging denunciations, the exposing of distressing conditions and passions which find their outlet in expression are in fact assimilated by the occupying power in a cathartic process" (239).

As domestic dependent nations, indigenous tribes in America have political means to assert their positions as separate, contemporary, and semi-sovereign peoples. Yet at the same time, these positions—while necessary and even powerful in some ways—nonetheless remain fundamentally subordinate to the United States government, subject to any number of directives within a guardian-to-ward relationship, including termination. Thus, Vine Deloria Jr. and Clifford M. Lytle conclude: "Since [tribal self-government] will never supplant the intangible, spiritual, and emotional aspirations of American Indians, it cannot be regarded as the final solution to Indian problems" (Deloria and Lytle 1984, 13). Likewise, drawing from the Haudenosaunee tradition that asserts an egalitarian "brother to brother" relationship between their nations and others, Mohawk political philosopher Taiaiake Alfred concurs, writing that "any notion of nationhood or self-government rooted in state institutions and framed within the context of state sovereignty can never satisfy the imperatives of Native American political traditions" (Alfred, 1999, 72).[6] In Australia, too, according to Mudrooroo, the Fanonian struggle for complete Aboriginal independence has become muted by Aboriginal demands within a state structure. Mudrooroo writes that "the stage of active struggle for an independent identity may be passing. . . . It might even be said that Aboriginal affairs is entering a stage of post-activism in that any separate goals are being replaced for those of equal opportunity in the wider Australian community" (Mudrooroo 1990, 14). Because many tribes have found stability and occasional prosperity in their legal status as wards of the federal government, the eighteenth-century struggle for complete independence has been replaced by the demands for increased self-determination, better government programs, and proper representation both in American culture and government.

Nonetheless, the dream of eventual independence for indigenous peoples remains with writers such as Alfred, Mudrooroo, and Young Bear. In fact, *Black Eagle Child*, perhaps more than any other indigenous novel in the United States, corresponds to Fanon's vision of third-stage or "fighting" literature, for the novel directly questions the validity and efficacy of a fundamentally subaltern relationship with the federal government. In the afterword to his novel, Young Bear writes:

> Historically, there was equality in the First-Named systems, but materialism and greed spawned novel methods by which to manipulate others. The day divine leadership was deemed unimportant was when the sacred myths began to crumble under the wheels of suzerainty. (Young Bear 1992a, 260)

Within the novel itself, external impositions of power on the community always result in the further deterioration of the community—for instance, boarding schools that removed indigenous children from their homes for years at a time, and elected governments that superseded traditional clan structures. Resisting external forms, Young Bear's novel employs a circular "journey of words," derived from oral traditions, to demonstrate the possibility, or at least the hope, of a reconstitution of traditional forms of identity and especially governance. Disrupting the "literary themes and styles" of American literature (in fact, Young Bear rarely reads other writers), *Black Eagle Child* asserts oral traditions as relevant and effective in the process of reinvigorating the desire for independence. As Fanon says of the fighting stage of literature: "the oral tradition—stories, epics, and songs of the people—which formerly were filed away as set pieces are now beginning to change. . . . The storyteller once more gives free rein to his imagination; he makes innovations and he creates a work of art" (Fanon 1963, 240–41).

Black Eagle Child is a reminder that the long story of indigenous peoples is not finished, and that we may yet have something to say about our destinies. Only a few generations ago, indigenous peoples lived as true sovereigns in this hemisphere—not as race-based, dependent nations, a legacy of Collier's Indian Reorganization Act, but instead, in Phyllis Peres's formulation, as changing, therefore "hybrid" and sometimes contested nation-spaces. *Black Eagle Child* reflects this older vision of indigenous cultural complexity, incorporating not only contested concepts of "race" in the formation of tribal identity, but also several different accepted religious practices, including Christianity. For instance, a venerated grandmother Nokomis respects both Christian and indigenous beliefs, telling the narrator: "To believe in two, three, / or even four is by far a better means to pray. / Combined, the religions brought your uncles / back from the Germans and Japanese" (Young Bear 1992a, 63). Consistent with Fanon's critique of certain movements in Africa, the novel demonstrates the difficulty of crystallizing tribal consciousness around the irresolvable questions of "race" or culture, but offers instead the possibility of tribal nations engaging such questions within the process of their own perpetual metamorphosis, free from external impositions of power and governance.

Given the ethos of unity in America in the form of *E Pluribus Unum*, most spectacularly displayed in the Civil War, and given the changes in policies in the nineteenth and twentieth centuries—Allotment, the Indian Reorganization Act, Termination, Relocation, and most recently Self-Determination—that further inscribe native nations into a system of dependency, the possibility that indigenous tribes in America will see independence and equality seems quite small. Yet these changes in policies also remind us that indigenous people will likely see many more such upheavals in the next century as well. Who knows what will happen if indigenous peoples crystallize their thoughts on independence in the next hundred years, among new generations of peoples from all backgrounds who will think about the world quite differently than we do today, and who may have a far different approach to the deep injustices of American history?

This study is the result of my years of teaching indigenous literature to diverse populations of students. I hope that these chapters will provide other teachers and readers of indigenous literatures with some useful ideas for thinking about and discussing oral traditions and indigenous writing, and also will provide ways to consider a permanent place in this hemisphere for indigenous communities. In my classes, I have attempted to help students appreciate the aesthetic innovations and the political consequences of indigenous fiction by writers who have in profound ways refashioned the English language and Western genres into new forms, or at least the possibilities of new forms, of indigenous literature. I also try to impress upon students that all of our cultures—not only indigenous cultures—have changed drastically over the past five hundred or even fifty years, and anxiety about the loss of culture understandably motivates indigenous (and nonindigenous) people to become conservative and suspicious of change. Yet circumstances surrounding indigenous communities continue to change at such incredible rates that it is becoming more imperative than ever that indigenous people be proficient at negotiating between progressive and conservative forces, both within and outside their tribal communities. Indeed, many gifted indigenous people such as Ray Young Bear and Louise Erdrich refuse the alternatives of museums or melting pots, and instead they create from a history of tragedy and ruin works of literature that stand as testaments to the continued existence and power of Native thought in our lives and in our dreams.

Assimilation or Appropriation? The Idea of the Center in N. Scott Momaday's *Way to Rainy Mountain* and Leslie Marmon Silko's *Ceremony*

everal years ago, the *National Geographic* published a large photograph showing an Indian youth sitting in a tipi watching television. It must have come as a pleasant shock to the photographer, this juxtaposition of two very dissimilar cultures—a moment of Barthesian *frisson* or *jouissance*, perhaps. Yet, had several of the indigenous youth's friends happened by, it is unlikely (although possible, if they were being highly ironical) that they would have exclaimed in a burst of ontological distress: "A television in a tipi!" More likely they would have asked, "Is the basketball game on yet?" Similarly, in his *Marvelous Possessions*, Stephen Greenblatt relates his initial disappointment when he witnessed a moment of indigenous assimilation upon seeing a group of Balinese watching television on a *bale bajar*, "the communal pavilion in which I knew—from having read Clifford Geertz and Miguel Covarrubias and Gregory Bateson and Margaret Mead—that the Balinese gathered in the evenings" (Greenblatt 1991, 3). As he approached the pavilion, however, Greenblatt saw that the Balinese were watching and immensely enjoying a taped recording of "an elaborate temple ceremony," with some of the recorded dancers themselves joining in this celebratory moment. Greenblatt offers his observation to explain that ethnological fieldwork frequently comprises a collection of such anecdotes, and these anecdotes then become understandable only within a "larger progress or pattern that is the proper subject of history" (3). Greenblatt thus implicitly critiques ethnology's claim to objectivity with its observations and classifications, showing how each observed object or anecdote accrues meaning and value only within larger narratives and strategies of interpretation.

Because the television has become a powerful sign of progress, both anecdotes appear to fall within the conventional and thus comprehensible "patterns" of progress and assimilation. At the same time, however, because indigenous peoples use the television for their own purposes, these anecdotes could just as easily suggest the pattern of appropriation. While assimilation and appropriation reflect quite different strategies for interpreting these anecdotes, neither is "right" in a logical sense, for reasoned arguments about the validity of one side or the other only serve to demonstrate the aporetic relationship between them. That is, the colonial concept of assimilation cannot escape the image or specter of the indigenous subaltern, nor can the resistant concept of appropriation escape the complications and potential destruction associated with assimilation. Rather, these different patterns of interpretation are dominant (in Brian McHales's use of the term) for different cultural groups, depending on their usefulness in legitimating certain beliefs, policies, or aims.[1] For example, in America, the dominant pattern of interpreting indigenous peoples remains within the language of assimilation, where indigenous peoples are forever fighting a losing battle against settlers and civilization, attempting to maintain older cultures while becoming inevitably absorbed into a modern world. In the discourse of assimilation, the only accurate descriptions of changing indigenous cultures fall within the binary alternatives of true and false, the authentic and inauthentic, where any evidence of cultural change is a sign of debasement, impoverishment, or impurity. This strategy of interpretation remains dominant in America, the historian James Wilson observes, because it provides compelling and guilt-free narrative or alibi for the disappearance of authentic indigenous peoples from the landscape of America. He writes: "Native Americans are expected to demonstrate their authenticity by vanishing before the irresistible tide of Progress. If they *fail* to vanish, if they change and adapt instead, then, by definition, they are not really Native Americans" (Wilson 1999, xxiii).

In contrast, indigenous writers of contemporary fiction are generally less concerned with assimilation than they are about the power of appropriating and revising nonindigenous forms to create a literature of resistance. Indeed, in his essay "Toward a National Indian Literature: Cultural Authenticity in Nationalism," Simon J. Ortiz argues that appropriation is not only a valuable tool for his Pueblo community, it is also a concept that emerges from the Pueblo traditions themselves. Furthermore, Ortiz appropriates the concept of authenticity itself away from its binary inflections, and instead toward a definition based on community acts of "strengths and continuance"—in other words, a conception of authenticity not as division of true or false, but as the continuum between these two (Ortiz 1981, 7). For example, he describes the feast days named for Catholic saints at his home, the Acqumeh Pueblo in New Mexico, when members of the community stand atop their adobe homes and throw food to persons waiting below who call their names. These feast days, Ortiz tells us, enact a "community fulfilled in its most complete sense of giving and receiving" (7). While outsiders may consider the use of Catholic saints and the Catholic calendar as examples of assimilation, Ortiz argues instead that the community has appropriated the religion to their own uses; indeed, he boldly claims that Catholic rituals "are Indian now because of the creative development that the native people applied to them" (8). What is more, these acts of cultural appropriation provide the broad outlines for a vision of indigenous nationalism that emphasizes creativity rather than the oppositional discourse of nativism and assimilation. Ortiz writes that "in every case where European culture was cast upon Indian people of this nation and there was similar creative response and development, it can be observed that this was the primary element of a nationalist impulse to make use of foreign ritual, ideas, and material in their own—Indian—terms" (8).

This process of communal appropriation is an ongoing, creative, and public process that not only offers resistance to forces of colonialism but also, according to Ortiz, ensures the psychological health of the community. In one particular event, for example, the Acqumeh people annually recall the destruction of their village in 1598 by reenacting the coming of both Santiago (the patron saint of the invading Spanish) and Chapiyuh (a figure of a Franciscan priest). Although both figures are grotesque in their costumes, Santiago "in ostentatious finery" and Chapiyuh stomping about and frightening the children, they are nonetheless a reminder of the destructive force that colonialism can continue to exert if left unchallenged. Ortiz writes:

> It is the only way in which event and experience, such as the entry of the Spaniard to the Western Hemisphere, can become significant and realized in the people's own terms. And this, of course, is what happens in literature, to bring about meaning and meaningfulness. This perception and meaningfulness has to happen; otherwise, the hard experience of the Euroamerican colonialization of the lands and people of the Western Hemisphere would be driven into the dark recesses of the indigenous mind and psyche. And this kind of repression is always a poison and detriment to creative growth and expression. (Ortiz 1981, 9)

The continued "health" of the center in the face of outside oppression is maintained not by excluding outside elements, nor by remaining unchanged over time, but through an understanding of outside elements, especially if these elements pose a psychological threat to the continued existence of the people. Indeed, it is perhaps this moment of cultural engagement that determines whether the use of non-Indian elements in Indian cultures is an act of appropriation and resistance, or a more dangerous instance of colonialism. If outside elements endanger the "health" of the center, as did the Chapiyuh, it is imperative that they be translated, remembered, and set in a proper context.

Finally, Ortiz considers the creative use of traditions within contemporary literature as a similar act of appropriation, resistance, and nationalism. Discussing the appropriation of the Catholic calendar and saints, Ortiz concludes, "Today's writing by Indian authors is a continuation of that elemental impulse" (Ortiz 1981, 8) Thus, although indigenous writers use nonindigenous languages (Spanish and English, for instance), these languages have the ability to offer a means of creating unity and resistance. He writes:

> Some would argue that this [borrowing of language] means that Indian people have succumbed or become educated into a different linguistic system and have forgotten or have been forced to forsake their native selves. This is simply not true. Along with their native languages, Indian women and men have carried on their lives and their expression through the use of the new languages, particularly Spanish, French, and English, and they have used these languages on their own terms. (Ortiz 1981, 10)

The combined use of the oral tradition (the cultural "encyclopedia" of the tribe) with writing is an example of the way American Indian cultures grow and change as they imagine both their relations within the group as well as their relations to outside, sometimes oppressive groups. In some ways, this claim about orality and writing is extraordinary, not because of its veracity (it is obviously true), but because it must be made at all. In African American literature, the use of the Black English vernacular by Zora Neale Hurston and Alice Walker rarely conjures questions of purity or authenticity; indeed, these authors are celebrated for establishing insightful and politically useful relationships between the spoken and written word.[2]

Although writers such as Ortiz, Momaday, and Silko offer rich alternatives to the discourse of authenticity, indigenous literatures continue to fall under the shadow of the ethnographic traditions of the late nineteenth and early twentieth centuries. In the context of the social sciences, indigenous cultures are objects of study rather than societies of equal human beings with whom one has ethical and political relations. Scientific studies of indigenous peoples emphasize authenticity and representation, with a particular emphasis on definitions and classifications. Even today, many anthropologists and literary critics consider indigenous traditions not as a source of power and resistance, but as a discrete subject of study, using terminology about indigenous traditions that assures their subaltern status: "myths," "legends," or "folk tales." They then classify them in any number of ways as a means of understanding them systematically and representing them authentically.

Yet because oral traditions constantly change in ways that Ortiz describes, representation within the social sciences remains forever out of reach. Indeed, in his *Voices in the Margin: American Indian Literature and the Canon*, Arnold Krupat argues that there is, in fact, no authentic representation of the oral tradition, since even "for a culturally prepared audience, narrators always modified and adjusted their tellings" (Krupat 1989, 225). Within the discourse of authenticity, oral traditions are similar to Heisenberg's electrons—always disrupted by the intrusive gaze of the observer or the pen of the ethnographer, forever a shadow of the original word.

At best, Krupat argues, indigenous oral traditions are represented by the works of ethnologists who use technological advances, such as taped recordings, or unconventional textual formats; yet even then, the results are suspect. Krupat writes that "we don't know what traditional story telling sessions were like; we don't even know what a 'real' telling even of some stories we have on tape or in translation. . . . would be like" (Krupat 1989, 225). To alleviate the perceived rift between past and present, between orality and text, Krupat refers to the work of Dennis Tedlock, who uses typography and marginal commentary in his books to indicate different actions on the part of the speaker, such as how long to hold vowels or when to raise the pitch (Tedlock 1978). For Krupat, this kind of work remains promising, for if an authentic text cannot be reproduced, then this kind of work can at least provide terms "more or less comprehensible" to outside readers (Krupat 1989, 228).[3] It is within this context of accurate and authentic representation that Krupat divides works produced by indigenous peoples into two general categories: "Indian literature," which consists of reproduced oral performances, usually in Indian languages; and "indigenous literature," which he also calls "mixed breed" (214)—literature written by American Indians in English. By establishing this taxonomy of indigenous culture, Krupat comes to terms with the crisis of representation by reifying the distinctions one often finds in anthropology and ethnology between "authentic" and cross-cultural texts. Indeed, it is a resolution using terms that address a crisis of its own making.

■ The Idea of the Center in the Oral Tradition

In contrast to the scientific methods of Tedlock and others, Leslie Marmon Silko, Laguna Pueblo novelist and essayist, challenges the distinctions crucial to the sciences: pure/impure, past/present, orality/writing. Instead, Silko suggests a much different approach to representing the oral tradition, conceiving of it not as an artifact for study, but, along with Ortiz, as a living tradition whose value and power expand and continue to have relevance for the present. Consequently, the oral tradition itself has, as Silko demonstrates, a fundamentally different way of conceptualizing itself than do the scientists who seek to represent it. In an address entitled "Language and Literature from a Pueblo Perspective," Silko says:

> Anthropologists and ethnologists have, for a long time, differentiated types of oral language they find in the Pueblos. They tended to rule out all but the old and sacred and traditional stories and were not interested in family stories and the family's account of itself. But these family stories are just as important as the other stories—the older stories. These family stories are given equal recognition. (Silko 1981b, 58)

In this conception of the oral tradition, hierarchical classifications between older stories and more recent family stories do not exist. The participants in the oral tradition receive the stories not as artifacts, but rather as changing sources of knowledge and entertainment. This conception of literature has little commerce with the distinctions most crucial to anthropological science: classifiable and determinate representations. Instead, Silko stresses that oral traditions perform a normative function that, like M. M. Bakhtin's centripetal concept of language, constantly pulls people and new concepts inward toward a relatively stable discursive community.[4]

Because the oral tradition constantly weaves relations between old and new stories, it may be termed a dialogic tradition—literally—for these stories are retold and remade by each generation of people in conversation with each other in the present moment. In her essay "Landscape, History, and the Pueblo Imagination," Silko writes:

> Communal storytelling was a self-correcting process in which listeners were
> encouraged to speak up if they noted an important fact or detail omitted. . . .
> Even conflicting versions of an incident were welcomed for the entertain-
> ment they provided. . . . The ancient Pueblo sought a communal truth, not
> an absolute. For them this truth lived somewhere within the web of differing
> versions, disputes over minor points, outright contradictions tangling with
> old feuds and village rivalries. (Silko 1986a, 90–91)

Thus, a Pueblo perspective suggests that literature is at once both a normative process and a changing process—continually re-creating meaning in
the present, creating a usable "communal truth." Furthermore, a storytelling
culture constantly moves toward integrating its individual elements—points
of view, old and new stories—into a complex, changing community. It does so
not only in spite of conflicting points of view but also *because of* these different
points of view, for they provide valuable correction and supplemental information. Silko says, "There is always, *always*, the dynamics of bringing things
together, of interrelating things. It is an imperative in Pueblo oral literature,
it seems to me, and it occurs structurally in narrative and in fiction" (64).
She writes: "The stories are always bringing us together, keeping this whole
together, keeping this family together, keeping this clan together. 'Don't go
away, don't isolate yourself, but come here, because we have all had these
experiences together'—this is what the people are saying to you when they tell
you these other stories" (59).

As a dialogic tradition, Silko's version of tradition coincides with
Bakhtin's theory of language and meaning, as his work is also predicated
upon orality—specifically, the interaction of two people in dialogue. For
Bakhtin, when two people speak to one another, they set aside the "noise" of
other languages that they possess (foreign languages, irrelevant languages,
archaic or otherwise incomprehensible languages, and so forth), similar to
the way people in storytelling cultures take various, sometimes conflicting,
points of view and move toward a consensus. With an active attempt of each
to "hear" the voice and subjectivity of the other, the result is a fragile moment
of clarity between two persons, which Bakhtin calls the "unitary language."
As Bakhtin says in "Discourse of the Novel," "Unitary language constitutes

the theoretical expression of the historical processes of linguistic unification and centralization, an expression of the centripetal forces of language. A unitary language is not something given [dan] but is always in essence posited [zadan]—and at every moment of its linguistic life it is opposed to the realities of heteroglossia" (Bakhtin 1981, 270). Similarly, in a storytelling culture, this "unitary language" exists for an entire group, where a stable center of value is created through the concerted efforts of speakers and listeners over time, sometimes millennia. Within this dynamic, the oral tradition maintains dialogical spaces where people can talk, learn, and live together in the continual creation of individual and group identity.

If the oral tradition is to remain useful, and thus "authentic" (in Ortiz's appropriated conception of the term), then it must by definition have some degree of hybridity or cultural interaction. For Silko and Ortiz, certainly, the impoverished language of purity and impurity fails to take into account the power of the oral tradition to encounter, translate, and transform outside elements into a changing tribal center—the same kind of power generally assumed for European cultures, as well as for individuals within those cultures who daily engage a changing world.

■ Centers of Identity in *The Way to Rainy Mountain*

One especially interesting work of literature that exists within this tension of stasis and change is N. Scott Momaday's *Way to Rainy Mountain*. Like Silko and Ortiz, Momaday writes frequently about the power of the oral tradition—especially the power of the word—to create meaning from either the emptiness of silence or from the chaos of fragmentation. At the same time, however, Momaday, like Silko, tells us that the tradition's malleability is also a sign of its fragility, for he says the oral tradition (and he has in mind specific tribal stories) is always one generation away from extinction (Momaday 1979, 171).[5] In *The Way to Rainy Mountain*, Momaday writes:

> The verbal tradition by which [the way to Rainy Mountain] has been preserved has suffered a deterioration in time. What remains is fragmentary:

mythology, legend, lore, and hearsay—and of course, the idea itself, as crucial and complete as it ever was. That is the miracle. (Momaday 1969, 4)

The "idea itself" that emerges from the fragmentary tradition is the capacity of the individual or group to think of itself as a whole—a unified entity. Like that of Ortiz and Silko, it is a conception of the self that is changing, "intricate in motion and meaning," and it always involves the past and present—"that experience of the mind which is legendary as well as historical, personal as well as cultural" (4). Indeed, I would argue that Momaday's description of this unity or wholeness is different from the normative aspect of Silko's perspective on storytelling only in degree, not in kind.

Along the narrative journey in *The Way to Rainy Mountain*, Momaday describes how the Kiowa people changed from a fragmentary, hunter-gathering society to one of the most distinct and powerful cultures on the Plains in the nineteenth century. This work traces the trajectory of the Kiowa people, who begin with a name, *Kwuda*, the "coming out"; who later acquire the Tai-me religion from the Crow Indians; and who at last obtain horses from the Europeans—all of which combined to give them a strong, indomitable sense of their own Kiowa identity. Momaday writes:

> The great adventure of the Kiowas was a going forth into the heart of the continent. They began a long migration from the headwaters of the Yellowstone River eastward to the Black Hills and south to the Wichita Mountains. Along the way they acquired horses, the religion of the Plains, a love and possession of the open land. Their nomadic soul was set free. In alliance with the Comanches they held dominion in the southern Plains for a hundred years. In the course of that long migration they had come of age as a people. They had conceived a good idea of themselves; they had dared to imagine and determine who they were. (Momaday 1969, 4)

Once the Kiowa people gained a "good idea" of themselves, the oral tradition maintained that identity in spite of changing times and considerable adversity, creating a center very similar to that discussed by Ortiz in relation to the invasion of the Spaniards. In one sense, we might say that the Kiowa of the plains were "mixed," for their horses and their religion were not original to them—and yet it also seems absurd to suggest that the Kiowa buffalo hunter on the plains is "inauthentic" or "impure" because of his lack of unmixed "origins" (an idea with its own mythical constructions). The discourse of "pure" and "mixed" (or "mixed blood") is therefore inadequate to express the complexities by which cultures come to fashion a center of identity—to imagine themselves as a people who persist over time.

For the Kiowa people, this cultural center gave them a means to refashion the events that might otherwise have left them completely devastated. In 1833, two events seriously threatened the fabric of the Kiowa culture: a spectacular, terrifying meteor shower, and the loss of the Tai-me to the Osage. Momaday writes: "The terrified Kiowas, when they had regained possession of themselves, did indeed imagine that the falling stars were symbolic of their being and their destiny. They accounted for themselves with reference to that awful memory. They appropriated it, recreated it, fashioned it into an image of themselves—imagined it" (Momaday 1981, 169). Just as Ortiz discussed the ability of the Pueblo people to use their traditions to dispel the negative effects of their encounter with the Spanish, so too does Momaday explain how the oral tradition allows the Kiowa people to understand and translate what appears to be a natural disaster into their own terms. Momaday tells us:

> Only by means of that act could they bear what happened to them thereafter. No defeat, no humiliation, no suffering was beyond their power to endure, for none of it was meaningless. They could say to themselves, "Yes, it was all meant to be in its turn. The order of the world was broken, it was clear. Even the stars were shaken loose in the night sky." The imagination of meaning was not much, perhaps, but it was all they had, and it was enough to sustain them. (Momaday 1981, 169)

So long as the oral tradition is able to translate meaninglessness or potential disaster into a Kiowa vision of the world, the Kiowa people endure. Therein, Momaday tells us, lies the power of the oral tradition as a force of stability and an interpreter of change. Like Silko and Ortiz, Momaday does not rely on the binary oppositions essential to the discourse of "mixed-ness," but instead posits a worldview that makes a powerful dual claim for tribal unity through the appropriation of both indigenous and nonindigenous sources.

In this regard, Momaday's position is quite similar to that of Vine Deloria Jr. and Clifford M. Lytle, who, in *The Nations Within*, argue that the "idea of the people" is the key concept in understanding decisions made by American Indian people throughout history and even today. (Deloria and Lytle 1984, 8) Deloria and Lytle explain this idea of the people in strikingly similar terms to those used by Momaday. They write:

> The idea of the people is primarily a religious conception, and with most American Indian tribes it begins somewhere in the primordial mists. In that time the people were gathered together but did not yet see themselves as a distinct people. A holy man had a dream or a vision; quasi-mythological figures of cosmic importance revealed themselves, or in some manner the people were instructed. They were given ceremonies and rituals that enabled them to find their place on the continent. Quite often they were given prophecies that informed them of the historical journey ahead. In some instances the people were told to migrate until a special place was revealed; in the interim, as with the Hebrews wandering in the deserts of Sinai, the older generation, which had lost its faith, and the cynics and skeptics of the group would be eliminated until the people were strong enough to receive the message. (Deloria and Lytle, 1984, 8)

The "idea of the people," Deloria and Lytle argue, is an often misunderstood but fundamental tenet in American Indian thought, and explains why treaty agreements have such resonance for Indian people. More than the spelling out of special provisions accorded to tribes, or the demarcation of a small portion of land to indigenous peoples, Deloria tells us, treaties are documents that in principle establish the existence and legitimacy of Indian tribes as independent groups in relation to the United States. This concept, fundamental to American Indian political thought, is also crucial to the conception of the group center for Silko, Ortiz, and Momaday. Indeed, we can say that Deloria and Lytle's political "idea of the people" coincides with an important tradition in American Indian literature that finds its roots in indigenous oral traditions.

Yet, one scholar of indigenous literature forcefully argues that Momaday's approach to writing actually forecloses on the dynamics of oral traditions. In his *Voice in the Margin*, Arnold Krupat asserts that while Silko includes the voices, the stories, and the perspectives of other members of her community in *Storyteller*, Momaday subsumes these other perspectives into his own particular voice and mythic perspective in *The Way to Rainy Mountain*. Using terminology derived from Bakhtin, Krupat asserts that Momaday is the "Native American most committed to hegemonic monologue to the all-encompassing voice of lyric or epic, romantic or modernist art-speech" (Krupat 1989, 177). Furthermore, Krupat tells us that in spite of Momaday's attempts to silence all voices not his own, he ultimately fails in this endeavor, for the voices of other writers—especially the anthropological/historical voices of James Mooney and George Catlin—nonetheless emerge surreptitiously in the work.

Perhaps because *The Way to Rainy Mountain* is sometimes considered an autobiography,[6] Krupat emphasizes the individual voice within this generic form. In fact, *The Way to Rainy Mountain* resists easy classification into any existing genre: it is in a sense the development of the individual, yet at the same time the book offers a parallel sketch of the long journey of the Kiowa people. In constructing these parallel narratives, the book combines different generic forms within the visual space of an open page—in Momaday's words, "three distinctive narrative voices": "the mythical, the historical, and the immediate," the latter two being "commentaries" on the oral tale (Momaday 1981, 170). *The Way to Rainy Mountain* contains twenty-four such tripartite groupings, including stories about Kiowa origins, the buffalo, the horse, and Momaday's own family. This combination of forms allows Momaday to place in the same rhetorical space three sometimes closely related, sometimes disparate discourses into a larger, unified narrative (metanarrative)—the migration of the Kiowa people from Montana to Oklahoma, and in some sense Momaday's own understanding of himself as a Kiowa. His method shows that just as the Kiowa gained a "good idea" of themselves with their origin story, religion, and the horse, so too does the poet create a "good idea" of himself in relation to the oral tradition and textual history. The self, then, rather than subsuming the other two languages as a kind of binary confrontation, instead becomes a linguistic center or site within the larger center of the history and culture of the tribe, or a circle within a larger circle. In other words, Momaday shows how the individual creates a unified language of the self, which in turn interacts with the larger unified language of the tribe and the language of textual history. Indeed, Momaday's unmistakable, highly rhetorical voice, rather than being an opprobrious moment of monologic self-indulgence, is a function of his commitment to the belief that individuals and groups imagine their changing identities through words and stories into a unified "voice."

For example, in his essay "Man Made of Words," where he discusses *The Way to Rainy Mountain* in some detail, Momaday poses the question "What is an Indian?" and replies with his famous response: "The answer is of course that it is an idea which a given man has of himself" (Momaday 1981, 162). Because of his desire for a clear taxonomy, Krupat comments that this answer is "hopelessly vague" (Krupat 1989, 207), but Momaday's statement becomes much clearer when read in the context of the rest of the essay, and especially in relation to Momaday's discussion of the way he or anyone else creates the "good idea" of the self that he ascribes to his tribe and individuals.[7] Later in the essay, for instance, Momaday uses the story of the Arrowmaker (section 13 in *The Way to Rainy Mountain*) to demonstrate this unifying dynamic, for the story shows that identity, and indeed survival itself, often depends upon the ability to determine the boundaries of one's own linguistic sphere. In this now famous story, an arrowmaker sees between the folds of his tipi a figure, perhaps an enemy, standing outside, and in this moment of potential danger places his fate in linguistic boundaries. After saying to his wife, "Let us talk easily, as of ordinary things," the arrowmaker then says, "I know that you are there on the outside, for I can feel your eyes upon me. If you are Kiowa, you will understand what I am saying, and you will speak your name" (Momaday 1969, 46). The enemy remains silent, and the arrowmaker sends an arrow through his heart.

For Momaday, this story is significant because it emphasizes the degree to which our conception of ourselves and others is profoundly linked to language—specifically, being understood within a particular, unified center of common language. This idea is precisely what the arrowmaker comprehends

when, with the help of his wife, he risks everything to determine that crucial
border between the language of their everyday lives and that of the potential
enemy. Momaday writes:

> And of the ominous unknown he asks only the utterance of a name, only the
> most nominal sign that he is understood, that his words are returned to him
> on the sheer edge of meaning. But there is no answer, and the arrowmaker
> knows at once what he has not known before; that his enemy is, and that he
> has gained an advantage over him. (Momaday 1981, 172)

The husband and wife's personal language—powerful in its ordinariness—
provides the means by which the arrowmaker can come to terms with the
outside world and thus effectively deal with it. Indeed, establishing this sense
of self and its relationship to outside elements works at every level of the book:
it is the story of The Way to Rainy Mountain, the Kiowa people (or any people),
the arrowmaker, and Momaday himself. Rather than being "monologic,"
then, Momaday is showing the power and indeed the necessity of creating
or positing a "unitary language" in which a group, family, or individual in
internal dialogue uses a particular language at a particular time to establish a
place for communication. It is worth returning here to Bakhtin's construct: "A
unitary language is not something given [dan] but is always in essence posited
[zadan]—and at every moment of its linguistic life it is opposed to the realities of heteroglossia" (Bakhtin 1981, 270). Here, the arrowmaker offers the
everyday language of his tribe to the unknown person as a kind of invitation
to demonstrate that he is part of that circle. It becomes, in short, a strategy
that creates both strength and resistance.

Just as the arrowmaker determines his relationship to the outside observer, so does The Way to Rainy Mountain explore the relationships among
the different languages—the personal, the historical, and the oral. More often
than not, far from being "monologic," the relationship of the narrator's own
stories (the "immediate," personal reflections) to the other two languages,
especially the myths, is tenuous, even tangential. For example, section 16
provides three buffalo stories: the first a wondrous story about the coming
of a buffalo with steel horns, the second a historical account about a pitiful

attempt to reenact the buffalo hunt, and the third Momaday's reflections on a childhood encounter with a mother buffalo near her calf at a park in Oklahoma. In this third section, Momaday writes:

> Then she came at us, and we turned and ran as fast as we could. She gave up after a short run, and I think we had not been in any real danger. But the spring morning was deep and beautiful and our hearts were beating fast and we knew just what it was to be alive. (Momaday 1969, 55)

Although the oral tradition seems part of a distant, magical past, Momaday makes a connection, however tangential, by affirming the fear and wonder inspired by an animal that figures so prominently in his tribe's history and identity. Like the reenactment of the buffalo chase, which also figures into the tripartite relationship, this gesture of affirmation is tenuous and personal; but it is also honest, hence powerful in its understanding of being alive within a tradition. Rather than absorbing the other two languages into his own, Momaday is exploring the relationship among these three different languages, showing how his own personal voice is, in this case at least, quite distant from the older tradition.

Also crucial to this discursive interaction is Momaday's complex relationship to ethnology. He indicates that although this field of study may have different ideas about meaning and truth than the oral tradition, he will not monologically exclude or demonize ethnology. In fact, he shows that the language of science is also useful to him, a twentieth-century indigenous writer, in pulling together a sense of his relationship to the migration story of the Kiowa people. In addition to the oral tradition (which Momaday gained through interviews with the help of his father), he presents, values, and dialogically engages the language of a quite different, scientific tradition. Krupat, however, in his critique of Momaday's work, argues that Momaday's own language usurps that of ethnology because he changes and paraphrases James Mooney's *Calendar History of the Kiowa Indians* (1895–1896) and George Catlin's *Letters and Notes on the Manners, Customs, and Conditions of North American Indians* (1844). Krupat suggests that first, Momaday should have been more forthright in his use of these anthropological texts, and that second, in revising these texts Momaday is imposing his own monologic voice onto these sources. In fairness, it is important to point out that Momaday has never made any secret of using either Mooney or Catlin, citing both later on in the text itself (which Krupat acknowledges in a footnote). More significantly, because ethnology is a field in its own right, with its own unitary rules and boundaries, and because Momaday is interested in the relationships among different languages (as with the arrowmaker and the enemy), he leaves the language of ethnology more or less intact, designating those sections "historical," setting them off with a different type face, and maintaining (with minor revisions) their scientific, factual tone. (Dates appear only in these sections, for example.) I would argue that instead of employing subterfuge or deceptively monologic writing, Momaday uses the ethnographic sources in a way consistent with the philosophical project of the book—namely, the creation, value, and exploration of the relationships among more or less sovereign, interdependent discursive groups.

The story that both Momaday and Deloria tell to explain how these groups began—from a fragmented people to a unified group—demonstrates why Momaday began *The Way to Rainy Mountain* with a sense of personal alienation from the landscape, for section 1 is the initial stage in his own journey toward establishing a relationship to his tribal past.[8] Momaday writes:

> I remember coming out upon the northern Great Plains in the late spring. There were meadows of blue and yellow wildflowers on the slopes, and I could see the still, sunlit plain below, reaching away out of sight. At first there was no discrimination in the eye, nothing but the land itself, whole and impenetrable. But then the smallest things begin to stand out of the depths—herds and rivers and groves—and each of these has perfect being in terms of distance and silence and of age. (Momaday 1969, 17)

The general narrative in *The Way to Rainy Mountain*, "the coming out" for the narrator, is a working out of his relationship to the landscape of his past that may in fact be profoundly "impenetrable" as he starts his personal journey—for he starts off alone, separated from the Kiowa stories. As with the

Kiowa themselves, the narrator must discover a means to imagine himself as a unified idea. Each step—the coming out, the going on, and the closing in—represents stages not only in the life of the Kiowa people, but also in the narrator as he further defines himself in relation to the past. (Indeed, a stronger critique of Momaday's project would point out that, in spite of his uses of multiple languages and unconventional format, ultimately the work is figuring, and perhaps subsumed into, the larger form of classic tragedy.)

Yet Krupat argues that it is especially evident in section 1 that Momaday demonstrates his commitment to hegemonic monologue, and that as a consequence, Momaday shows that he lacks the sensibilities of an indigenous writer (or an indigenous writer named Silko). Krupat writes, "I have seen no Native American autobiography that ever took such aloneness-with-the-landscape as definitive or instrumental in the shaping of a world view of the personal self" (Krupat 1989, 179). In fact, Krupat goes on to say that section 1 of the book suggests a perspective more "Western than Native American," and displays notions that are "quite foreign to indigenous conceptions" of the world. Furthermore, Momaday's use of the concept of "penetrating" the land, Krupat writes, is the province of "a fairly typical American (not Native American) male" (Krupat 1989, 179).

However, such judgments about Momaday's "authenticity" as an indigenous writer, based on the first section, take Momaday's observations out of narrative context, ignoring the general narrative and philosophical approach of the book. Furthermore, Krupat's critique highlights the weakness of an approach that creates a binary opposition between the Bakhtinian concepts of monologism and dialogism, placing one in hierarchical contradistinction to the other, suggesting that dialogism has a larger claim to "authenticity" than the other. In *Problems of Dostoevsky's Poetics*, Bakhtin emphasizes that the polyphonic novel is neither in opposition to nor a replacement of monologic enterprises. Indeed, monologic perspectives—because they yield shared codes, iteration, and hence clarity—often provide an important source of meaning and value. Bakhtin writes:

> Thus the appearance of the polyphonic novel does not nullify or in any way restrict the further productive development of monologic forms of the novel

> (biographical, historical, the novel of everyday life, the novel epic, etc.), for there will always continue to exist and expand those spheres of existence, of man and nature, which require precisely objectified and finalizing, that is monological, forms of artistic cognition. But again we repeat: *the thinking human consciousness and the dialogic sphere in which this consciousness exists,* in all its depth and specificity, cannot be reached through a monologic artistic approach. (Bakhtin 1984, 271)

Dialogism invalidates neither the usefulness nor the value of different monologic presentations, though it does show that each local group has no particular ownership of universal truth. Different "frames of reference," to use Bakhtin's frequent analogy from physics, have a certain truth value within the structure of their own rules for producing meaning and value—a truth entirely appropriate to the history, traditions, language, and quite possibly the geographic landscape of a people. Each of these frames of reference (personal, tribal, linguistic) may have elements of monoglossia or unity—the repetition of shared language (the Arrowmaker story), ideas (the Tai-me religions), and customs (the Sun Dance) that maximize a unified identity and communication.

Consequently, the use of the terms *monologism* and *dialogism* as measures of Indian authenticity surely misses the way that these concepts interact with each other, and how they are in fact dependent upon one another. When this binary approach is applied to Momaday (or any writer), it demands that we place him in the camp of the dialogic or monologic, but not both at once, even though is quite evident that Momaday is interested in exploring the dynamics of both monoglossia and polyglossia in *The Way to Rainy Mountain*. Used in a different, less polarized way, however, Bakhtinian terminology is useful in showing how individuals or groups create a unitary language—a shared culture—sometimes over hundreds of years, through writing, through the oral tradition, or both. This shared language or center of culture exists always in relation to the forces of fragmentation, dispersal, or, in Bakhtin's term, the "realities of heteroglossia." In precisely this same way, *The Way to Rainy Mountain* enacts a dynamic in which individuals and groups posit their own centers of identity, an approach that places him in a tradition of indigenous letters along with Ortiz, Silko, and Deloria. The discourse of authenticity, with its binary constructions of purity and impurity, in fact parallels the discourse of colonialism, severing as it does the past from the present and the oral from the written. Discarding the roadblock of authenticity, these writers turn to the oral tradition, not only as a source of cultural information, but for interpretive strategies and theories of reading that contribute to the continued health and sovereignty of indigenous centers of culture.

CHAPTER TWO

"Authenticity" and Leslie Marmon Silko's *Ceremony*

I n the brief history of indigenous fiction in America, the novels of authors such as N. Scott Momaday, Leslie Marmon Silko, and James Welch have attained a kind of canonical and even authentic status, in part because they often employ conventional, modernist forms of fiction when writing about contemporary indigenous life. Silko's *Ceremony* is somewhat different, however, because it successfully combines elements from the modernist tradition (for example, stylistic fragmentation through time and psychological flashbacks) with thematic and structural patterns from Pueblo oral traditions. In fact, the novel parallels a tradition of stories that have a similar narrative trajectory: drought (often caused by some inappropriate action), ceremony, and harmony or balance, which exists until the next turn of the wheel. Thus *Ceremony* not only offers an exceptionally rich meditation on Pueblo life but also offers a narrative that resists the destructive, drought-inducing philosophies of colonialism, using both a form and substance derived from Pueblo oral traditions. Nonetheless, indigenous critics such as Jack Forbes and Jana Sequoya Magdaleno question whether *Ceremony* should be considered an authentic indigenous text, because, they argue, the novel finally cannot overcome the restrictions of its ontological form, namely, a work of written fiction whose audience is primarily nonindigenous. For example, because *Ceremony* breaks up oral stories and intersperses them throughout the novel, Magdaleno questions how a text can claim any kind of authenticity when it fragments the traditions it purports to represent and presents them in a discursive space (published writing) that is alien to its original form.

As Kalpana Ram argues, however, perhaps the very concept of authenticity places theoretically untenable restrictions on constructions of indigenous identity, culture, and literature. In an essay on Australian Aboriginal literature, Ram writes that, while the colonialist discourse of authenticity places indigenous cultures in "an ontology of fixed and unchanging meanings," it is precisely the colonial powers that "are simultaneously inflicting unprecedented change on the cultures" (Ram 2000, 359). Combined, the philosophical imperatives of authenticity and the realities of colonialism prevent Aboriginal people from having even the possibility of a cultural or ideological presence in contemporary Australia. Ram writes: "'Authenticity' becomes impossible to obtain under such conditions yet, at the same time, impossible to avoid since it is a state-imposed criteria for group identity" (359–60).

A similar dynamic between authenticity and change exists in America as well, where the concept of an authentic indigenous culture remains a powerful component of the nation's ideology. For example, in his study *Predicaments of Culture*, James Clifford considers how the parameters of authenticity prevented a Boston jury in 1977 from finding that the Mashpee Wampanoags of Massachusetts constituted an indigenous tribe of people (Clifford 1988). Although the trial was ostensibly about legal definitions of a tribe, Clifford argues that the trial was also an ideological struggle between the commonly accepted and frequently reproduced image of authentic Indians as "proud, beautiful, and 'vanishing,'" and the image of a contemporary tribal people forced by Europeans and Americans to reinvent their culture. Clifford argues that because "authentic Indian culture" refers to a previous age in American history, the jury was unable to understand that the Mashpee, to survive a terrible history of colonialism, were forced to reinvent their individual and cultural identities several times over (a reinvention that Frances Fitzgerald argues is fundamental to Protestant America).[1] Clifford tells us that the history of the Mashpee "is a long relational struggle to maintain and re-create identities that began when an English-speaking Indian traveler, Squanto, greeted the Pilgrims at Plymouth"; indeed, the "struggle was still going on three-and-a-half centuries later in a Boston Federal Court" (339). What makes the Boston jury's decision particularly ironic is that while the Pilgrims—America's mythical forebears—have remained a constant (even if somewhat erroneous) symbol of religious freedom throughout America's changing history, the Pilgrims survived only at the expense of the freedom of other peoples, including the Wampanoags, who were removed from the landscape by death or by being sold into slavery, who were erased from history, and whose ancestors were legally removed from consideration as an indigenous tribe.

Ram also emphasizes that authenticity is neither fixed nor natural, for its relation to its defining opposite, the inauthentic, is an uneasy construction, logically uncertain and historically determined.[2] Citing Jacques Derrida's deconstruction of the metaphysics of presence, Ram writes that the concept of authenticity is a "variant of the discredited metaphysics" of truth as essential, present, and understandable. Ram offers an alternative reading of this opposition, arguing that neither term in putative opposition finally offers the fullness of meaning one might hope or imagine, for both sides contain the traces of the other and render any verdict about authenticity or inauthenticity ultimately ambiguous. For instance, even prior to contact with Europeans, indigenous communities changed—sometimes dramatically—as a result of both their relationship to a changing environment and their relations with other tribal groups through cultural exchange and sometimes warfare. As Larry Shiner tells us: "The notion that 'traditional societies' are or were self-contained and unchanging ('without history' in Hegel's terms) is simply false, as recent work on African, Pacific, and Native American history has shown" (Shiner 1994, 228).[3] Similarly, Charles Lindholm writes that the "romantic anthropological quest to experience the 'truth' of exotic peoples" has consequences: the "most serious" is "that the search for a genuine culture has encouraged a reification of the 'primitive' as a monolithic entity, an essential-izing of others, and a foolish refusal to accept the actual mobility and fluidity of the social world" (Lindholm 2002, 334). The very desire to locate a kind of truth in the opposition between authenticity and inauthenticity guarantees its own failure, for the terms themselves do not provide any positive ground, only their differences (or *différances*). As Jonathan Culler writes of Derrida's investigation of language: "A scrupulous theory must shift back and forth between these perspectives, of event and structure or *langue* and *parole*, which never lead to synthesis. Each perspective shows the error of the other in an irresolvable alternation or aporia" (Culler 1982, 96).

Although authenticity, like "race," is theoretically elusive, it nonetheless has tremendous resonance in the American discourse of Indianness, in both the policies that profoundly affect the lives of indigenous peoples, and also the resistance to these policies by indigenous peoples. Ram suggests that we might use as a guide Gayatri Spivak's well-known concept of "strategic essentialism," a highly self-conscious position that utilizes the discourse of essentialism/authenticity to respond to destructive public policies—what we might call "strategic authenticity." As a practical matter, however, such an approach is as dangerous as it is unavoidable, for sometimes those using strategic approaches forget that the strategy is not the game. Spivak herself says she no longer uses the term, because it has become a "union card" for essentialist positions that are not especially strategic—in other words, that forget the theoretical difficulties and thus the potentially dangerous conse-quences of assigning essentialist identities (Spivak 1993, 35). Nonetheless, for indigenous peoples struggling for the recognition of individual and tribal justice, strategic authenticity or essentialism provides a theoretical ground for confronting colonial discourse on its own terms—that is, terms that are comprehensible within a colonialist ideology and that may, therefore, have some effect on existing social conditions. Especially in the discourse of Fed-eral Indian Law, strategic authenticity helps to assert certain prerogatives for indigenous peoples under the umbrella of the federal "trust status," but these prerogatives are available only if the tribes and members accept the federal guidelines for authenticity (and indeed implicitly accept the United States' ultimate authority for all matters pertaining to indigenous peoples).

For example, the Indian Arts and Crafts Act (Public Law 101–644, 1990, a revision of a similar act from 1935) intercedes in the question of "authentic" Indian identity with the intent to prevent non-Indian craftsmen and sellers from representing themselves and their goods as "true" or "real."[4] The federal standard for authenticity is enrollment in a federally recognized tribe, a standard that normally depends upon some degree of blood quantum originally determined by racially constructed rolls collected at the turn of the nineteenth century. According to the Federal Register, the Arts and Crafts Board distributed a draft of the act "to interested parties, including every Federally-recognized Indian tribe," from which the board received thirty-nine responses, some positive, some concerned about how to represent their indigenous heritage even though they were not documented members of tribes. For many indigenous artisans—from those who earn a modest living by traveling to indigenous conferences and powwows, to those who have high visibility and potential for large profits in galleries such as those of Santa Fe, New Mexico—the Arts and Crafts Act constructs a form of authenticity through federal recognition that distinguishes artisans' works as exceptional because of their origin in a racial identity. As a positive consequence, the Arts and Crafts Act likely helps their economic enterprises through the twin forces of supply and demand, and quite possibly helps support and maintain certain indigenous artistic practices. Because this form of authenticity is primarily dependent upon enrollment in a federally recognized tribe (there is a provision in the act for a tribe to include non-member artisans), the Arts and Craft Act further supports the domestic dependent (semi-sovereign) status of Indian nations in their ability to determine their own membership. Furthermore, as Elizabeth Burns Coleman points out, discarding the concept of authenticity altogether would also theoretically eliminate indigenous claims to cultural property rights. She writes that "as these claims also contain arguments for collective ownership of cultural property beyond those provided by Western legislative systems, the denial of authenticity may be used to undermine demands for the reconsideration of intellectual and cultural property rights" (Coleman 2001, 387).[5]

While the Indian Arts and Crafts Act is successful in some ways in helping indigenous artists and craftsmen, it also demonstrates, in a particularly public way, the power of the federal government to regulate all aspects of indigenous life, including what indigenous people may consider "real" or "authentic." The Arts and Crafts Act further shows that strategies of authenticity carry enormous risks, especially when the strategy takes on the imprimatur of natural truth. Although the Arts and Crafts Act appears to defer to semi-sovereign American Indian tribes to determine indigenous identity, the tribes themselves are ultimately restricted by the federal government as to whom they may include as tribal members. In *The Rights of Indians and Tribes*, Stephen Pevar writes: "To be considered an Indian for federal purposes, an individual must have Indian blood. A non-Indian who is adopted into an Indian tribe is not an Indian under federal law" (Pevar 1992, 13). Depending on blood as a sign of genetic authenticity, the federal government has made the strategy into a game—a game whose rules are constructed in the discredited science of blood quantum. In an essay on nineteenth-century science and blood quantum, David Beaulieu writes that blood is historically a corrupt sign for authentic identity, for the science of determining "mixed bloods" and "full bloods" often depended on the unpredictable methodology of appearances (someone "looked full-blooded," for instance), or dubious methods such as the skin scratch test, where blood quantum was determined by the color of an indigenous person's skin after it was scratched (Beaulieu 1984). For the federal government, assigning identity based upon spurious fractions of "Indian blood" offered the illusion of truth and authenticity in the language of science and mathematics, thus framing indigenous peoples as a problem with a resolution, rather than as complex societies with whom one should have a just and equitable political relationship.

■ *Ceremony:* **A Contest of Narratives**

As a novel about returning war veterans, Silko's *Ceremony* demonstrates both the necessity and the danger of constructing strategic identities against an enemy; at the same time, as a novel of resistance, *Ceremony* rejects essentialized, authentic, and thus unchanging constructions of indigenous identity based on such oppositions. Consonant with the tribe's longstanding oral traditions, the novel insists that an oppositional psychology of warfare is always temporary and strategic, existing only as long as the duration of the war. Upon returning home, these veterans must undergo ceremonies so that they move away from oppositions toward more dialogic relationships within a family, in a community, with the natural world and the world of spirits. For returning war veterans from both long-ago wars and from contemporary wars, the book tells us:

> They had things
> they must do
> otherwise
> K'oo'ko would haunt their dreams
> with her great fangs and
> everything would be endangered. (Silko 1977, 37)

The Pueblo peoples have long theorized about the transitions from war to peace, having engaged in conflict with tribes in the area prior to conflict with Europeans, and then later having defended themselves against the Spanish and then the Americans. Silko's novel shows that the stark logic of warfare— the binary opposition par excellence—demands that participants clearly determine the identity of people on both sides of the opposition, denying their commonalities of appearances, histories, and even their common humanity. Only by creating this uncomplicated opposition will soldiers be able to demonize or dehumanize the enemy so that killing becomes justifiable, and thus possible. Although returning Pueblo war veterans traditionally undergo ceremonies to turn their thoughts from a mindset of war (opposition) to a mindset of peace (dialogue), many of the veterans from World War II abjure the traditions of the community: their temporary successes in American culture cause them to devalue their homelands in relation to the material wealth of Americans. As the dangerous war veteran Emo says, "us Indians deserve something better than this goddamn dried-up country around here" (Silko 1977, 55). Rather than resist colonial narratives that are destructive to indigenous peoples, the returning war veterans continue to rehearse war stories that placed them in opposition to the Japanese and to their own people—stories that, for a time at least, positioned them on the same side with Americans, where they found equality in the second skin of the uniform. Worse, at the conclusion of the war, in the absence of a common enemy, these strategic differences of the uniform were no longer necessary, and the essentialized difference of racism once again prevented them from obtaining any kind of American success.

The growth of this oppositional philosophy, the novel tells us, threatens much more than the health of this indigenous community. Expressing the tremendous anxiety in the 1970s about the potential for global annihilation, and entering a market for a primarily nonindigenous audience, *Ceremony* warns readers that a world embracing a philosophy of opposition will indeed destroy itself, given the enormous nuclear weaponry possessed by countries in conflict with each other. Although Laguna is a small community in New Mexico, this indigenous space is the both the origin of oppositional narratives and also the source of the fuel for a potential nuclear holocaust. From a competition among old-time witches, each attempting to appear more powerful than the others, *Ceremony* describes a particular witch of unknown race or origin who gives compelling form to oppositional discourse—a discourse that eventually becomes a dominant philosophy in American westward expansion, and later the global oppositional stances of the Cold War. Silko writes:

> *They will take this world from ocean to ocean*
> *they will turn on each other*
> *they will destroy each other*
> *Up here*
> *In these hills*
> *they will find the rocks,*
> *rocks with veins of green and yellow and black.*
> *They will lay the final pattern with these rocks*
> *they will lay it across the world*
> *and explode everything.* (Silko 1977, 137)

The novel foreshadows this apocalyptic denouement to the witch's story when Tayo's grandmother, who is old and almost blind, sees the bright flash from the first nuclear test explosion at the Trinity Site in New Mexico (Silko 1977, 245). The book suggests that the world is at a moment in history when it is precisely balanced in its choice between the oppositional narrative of war and the dialogic narrative of peace, and this balance is figured into the character of the protagonist, Tayo. Thus we can read *Ceremony* as a call or even a prayer for the world to move toward dialogue rather than oppositional narrative structures.

As a kind of literary ceremony for returning war veterans, *Ceremony* can perhaps only tell a story of peace; but for many indigenous peoples, a struggle and perhaps even a war continues for social justice, for the return of indigenous lands, and for the freedom to live as sovereign peoples. When Tayo contemplates the enormous land and wealth taken by nonindigenous peoples, Betonie offers him various explanations: that the theft was part of a larger pattern or story, that indigenous people had fought as much as they "could do and still survive," and finally, that ownership is an illusion. Betonie says: "The deeds and papers don't mean anything. It is the people who belong to the mountain" (Silko 1977, 128). Because *Ceremony* thematically moves from war to peace, from opposition to harmony and balance, Betonie's explanations are consistent with the trajectory of the novel. Rather than reinscribing the oppositional and isolating philosophy of war that nearly destroys Tayo, the novel instead opens up its internal stories and traditions to both indigenous and nonindigenous readers, creating a dialogue that makes room for mixed-blood identity, cultural exchange, and the possibility of peace. In the discourse of warfare, such dialogue is unthinkable, even treasonous; but in the discourse of peace, shared discourse among groups is essential. Thus Betonie affirms what Tayo believes later, that regardless of race, "human beings were one clan again, united by the fate the destroyers planned for all of them" (246). Betonie's long-ago grandmother likewise affirms the importance of uniting all races against witchery: "We must have power from everywhere. Even the power we can get from the whites" (150).

Despite Betonie's belief in an abiding resistance rather than an overt oppositional stance toward colonialism, some indigenous critics find this literary approach to be inadequate to the survival of indigenous communities. For example, in his essay "Colonialism and Native American Literature,"

Jack Forbes argues that the novels we usually associate with indigenous literatures, in particular *Ceremony* and *House Made of Dawn*, offer little to change harmful social conditions; instead, these works address and satisfy a predominantly nonindigenous readership, using "modern-day chants and lots of symbolic beads and feathers" (Forbes 1987, 22). Indeed, Forbes writes that "Native literature today must be regarded as a colonized and submerged literature" because it inadequately expresses the contemporary indigenous concerns and desires that are "internal to the culture" (19, 22). This "authentic 'core'" of indigenous writing, Forbes tells us, is not found in contemporary fiction but in tribal newspapers, journals, small presses, and even in oral stories translated by anthropologists. While *Ceremony* insists on a dialogic communication among various cultural groups, Forbes counters that indigenous writers should instead write specifically for indigenous communities, both rural and urban, which have their own culture, language, history, and therefore their own particular social and political concerns. Forbes writes: "This definition becomes clearer if we substitute 'Navaho Literature' for Native American. Navajo literature is that literature created by people of Navajo identity and/or culture primarily for other Navajos" (19).

While Forbes acknowledges "the fine creative ability of Leslie Silko" and her accurate depiction of problems in American Indian life—"race mixture, alienation, alcoholism, and disruptive cultural change"—he faults the novel because it falls short in the "remedies" it prescribes for these ills (Forbes 1987, 22). For example, Forbes argues that the "shamanistic" healing of the protagonist at the close of the novel is insufficient to solve real-world problems resulting from a "total disruption of Indian cultures by conquest and colonialism" (22). Forbes writes:

> Silko's ending for *Ceremony* is acceptable within the context of her approach, but what if she were to have envisioned a more political conclusion? What if she were to have identified the colonial network surrounding her people and developed a solution which challenged that network? (Forbes 1987, 22)

By making the argument that indigenous literature should support the political aims of indigenous peoples, Forbes offers a crucial reminder that many indigenous readers will have little patience for literary works or reading theories that do not offer some strategic ground upon which to confront oppressive policies and ideologies. Forbes's critique is especially compelling because many indigenous readers have become disillusioned with the unfulfilled promises of the federal "trust relationship" for adequate opportunity, education, and health care in both urban and reservation communities.

Yet Forbes's vision of an "authentic 'core'" of indigenous literature, like the concept of authenticity itself, is once again inseparable from inauthentic elements outside the metaphoric "core." In his conception of a cultural core, Forbes does not employ the usual boundaries of separation—geography, language, culture, or "race." Instead, likening tribal communities to countries with longstanding traditions, such as France, Forbes suggests that literature from any culture has an intended audience of those who live within that culture. Thus Forbes identifies as authentic indigenous literature those forms of writing that appear frequently within indigenous communities from indigenous-controlled means of publication, or from edited and transcribed collections of older indigenous oral stories. Yet in each case, the "core" examples of indigenous literature are always inextricably connected to the "non-core" American culture. For instance, while tribal newspapers have a larger circulation in indigenous communities than novels, these newspapers frequently address outside audiences, not just in news articles but also in advertisements, in letters to the editors, and especially in editorial opinions. As editor of *Indian Country Today*, Tim Giago's long-running resistance to the use of American Indian mascots for sports teams is just one example of an indigenous writer attempting to engage a nonindigenous audience through journalism. Likewise, translated collections of indigenous oral stories inevitably take on contentious issues of linguistic and cultural translation through nonindigenous editors. Forbes cites John G. Neihardt's *Black Elk Speaks* (1932) as a work that makes a "useful contribution," but Clyde Holler demonstrates that Neihardt, in an apparent attempt to re-create Black Elk's authentic Indian past, "which the white man has not yet been able to influence or corrupt," omits any references to Black Elk's work as a Catholic catechist for the latter half of his life. (Holler 1984). Finally, Forbes does not address the highly contentious question of who might constitute an indigenous audience (who is, or is not indigenous), particularly in urban settings. Nonetheless, Forbes's essay is an important reminder that a fundamental goal for resistant indigenous literatures is to assert the existence of indigenous peoples as nations of the world, even in the construction of its literatures.

Jana Sequoya Magdaleno echoes Forbes's critique of *Ceremony*, arguing that the novel not only provides for an accessible and mostly guiltless experience of literary tourism for nonindigenous readers, but also offers examples of decontextualized, fragmented oral traditions as evidence of its own authenticity. Unlike Forbes, however, Magdaleno both historicizes and critiques the concept of authenticity as it is frequently applied to indigenous peoples and their literatures. Drawing from Vine Deloria Jr., Magdaleno divides contemporary indigenous identity in America into two general categories—tribal, suggesting a legal or political affiliation with a tribe; and ethnic, reflecting the complex diaspora of indigenous experience. Of the two, Magdaleno observes that enrollment in a tribe—almost always based on "blood quantum"—generally connotes a more authentic identity among both indigenous and nonindigenous peoples, although ironically and "until quite recently the tribal roll was a preeminent sign of a colonialized identity" (Magdaleno 2000, 280). In contrast, ethnic identities, which do not fall within the "official narratives of nationhood (be they tribal or federal)," remain excluded from claims to indigenous identity, thus denying complex stories of identity that emerge in the difference between tribal and federal requirements for legitimacy (280). Although Magdaleno does not offer specific examples, we know anecdotally from family stories that many indigenous peoples remain outside the official constructs of identity because their ancestors refused to participate in nineteenth-century land allotment programs, or because their families moved to areas away from other forms of federal interference, sometimes as far away as Mexico or Canada. Rather than fall into these official narratives, Magdaleno argues, indigenous writers "must be particularly attentive to the multiple relationships out of and into which we write," because unlike the wide range of possible identities for European Americans, authentic indigenous identities in America remain severely constrained.

Because *Ceremony* creates a liminal narrative space within traditional Pueblo oral traditions for the diasporic condition of the protagonist, Tayo,

Silko's novel appears to coincide with Magdaleno's critique of binary structure of indigenous identity. But Magdaleno offers one other important consideration: the danger of using sacred oral traditions for purposes beyond the boundaries of indigenous control. Specifically, while critics often cite the use of Pueblo oral traditions in the novel as a sign of its "authenticity," Magdaleno points out that the very means by which such authenticity is achieved betrays the community's desire to keep these stories within a sacred, noncommercialized context. In other words, claims for authenticity in indigenous texts through the use of tribal secrets create a logical impasse: the more accurately a novel represents sacred aspects of an indigenous community, the more it invades the community's private relationship to these sacred traditions. Thus, Magdaleno concludes that *Ceremony* and N. Scott Momaday's *House Made of Dawn* do not accrue authenticity because they include stories from indigenous traditions; on the contrary, these works reflect the desires of a much different cultural and scientific tradition, namely, the "canonical esthetics of the privileged imagination mediated by ethnographic material" (Magdaleno 2000, 286). Indeed, because Momaday and Silko use sacred story fragments from the "already alienated context of anthropological archives," Magdaleno argues that their projects constitute "textual necrophilia" (292), suggesting that these works confirm, rather than resist, the colonial discourse of the dying or vanishing Indian.[6]

Furthermore, Magdaleno argues, just as *Ceremony* confirms its own status as an authentic indigenous text, so too does the novel confer "cultural authenticity to the racially hybrid position" in the figure of Tayo (Magdaleno 2000, 292). While this liminal figure counters the image of authentic Indians in such forms as sports mascots or the discredited science of blood quantum, Magdaleno cautions that such a figure of "revival and invention" offers an all-too-comfortable vehicle for literary tourism for nonindigenous readers, affording the "disaffected reader with an accessible (albeit male-gendered) structure of identification," particularly readers who envision indigenous peoples as the stereotypical spiritual healer for America (291). In addition, Magdaleno warns that as a kind of ideal—as a figuration of Hegelian synthesis between colonizer and colonized—this mixed-blood figure (not actual people) should be taken "with a grain of salt," a statement I interpret to mean that the mixed blood is not a figure of higher-order synthesis (along with the teleological implication), but is instead a mediator and a sign of difference. And because it is not an ideal (that is, it should not be read as such), the figure of the mixed blood is an empty sign that readers and academics frequently invest with considerable emotion, meaning, and accessibility. Thus Magdaleno refers to the mysterious word "croatoan" carved in a tree at the abandoned Roanoke colony as the "first move toward such literature" because it signifies only an absence of knowledge with some perception or coloration of Indianness, yet has induced an enormous amount of speculation about its meaning (292). In the terminology of deconstruction, then, the figure of the mixed blood is not a presence, but an aporia, an irresolvable back-and-forth movement between sign and signified, between indigenous and nonindigenous structures of identification, which are themselves constantly changing.

Magdaleno's claim that *Ceremony* ascribes "authenticity to the racially hybrid position" is similar to Paula Gunn Allen's well-known earlier assessment that the novel is "a plea for inclusion by a writer who felt excluded and compelled to depict the potential importance of breeds to Laguna survival" (Allen 1990, 383). Certainly, *Ceremony* does offer the possibility of a kind of stable, liminal, yet isolated position in the characters of Night Swan and Betonie. Night Swan, for instance, although not a trickster in the traditional sense of Pueblo *koshari*, has important trickster qualities, for she lives on the fringes of the indigenous community in a room above the local bar, and she also serves as an uncomfortable reminder to the community of the precarious, fragile nature of their conventional rules and obligations. Likewise, Betonie lives in an isolated hogan apart from both indigenous communities and the city of Gallup, where he performs curative ceremonies for those willing to accept the changes he makes to traditional medicines. Like his helper Shush, a boy who grew up with bears and now lives in the difference between animals and man, Betonie exists in the borderlands between cultures. Thus he is not circumscribed by tradition and convention, and as a consequence, he is more able (in the spirit of the novel) to know how to change traditional medicines so that they are effective in a radically changing world. In fact, Betonie himself suggests that those people who advocate for a kind of "authenticity" in untouched or unchanged ceremonialism (nativism) do not understand that everything changes over time to some extent, "if only the aging of the yellow gourd rattle or the shrinking of the skin around the eagle's claw" (Silko 1977, 126). He further tells Tayo that despite warnings by some purists, ceremonies too must change if they are to live: "things which don't shift and grow are dead things" (126). In this context, authenticity in a past cultural purity itself becomes a kind of necrophilia, similar to how Emo wishes to relive his past glories in the war when he plays with the teeth taken from enemy soldiers.

While *Ceremony* shows the "racially hybrid position" of Night Swan and Betonie to be crucial to Tayo's narrative of healing, the novel also shows this liminal position for other characters to be aporetic, that is, a temporary site of difference between indigenous and nonindigenous structures of identification. As Kimberly Blaeser observes, the mixed-blood protagonist in most contemporary indigenous fiction (unlike the major figures in Gerald Vizenor's fiction, for example) ultimately succeeds when he or she can escape from the unstructured and thus incomprehensible margins of existence and return to a "physical center, sometimes to a spiritual, ancestral, or community center" (Blaeser 1996, 158). Thus for most characters in *Ceremony*, the indeterminate hybrid space is uninhabitable, treacherous, even fatal. For example, Tayo denies the possibility of his own presence while in a military hospital as he makes his transition from the United States Army to his Laguna home, believing that he is invisible—"white smoke" that has "no consciousness of itself" (Silko 1977, 14). Later, Betonie tells him that, as a nonentity in the hospital, he "might as well go down there [to Gallup], with the rest of them, sleeping in the mud, vomiting cheap wine, rolling over women" (123). In contrast to the peaceful isolation of Night Swan and Betonie, the hybrid positions for characters such as Helen Jean, Laura, Emo, and the impoverished indigenous people living on the fringes of Gallup remain in a nightmare of fragmentation. Each of these characters desires to pass through this space of difference as quickly as possible—some wishing to move on to American society and others wishing to return home. Yet, for reasons sometimes beyond their control or understanding, they find the doors to American society and even to their homes closed and locked. Tayo, for instance, knows that he must accept Betonie's help because the community "didn't want him at Laguna the way he was" (118).

In *Ceremony*, the hybrid or mixed-blood position is thus neither authenticated nor denied by the novel; rather, this liminal position is a source of both creative and destructive power, characteristics of almost all traditional indigenous trickster figures. As Josiah says, "Nothing was all good or all bad either; it all depended" (Silko 1997, 11). Moreover, *Ceremony* critiques the very oppositions upon which the discourse of authenticity depends: real/unreal, true/false, pure/impure, past/present, orality/writing. In each of these cases, *Ceremony* deconstructs the apparent naturalness of these oppositions, disclosing how the promise of clarity and understanding actually masks the impossibility of the project. For example, readers might attempt to locate an authentic Laguna culture in the figure of the medicine man Ku'oosh or in the traditional space of the kiva, but neither man nor sacred space can ever escape traces of the "inauthentic." Such traces include Ku'oosh's use of English when he prays, or the use of folding chairs in the kiva with, ironically, a church's name ("St. Joseph Mission") stenciled on them. But these traces do not invalidate the cultural vitality of either the healer or the sacred space; on the contrary, the novel shows that the strength of a tradition is its ability to adjust to sometimes devastating circumstances while maintaining the integrity of its most fundamental narratives. Regardless of how far back in time one might go to make a claim for an authentic Laguna culture, traces of the inauthentic will always remain in some form, for authenticity or cultural purity is necessarily deferred. *Ceremony* itself demonstrates this aporia through the series of stories—some quite old—that are both similar and different in their predecessors. Claims for cultural authenticity at any point along the continuum of stories—Reed Woman and Corn Woman, Fly and Hummingbird, Gambler stories, and even Tayo's story—are always mitigated by the changing nature of the oral tradition. Any attempt to locate the "authentic" at any point in the past always defers to yet another older story from the tradition.

Magdaleno is undoubtedly correct that some readers will interpret the mere appearance of sacred story fragments in *Ceremony* as a sign of "authenticity"; but it is also true that any number of images of, or concepts about, indigenous peoples have a similar synecdochic function in reductive readings that substitute the sign for the system. Forrest Carter's *Education of Little Tree*, for example, a book frequently taught in secondary schools as an example of

American Indian literature, appears to many readers as an "authentic" text because it contains certain signs or markers of Indianness—among others, the appearance of wise elders, the boarding-school experience, the oral tradition, a love of the environment, and a nature philosophy the novel calls "The Cherokee Way." About *Little Tree*, Werner Sollers comments:

> Such markers are of course all the more easily faked if the primary interest in reading ethnic texts is to find in them the very sign of authenticity that good writers can simulate so well. In fact, one could go a step further and say that the ideal text to study for the group-by-group approach would be the ones that were faked by outsiders but were believed to be insiders, because they are likely to contain the richest agglomeration of those signs that are taken to establish ethnic verisimilitude. (Sollers 1996, 154–55)

Although "outsiders" may interpret these signs as reflections of indigenous experiences, the markers for Indianness in *Little Tree* only reflect a canon of images acceptable to American readers, and actually offer very little about the changing, complex histories and philosophies of the Cherokee people. In fact, Shari M. Huhndorf argues that rather than offering insight into Cherokee beliefs, the novel's Darwinist concept of "The Way" has the effect of placing indigenous people comfortably within the national narrative of the triumphant settlers and the Vanishing Indian. She writes: "Not only does the story imply that Natives will 'naturally' succumb as society progresses, it implies that they accept this fate without question" (Huhndorf 2001, 155). In *Little Tree*, as in many popular depictions of indigenous people in movies and television, the signs have accumulated such ideological weight that for many readers, they are sufficient for fiction (or other representations) to pass as authentically indigenous, and worse, become part of a national discourse that actually contributes to the belief that indigenous people must inevitably pass away.

Perhaps part of the reason these signs are taken for wonders, to use Homi Bhabha's phrase, is that they sometimes do, in fact, have a place within indigenous communities and some indigenous literatures, although not necessarily as markers of authenticity. Rather, those aspects readers normally associate with indigenous peoples—for instance, the elders, language, the environment, the earth, and the oral tradition—are only part of a changing and irreducibly complex system of relationships within indigenous communities. Certain works of fiction such as Ray Young Bear's *Black Eagle Child*, Louise Erdrich's *Love Medicine*, and Silko's *Ceremony* intimate such an intricate connection between the part and the whole, incorporating these ideologically laden elements into systems of historical, cultural, and familial relationships, suggesting (but not necessarily representing) a sense of a communal and variable indigenous life. In *Ceremony*, for instance, the elders are not a unified sign standing for traditional wisdom; rather, the elders Ku'oosh, Josiah, Betonie, and Descheeny have varying, sometimes quite different perspectives on the proper approach to changing ceremonialism and thus Tayo's healing. The environment, too, in *Ceremony* is not an easily comprehensible sign evoking our reverence, but is instead comprised of differing ecosystems that vary from the extremely dry climate of New Mexico to the extremely rainy climate in the jungles of the Philippines, each offering the potential for great good or great harm. Similarly, while a reverence for the earth may reflect its importance as the origins of a people or the source of life, the earth also has the potential for unimaginable destruction in its swirling patterns of uranium ore.

In this same way, the oral stories interspersed throughout the novel do not constitute, as Magdaleno claims, a unified, readable sign standing for authenticity. Rather, the narratives in *Ceremony* become living entities as they are told, and most importantly as they are believed, by Tayo. Furthermore, these narratives are especially powerful because they contain philosophies that can either bring healing or balance to the community, or result in warfare, violence, and destruction. These two narratives are part of the larger metanarrative of this indigenous community that follows a cyclical plot, beginning with a drought (narratives of destruction), moving through a ceremony (narratives of healing, the novel itself), and finally ending with a return to a temporary balance or harmony. Just as with the older oral stories interspersed throughout the novel, *Ceremony* itself begins in a drought, both in the landscape of the community and in the spiritual malaise of the protagonist, Tayo. For the most part, these droughts result from a disruption of the delicate balance of traditional and sacred spaces—for instance, the story of Corn Woman and

Reed Woman, the story about the Ck'o'yo medicine man, and Tayo's story. In the story of the Corn Woman and Reed Woman, the balance between their two roles—food and water—becomes disrupted when Corn Woman complains that she must work all day, causing Reed Woman to leave. In the story of the Ck'o'yo medicine man, two brothers neglect their duty to care for the mother corn altar when they pursue the illusion of Ck'o'yo's magic. In the novel itself, Tayo curses the torrential rains in the Philippines that contribute to his cousin Rocky's death, forgetting that his curses might affect the crucial environmental balance between the Philippines and his Laguna home, where prayers and ceremonies often ask for rain. Tayo forgets, too, the important lesson from Josiah that everything has its place, that nothing, even jungle rain, "was all good or all bad"—"that it all depended" (Silko 1977, 11). Following the introduction of droughts in the narrative, both the novel itself and the various oral stories within the novel demonstrate the lengthy and sometimes arduous steps required for a ceremony to cure the drought: fly and hummingbird must journey underground to find tobacco, and Tayo, among other tasks, must locate and bring back Josiah's spotted cattle from the fenced-in lands of white ranchers.

As a mixed blood brought up in a predominantly Christian household, Tayo has a marginal relationship to the traditions of the indigenous community, and yet so much depends upon his ability not only to understand the traditions of the community but also to inscribe or "author" the story of his life into the community metanarrative of drought, ceremony, and balance. Thus the community's relationship to Tayo is perhaps an example of what the anthropologist Charles Lindholm calls "authoritative worldviews" that "provided human beings with the legitimization of their daily orientation to action" (Lindholm 2002, 331). Tayo's task is especially difficult because the competing American narratives of progress, success, and failure call to him or interpellate him from powerful and compelling voices—his aunt, who raised him; his cousin Rocky, whom he loves; and his fellow war veterans, who goad him into acts of violence. These nonindigenous narratives are compelling too, because for a time, at least, Tayo and the other veterans did in fact experience the rewards of success when they wore American uniforms: sex, money, and, most important, equality. Such narratives of success, however, necessarily include a philosophical insistence on ranking people and nature hierarchically—by occupation, religion, culture, "race"—reinscribing vertical power structures and creating worlds of imbalance that lead to drought. If these narratives supersede the narratives of the indigenous community, they would then threaten the community's philosophical and cultural existence; as the novel tells us in its opening pages, "You don't have anything if you don't have the stories" (Silko 1977, 2). The elders in the community understand the stakes of narrative encroachment: they know that K'oo'ko may haunt the dreams of the war veterans and that "everything would be endangered" (2). Consequently, they inform Robert that if Tayo does not find his way back to the ways of the community, he risks being sent away (106). Whether his fellow war veterans are aware of it or not, the destructive narratives of death and self-loathing have become their lived realities and thus have the potential to become the lived realities of this community.

The oral stories in *Ceremony*, then, remind us that ideological narratives involving progress and civilization often have powerful effects on everyday life, especially when these narratives become naturalized, attaining the imprimatur of "common sense." Within these frequently naturalized plots, indigenous peoples inhabit the earliest stages of evolution, ambivalently representing either a savage past or lost innocence from which America must emerge. The only possibility for indigenous people to succeed in America is to forego tribal stories (like Rocky, Auntie, and the returning war veterans) and to accept some other competing narrative of identity in the American landscape. Social theorists Margaret R. Somers and Gloria D. Gibson take this concept a step further, arguing that all people (not just indigenous peoples) inevitably locate their identities within given social narratives: "It matters not whether we are social scientists or subjects of historical research for all of us to come to be who we are (however ephemeral, multiple, and changing) by locating ourselves (usually unconsciously) in social narratives *rarely of our own making*" (Somers and Gibson 1994, 59). They cite several different kinds of narratives that are inextricably part of identity formation: public narratives such as the working-class hero and metanarrative or master narratives such as "Progress, Decadence, Industrialism, Enlightenment" (63). Somers and Gibson tell us that identity formation is never fixed, but is always in the process of becoming in relation to others and to other parts of the story. They write: "Joining narra-tive to identity introduces time, space, and analytic rationality—each of which is excluded from the categorical or 'essentialist' approach to identity" (65).

In *Ceremony*, Tayo finds himself drawn to several narratives that are not of his own making: the angry war veteran, the drunken Indian, the tragic mixed blood, and the narrative of the indigenous ceremony. As with the older stories in the novel, Tayo requires the help of knowledgeable elders to understand the way out of his spiritual drought and confusion, specifically his difficulty in finding peace in the heteroglossia of the many voices and stories that call to him—for instance, the voices of the Japanese, English, and Pueblo peoples, and the loud music of the jukebox (Silko 1977, 6). Ku'oosh is helpful to some extent, but his limited knowledge of the power of modern warfare appears to prevent him from curing Tayo completely; for Ku'oosh, the mortars and atomic bombs would be "too alien to comprehend" (36). The novel thus suggests that it is imperative to know the full implications of the different stories (ideologies) that affect the community before healing can occur. Fortunately, Betonie not only helps Tayo understand the different nar-ratives at work in his life, he also helps Tayo appreciate the ontological power of stories in the creation of lived narratives. In other words, like the stories of Thought Woman that begin the novel ("whatever she thinks about appears"), Tayo's life becomes a kind of aesthetic work that he authors—a work of art that has the potential to end in tragedy or harmony, in disaster or great beauty. The power of stories to create realities is particularly evident in the rendition of the witches' competition, where the story of opposition between man and nature creates the predominating ideology for the colonization of the Ameri-cas; indeed, it is the oppositional ideology of war that creates the potential destruction of the world.

In *Ceremony*, as in other novels by indigenous writers I will discuss later, the oral tradition is not a metaphoric sign, or even a unitary sign for authen-ticity or truth, but is instead the possibility of truth itself, the possibility of a future for indigenous peoples. Consequently, in the brief history of indigenous writing in America, indigenous writers have often found the conventional forms of written American and European fiction to be inadequate, even coun-terproductive, as expressions about indigenous life. For precisely this reason,

Ceremony and novels such as Louise Erdrich's *Love Medicine*, Gerald Vizenor's *Bearheart*, and Ray Young Bear's *Black Eagle Child* do not appear in the form of traditional literary genres, and instead resist the authenticating narrative forms and images of "Indians" from American ideology. In the next chapter, I will discuss some of the ethical issues of using indigenous oral traditions in contemporary works of literature, and in the following four chapters, I will offer readings of novels by indigenous writers who, like Silko in her use of oral traditions in *Ceremony*, employ the traditions from their own indigenous backgrounds to create contemporary fiction that intimates the "powers inherent in the process of storytelling."

CHAPTER THREE

The Ethical Use of Indigenous Traditions in Contemporary Literature

I n Frantz Fanon's vision of resistance literature, subaltern writers use updated and revised indigenous oral traditions as a means to inspire and crystallize indigenous populations in the quest for freedom from colonization. "The storyteller," Fanon tells us, "replies to the people by successive approximations and makes his way, apparently left alone but in fact helped on by his public, toward the seeking out of new patterns, that is to say national patterns" (Fanon 1963, 241). For instance, Leslie Marmon Silko's *Ceremony* offers a pattern of literature, based on successive iterations of indigenous oral traditions, that restores balance to the protagonist, including a balance between the past and present traditions. While an American pattern of progress moves the country "innocently" away from its savage past, including an erasure of indigenous peoples and their cultures, the traditions in *Ceremony* suggest that the past is not an essentially lesser stage from which a more advanced or civilized present emerges or escapes through further enlightenment of the workings of a dialectic. Instead, the past in the form of oral traditions remains an equal source of power and knowledge—one reason why Silko and other indigenous writers often turn to them as patterns for their works of contemporary fiction and, in a political sense, assert the fundamental equality and viability of indigenous cultures and practices in the contemporary world.

And yet many indigenous writers point out, including David Treuer, Jana Sequoya Magdaleno, and Paula Gunn Allen, that the use of tribal traditions outside tribal contexts carries enormous risks, for many indigenous practices (like the practices of some European religions) are private, even sacred. Once these traditions enter the marketplace of fiction, they become commodified and consumed in ways that run counter to the sanctity and purpose of these traditions. Treuer argues, for instance, that tribal traditions in Leslie Silko's *Ceremony* and Louise Erdrich's *The Antelope Wife* do not represent indigenous practices or beliefs, but rather they represent the desire for fiction to appear authentically native. Emblematic of this attitude, Treuer observes, is Erdrich's use of Anishinabe language, which appears as an artifact because it is translated and sometimes ungrammatical, suggesting a decorative rather than an essential function in the book. (The German language, Treuer points out, is not translated in the novel.) Consequently, because the Anishinabe language appears to be a sign for culture rather than an expression of culture, it becomes a second-class tradition in the context of the novel. In other words, Treuer argues that it has "no purpose except, at best, in bits to function as a 'gang sign,' and, at worst, as static, dioramic museum pieces" (Treuer 2002, 55). Because contemporary novels by indigenous writers sometimes offer traditions as exoticized and thus commodified displays of culture rather than as expressions of indigenous thought, Treuer tells us that they "function as 'Native Informants'," hauntingly similar to museums or anthropological studies, both of which have a long history of hoarding and exploiting indigenous sacred artifacts and even human remains.[1]

Similarly, Magdaleno argues that while canonical indigenous authors frequently employ traditions as signs of authenticity, the use of sacred traditions may in fact be prohibited by indigenous communities, thus rendering them inauthentic from a tribal perspective. Magdaleno writes: "Surely to many Indian-identified students it seems ironic at best that academic commentary on these works cites the literary incorporation of fragments of sacred story as evidence that they are authentically American Indian" (Magdaleno 2000, 286). For instance, while oral traditions provide crucial structures of identity for the protagonists in N. Scott Momaday's *House Made of Dawn* and in Silko's *Ceremony*, Magdaleno points out that this act of literary recuperation is mitigated by the use of sacred traditions that overlook the indigenous context for these stories—a context that relies on "a logic of space rather than of place." Magdaleno explains that indigenous peoples maintain a "geocentric sense of identity" in which "ancestral events, customs and values" are "sustained by the territorial features of the homeplace" (288). Within the logic of place, traditional indigenous stories perform the function of bringing members together into a "communal place." In contrast, in the logic of space, indigenous stories in contemporary fiction become dispersed though the publishing industry and thus undergo "assimilated pressures" from various institutions, thus further eroding the intellectual and perhaps the political sovereignty of indigenous people (289). Magdaleno points out that indigenous peoples are so concerned about keeping sacred traditions within a tribal space that, according to Leigh Jenkins, director of the Hopi Cultural Preservation Office, "the tribe would prefer to lose its traditions" (287) rather than have them become part of university curricula.

Like Treuer and Magdaleno, Paula Gunn Allen discusses the potential for abuse of indigenous traditions, with particular emphasis on her role as a teacher and an academic. In her essay "Special Problems in Teaching Leslie Marmon Silko's *Ceremony*," Allen writes that her Pueblo upbringing teaches her to question the use of indigenous oral traditions in contemporary literature:

> But to use the oral tradition directly is to run afoul of native ethics, which is itself a considerable part of the tradition. Using the tradition while contravening it is to do violence to it. (Allen 1990, 379)

Allen refers specifically to four contemporary novels by American Indian writers: Mourning Dove's *Cogewea*, James Welch's *Fools Crow*, Momaday's

House Made of Dawn, and Silko's *Ceremony*. Each of these novels, Allen writes, "contains a number of references to arcane matters" (382) that she judges should not have been included in the novels. When teaching these novels, Allen is careful to avoid disclosing tribal secrets. She writes: "I shy away from answering many particular questions because I find them offensive" (382). Yet as a member of a profession that values open inquiry, Allen feels somewhat obligated to disclose everything she knows about a particular work to provide the context and knowledge for students to have a more comprehensive understanding of the books. Ultimately, however, Allen refuses to discuss oral traditions: "Ethically, as a professor, I see this kind of methodology as necessary; but ethically, as an Indian, I can't do it" (385).

Thus for Allen, the teaching of indigenous literature pits her against two strong ethical demands, similar to Magdaleno's distinction between the logic of place and space: on the one hand, the ethical demand to respect the privacy of tribal communities (in her terms, being "street smart"), and on the other hand, the ethical demand to teach indigenous literature thoroughly ("book smart"). Teaching Silko's *Ceremony*, for example, a "book smart" reader would certainly feel entitled to investigate the clan stories (that is, those stories within the province of a particular tribal clan) within the novel to examine how the protagonist, the novel, or the genre correspond to the oral traditions of the Laguna Pueblo. As a "street smart" tribal member, however, Allen not only questions Silko's use of clan stories, but she also reacts violently to non-tribal scholars researching these private traditions. She writes:

> I believe I could not more do (or sanction) the kind of ceremonial investigation of *Ceremony* done by some researchers than I could slit my mother's throat. Even seeing some of it published makes my skin crawl. I have yet to read one of those articles all the way through, my physical reaction is so pronounced. (Allen 1990, 383)

Allen's objection is not only a personal reaction, nor is it only a desire to maintain tribal control of stories within the logic of space. Allen points out that in certain tribal communities, any disclosures of private tribal information may result in disaster. She quotes Ray Young Bear when he discusses in an interview the fate of William Jones, who collected stories at Mesquakie and came to a bad end. She also suggests that certain disasters at Laguna and abroad—"the development of nuclear weapons near Jemez, the Second World War, jackpile mine, water and land poisoned by nuclear waste"—all may have resulted from "security leaks" (384).

In part, Treuer, Magdaleno, and Allen are responding to a history of indigenous studies, in particular the sibling fields of ethnology and anthropology, where a researcher's ethical imperative is to provide accurate (although mostly synchronic) representations of indigenous culture—religions, language, clothing, personal habits. Within this binary relationship between observer and observed, the sciences often dehumanize indigenous peoples rather than encouraging cultural interactions based upon mutual understanding and respect. Speaking of the reluctance of Don Talayesva to reveal Hopi ceremonies to outsiders, David Murray writes: "The way anthropologists deal with this reluctance has thrown into sharp relief their assumptions about whether the Indians are subjects in their own rights—and can make their own choices—or are objects of study, and can be coaxed, bullied, and deceived in the name of science" (Murray 1991, 75). Social scientists would do well to consider how they might feel responding to questions involving private matters such as their religion, spirituality, or their menses, and whether they might feel betrayed if, without their consent, such issues were brought to the public in print publications. In his well-known discussion of anthropologists in his *Custer Died for Your Sins*, Vine Deloria Jr. notes that indigenous communities find themselves constantly barraged by inquiries into their private affairs. Deloria writes:

> Academic freedom certainly does not imply that one group of people have to become chessmen for another group of people. Why should Indian communities be subjected to prying non-Indians any more than other communities? Should any group have a franchise to stick its nose into someone else's business? No. (Deloria 1969, 95)

While more social scientists (for example, Tyler 1987) are critically examining their own subject-positions as they observe indigenous peoples, questioning the myth of an objective representation of any peoples, in both scholarly and everyday discourse about indigenous peoples (and other peoples with respect to the United States), binary conceptions of cultural relations have by no means been erased.

Thus, even for the purposes of authentic representation, Allen resists the ethics of "book smart" research of sacred traditions that relies on the belief that indigenous peoples are (or at least should be) open to complete scrutiny, regardless of the imposition on personal and cultural privacy. Similarly, Magdaleno questions the construction of authenticity through the use of decontextualized and sometimes fragmented indigenous oral traditions, even when justified under the banner of cultural revitalization, for these fragments arise from an "already alienated context of anthropological archives—a sort of textual necrophilia" (Magdaleno 2000, 292). Treuer, likewise, not only critiques the use of indigenous traditions as signs of authenticity, but also wonders whether indigenous authors themselves play the role of "informants," the apt anthropological term describing indigenous people who offer private and sometimes sacred information to scientific investigators. Treuer writes: "Ironically, during the last thirty or so years, certainly since *Custer Died for Your Sins*, Native American authors have been honing their hatred and dismissal of anthropology and anthropologists, while at the same time creating novels that function as 'Native Informants'" (Treuer 2002, 55).

Indeed, when conceived as literary realism, indigenous literature shares with anthropology the concern for representation, especially in its use of accurate details from indigenous life—sometimes (unfortunately) including details from sacred traditions. Even when indigenous literature resists realism and representation through the use of magical realism, metafiction, and subjective voices, commentators frequently read indigenous literature as authentic representations of indigenous culture—in other words, as a kind of literary tourism or readable anthropology. Similarly, anthropology often shares with literature the concern for a coherent narrative, relying on approaches to writing culture from conventional realist fiction—for instance, character development of a protagonist, a linear plot, interesting and accurate details, and (perhaps unconsciously) an unreliable narrator. Thus, while indigenous writers often object to the aims and practices of anthropological studies, and while anthropologists would likely object to labeling their work as fiction, both enterprises converge in unavoidable and uncomfortable ways within the context of authenticity and accurate representation.

One particularly illustrative example is *Papago Woman* by Ruth Underhill, a student of both Ruth Benedict and Franz Boas, who lived with the Papago people (now known by their proper name, the Tohono O'odham) for three years, between 1931 and 1933. What is perhaps most remarkable about this publication is Underhill's desire to represent the life of her "informant," Chona, as an autobiography in section 2 of the book, even though it is unlikely that Chona would have known the scope or purpose of such a project. Indeed, the title, "Autobiography of Chona, a Papago Woman," indicates that this section reflects what Chona would reveal about her life had she a desire to see it published. Yet in a number of significant ways, the "Autobiography of Chona" undermines not only Chona's own desires about what she wishes to be revealed about her life and her community, but also the manner in which she talked about her life. For instance, Underhill writes that "Indian narrative style involves a repetition and a dwelling on unimportant details which confuse the white reader and make it hard for him to follow the story" (Underhill 1985, 33). As a consequence, Underhill takes the "repetitious confusion" of Chona's discussion and, through years of questioning, places the incidents into what she calls the "correct order," thus creating a coherent, readable narrative for a nonindigenous (and masculine) audience (33). To communicate Chona's life to an audience in a way that does not call attention to the stylistics of the text—in other words, to provide a transparent narrative—Underhill cannot write an unconventional narrative reflecting "Indian narrative styles," as do Mourning Dove, Ray Young Bear, and Louise Erdrich. Even her use of a conventional genre, the autobiography, provides a familiar, readable site for her audience, even while doing violence to Chona's own subjectivity (the work is obviously not an autobiography).

In fact, Underhill not only colonizes Chona's subjectivity, she also freely includes information in the text that is inappropriate according to Chona's own standards of ethics. For instance, although Chona tells Underhill that it is inappropriate for persons in her community to "tell if he had seen Coyote" (Underhill 1985, 52), she nevertheless entrusts Underhill with her dream about Coyote, including a song Coyote sang in the dream. In spite of Chona's explicit concerns, Underhill publishes both the dream and the song in the "Autobiography." Elsewhere, Chona says to Underhill: "You cannot ask any Indian woman about the harvest festival. That is a thing from which we keep far away" (82). Nevertheless, Underhill commits the next paragraphs to describing this very festival. Elsewhere, Chona and other women inform Underhill of one rule that cannot be broken, even by children (who are normally absolved from such rules): the "names of the dead must not be mentioned" (90). And yet in writing about the death of Chona's father, Underhill includes the following contradictory statement as part of Chona's life story: "After that, we never said his name, José María" (74). Magdaleno's criticism of indigenous literature is most clearly evident here in an anthropological narrative: the confusion of the logics of space and of place. Underhill makes it clear that she is interested primarily in the reception of her work by a non-Indian audience: "It is an Indian story told to satisfy whites rather than Indians" (33). Consequently, the moral or ethical concerns about privacy are perhaps far less important to Underhill than the communication of what she sees as different, perhaps exotic.

To avoid participating in these kinds of investigations as a teacher of indigenous literature, Allen chooses to "non-teach" *Ceremony*, focusing on the "plot and action" instead of providing more arcane contextual knowledge about Laguna traditions. In this regard, Allen probably does what many sensitive teachers of indigenous literature do as well: she refrains from discussing information in indigenous texts clearly not appropriate for public consumption. For teachers of indigenous literature, such issues present (or should present) difficult challenges in determining what may or may not be taught in our classes. Even if we use books such as *Cogewea*, *Storyteller*, and *Ceremony* to explore this very issue of ethics, their inclusion in our classrooms may run counter to the desires of community tribal members. In my chapter on *Cogewea*, for instance, I examine some of the ways the novel employs Okanogan traditions, yet in doing so run the risk of exposing what should be kept secret. Allen, too, has encouraged the study of tribal stories in her *Sacred Hoop*, where she presents a careful and thoughtful reading of *Ceremony* without referring to issues surrounding unethical disclosures. Elsewhere, in her collection of pieces in *Spider Woman's Granddaughters*, she not only reprints the Green Blanket Feet story in its entirety from *Cogewea*, she also presents four older versions of the Yellow Woman stories prior to publishing Silko's "Yellow Woman." I do not cite these examples as an attempt to expose a debilitating contradiction in Allen's important statements about the ethical use of the oral tradition; instead, I believe they indicate an ongoing critical concern for students of indigenous literatures working within the ethical imperatives of space and place.

■ Indian Literature without Indians: Erdrich's *The Beet Queen* and Hogan's *Mean Spirit*

Within the questionable context of authentic representation, indigenous literature must offer detailed and accurate examples of indigenous peoples and their cultures, even while avoiding detailed and accurate sacred information that is inappropriate for distribution outside the tribal community. For many readers of indigenous literature, authentic representation in fiction has become a moral imperative, offering a truth in fiction that counters demeaning, destructive, and self-serving depictions of indigenous peoples in American art, literature, film and television, such as mascots, ethnic sidekicks, and helpful shamans. But of course, indigenous fiction does not always fall within the context of authentic representation; in fact, some works challenge the necessity or even the very possibility of representation in fiction and even history. Louise Erdrich's *The Beet Queen*, for instance, uses a series of highly subjective and sometimes conflicting voices to critique the narcissism of both indigenous and nonindigenous people living in a community outside the reservation. Because truth and fiction in the novel become so highly intertwined in this novel, and because the novel foregrounds its own status as subjective artifice, the novel demonstrates that any attempt at an authentic representation of this community (and perhaps any community) would itself constitute a considerable fiction. Similarly, Linda Hogan's *Mean Spirit* employs the conventional methods of the mystery and melodrama to call attention to a horrific period in Osage history when tribal members were murdered for their wealth from oil revenues. Because the novel appears dedicated to a political awakening of its readers, it omits many details from the actual history that would perhaps dull the vivid political melodrama, where the distinctions between light and dark and good and evil are stark and compelling.

Without the traditional markers of authentic representation—correct cultural information, historical details, and oral traditions—these novels have attracted considerable controversy, especially from indigenous critics who understandably question the wisdom of revising indigenous history in fiction. In her review of *The Beet Queen*, Silko criticizes the novel because it does not satisfy the logic of place in North Dakota, especially with regard to the bigotry and racism that must have existed at that time. In fact, Silko tells us, it is very difficult to tell who in the novel is indigenous and who is not, a fact that would have mattered a great deal at that time and place. Silko suggests that instead, Erdrich has given herself over to postmodern wordplay, the logic of space, with her characters in the fictional town of Argus absorbed mostly in their own personal feelings of angst. Consequently, Silko argues, Erdrich has ignored her responsibility as an indigenous writer to address unpleasant truths that may not be especially appealing to her reading audiences:

> Good fiction need not be factual, but it doesn't obscure basic truth. In Erdrich's hands, the rural North Dakota of Indian-hating, queer-baiting white farmers, of the Depression, becomes magically transformed. Or maybe "transported." Rural New Hampshire seems a far more probable location for *The Beet Queen* and its characters, white and Indian, straight and gay. (Silko 1986b, 180)

Silko here ascribes the novel's geographical disorientation to Erdrich's connections (at the time of writing) to Dartmouth College in Hanover, New Hampshire, where (Silko suggests, perhaps optimistically) one might find less racism and homophobia than in North Dakota.

Silko is certainly accurate in her assessment that *The Beet Queen* does not contain overt references to racism, an omission that becomes more evident in light of Erdrich's later depiction of Argus in *Tracks*, where the rape of Fleur is largely motivated by racism. In *The Beet Queen*, however, Erdrich focuses on the nonindigenous attitudes of Argus, effectively critiquing this community that has lost its connection to the political and historical reality that Silko says is missing. As Dennis M. Wash and Ann Braley argue, Erdrich perhaps "intends not to show what is present in Argus but what is missing," creating a "white world devoid of spirituality, meaningful tradition, and ceremony" (Walsh and Braley 1994, 3).[2] Argus is indeed a "Fairy-Tale" world, where Adelaide leaves the realities of poverty and child-rearing to join an air showman named Omar; where her daughter Mary, after creating a kind of Rorschach blot in the ice by hitting it with her face, becomes a diviner of the future by "sending off for special offers and reading books on mental projection"; where the leader of the chamber of commerce, Wallace Pfef, creates a fictive life to hide his homosexuality; and where the principle means of economic development is the polluting, processed-sugar-beet industry, which, as Wallace Pfef says, "will make refined white sugar every bit as American as corn on the cob" (Erdrich 1986, 118, 160). The novel supports and even foregrounds Silko's contention that it is a "Fairy-Tale," not because Erdrich cannot or will not address unpleasant social conditions in North Dakota, but because the novel critiques how the characters themselves have created fictive lives through which they deny their pasts and their present realities.

One significant way *The Beet Queen* thematically underscores the "Fairy-Tale" nature of Argus is in its treatment of two quite different characters, Sita Kozka and Russell Kashpaw. Silko argues that Sita embodies "western ideals of beauty" and that the book appears to value her over the characters with dark hair and skin, Celestine and Mary. Yet the book clearly illustrates that Sita's attempts to use her beauty to succeed in love, friendship, and in her career ultimately end in failure. When, as young children, Sita's friend Celestine and her cousin Mary first meet and become easy friends, a young Sita tries awkwardly and unsuccessfully to win Celestine back from Mary by revealing her breasts. Later in her life, after she has left Argus and the butcher shop as far behind as she can, Sita makes her living by modeling in Minneapolis; but despite her rigorous efforts to preserve her youthful appearance, and despite frequent refresher courses at the Dorothy Ludlow Evening School of Charm, Sita knows she cannot stay young forever and must marry to survive. She waits in vain for a rich doctor, and instead settles for living her life with Jimmy Bohl, a steakhouse owner from Argus who knew her only as "Sita Kozka, daughter of Pete, the butcher" (Erdrich 1986, 86). This idea of preservation continues as Sita grows older: her house, her appearance, even her mind (by means of pills) all require careful maintenance to preserve Sita's fragile but ordered existence. Even in death, Sita is so well preserved that, as she rides with Celestine and Mary in the Kozka meat truck through the Beet Festival parade, she appears alive to spectators, who wave at her thinking she might be "an alderwoman or the governor's wife" (296).

While *The Beet Queen* foregrounds and critiques Sita's preoccupation with appearances, the book offers much less information about Russell, one of the most recognizably American Indian characters living in Argus. Silko argues that the brevity of references to indigenous characters in the book reveals Erdrich's unwillingness to confront social and political realities in this novel. If, however, *The Beet Queen* is primarily a critique of the self-absorbed characters in Argus, then it is appropriate that the book does not foreground indigenous characters such as Eli, who lives on the reservation, or Fleur, who survives poverty as a peddler. Where the novel describes Russell, Eli, and Fleur, it moves away from the fairy-tale language of Argus and instead shows how these characters are marked by the difficulties of life. For example, although Russell (a character similar to Silko's own Rocky in her novel *Ceremony*) excels for a time in the "Fairy-Tale" world of Argus, having "gone through high school as a football star," he too must confront harsh realities of survival (in his case the realities of war), but leaves, in complete contrast to Sita, visibly marked by his experiences, with "scars stretched up his cheeks like claw marks, angry and long, even running past his temples and parting his hair" (Erdrich 1986, 70). While Sita remains preserved in old age, Russell, because of his war injuries and his age, can neither speak nor care for himself, moving in his later years to the reservation, where Fleur and Eli care for him. Only once does he return to Argus to take part in the Beet Festival parade. There, surrounded by images of military death on the float honoring veterans, he dozes off in his wheelchair, awakened only when he hears someone shout: "He looks stuffed" (300). This contrast between Sita and Russell suggests that, to the beet-producing "Fairy-Tale" world of Argus, what appears to be alive is actually dead, and what appears to be dead—such as Russell, and perhaps Indian life in general—though not visibly apparent, is in fact very much alive. As Mary says, "We are very much like the dead . . . except we have the use of our senses" (263). This moment of reversed perceptions is, in fact, a critique of the characters' inability to distinguish truth from fiction, especially as truth and fiction appear in the parade and the crowning of the Beet Queen, which is itself a farce because Wallace Pfef has counterfeited votes to ensure Dot's election. But Dot rejects her coronation as the Beet Queen, just as she rejects Argus life in general. Wallace Pfef despairs that Dot rejects the values of Argus, but her outlaw behavior suggests that she understands, at least intuitively, that Argus offers only a simulacrum of life:

> Dot wore fishnet stockings and a vinyl skirt to classes, teased her hair into a nest, came home with merchandise she couldn't have purchased on her minimum wage at the Argus Theater. Her friends were hoods, drinkers, smokers, motorcycle riders, and assorted deadbeats who haunted the street of bars that did not donate to the Christmas Lighting Fund. (Erdrich 1986, 301)

Like her grandmother Adelaide, Dot initially responds to the intolerable situation of the Sugar Beet Festival through (literal) flight; unlike Adelaide, she eventually returns home to make a tenuous but significant connection with her mother, Celestine. Thus, while the novel critiques a world of "air seeders," Sugar Beet Festivals, and "one-stop-shopping," *The Beet Queen* also suggests that such affirmations of human connection, however brief or subdued, provide the possibility of redemption in what Silko calls a "post-modern" and "self-referential" novel—a textual world, Silko argues, that is "light years from shared or communal experience" (Silko 1986b, 179).

In spite of Silko's contention, such moments of communal experience are, in fact, fairly frequent in the fragmented world of *The Beet Queen*, and they have significant effect upon the characters when they occur. For example, Fleur rescues Karl from crippling injuries and possibly death when she takes him to the reservation; Fritzie and Pete take in Mary after Adelaide abandons her; Fleur and Eli take in Russell when he is infirm; Wallace cares for Karl when he is hospitalized or needs a place to stay; and Mary and Celestine make an instant and lifelong connection the first time they meet as girls and make cookies. Although Silko argues that Erdrich's style of writing does not reflect the "communal experience that underlies oral narrative," suggesting the kind of indigenous fiction Silko herself writes so well in *Ceremony* and *Storyteller*, *The Beet Queen* does in fact yearn for precisely the communal experience Silko values. Furthermore, although such moments of communal experience are certainly not the exclusive province of indigenous peoples, the reservation is a place of healing in the novel for Karl, for Russell, and in some ways for Dot, who discovers a place where she does not always need to rebel.[3]

As a kind of fairy-tale novel, *The Beet Queen* employs little imagery or cultural information that suggests its own authenticity as indigenous or representative. A more difficult example is Linda Hogan's *Mean Spirit*, which appears to represent a particular era of Osage history while at the same time taking liberties with this important and perhaps even sacred history. Using the mystery genre and techniques of melodrama, the novel provides a compelling account of several murders of oil-wealthy Osage people during the early years of the twentieth century (sometimes misnamed the "Osage Reign of Terror," for the Osage were terrorizing no one); yet in creating a novel that may generate political sympathies within readers, the novel overlooks significant details from both Osage history and traditional Osage practices. Perhaps because Hogan did not have access to actual Osage traditions, or perhaps because she chose, out of the kind of respect Allen demands, not to include these practices, the novel offers "bat medicine" as a central tradition for the Osage people in the book, even though, as Eric Anderson points out, bat medicine is not a traditional Osage practice (Anderson 2000). Instead, to heighten the dramatic tension in the novel, the bat medicine in the caves provides imagery consistent with the dark oil: both are powers beneath the ground that are not well understood by the Osage people in desperate trouble. Throughout the novel, characters constantly search for clues, ideas, horses, people—anything that will help them make sense of, or have some measure of control over, the incomprehensible forces of greed, corruption, and corporate power that surround them. The bat medicine offers no clear guidance for the searchers, but it does suggest that tradition, presented in the form of the "pure" Hill People, might offer possibilities of salvation.

In a review essay of Hogan's book, Osage tribal member Robert Allen Warrior takes issue with the novel's lack of fidelity to the facts of Osage history and spirituality. Warrior writes:

> She, in effect, de-Osaged the story, picking and choosing what she liked about the particulars of history and inventing new materials for what she didn't—sort of like, and I don't choose the analogy lightly, finding the Holocaust a rich source, but not finding Jewish people interesting enough to be the subjects of their own history. In place of Osage spirituality, for instance, Hogan uses a sort of pan-tribal New Age-ism with Southern Plains and Southeastern (Hogan is Chickasaw) features, presumably making it easier for her inter-tribal cast of characters to interact but losing the specificity of Osages in the process. (Warrior 1995a, 52)

Warrior is likely referring to the "Book of Horse," in which the seer Michael Horse adds his own name to the books of the Holy Bible, despite the protestations of Father Dunne. Such an addition to the Holy Bible suggest that history and even religion are not immutable or ahistorical sources of knowledge, but are instead human constructs that change with the demands of each generation, including perhaps the addition of *Mean Spirit* to Osage history. And yet, if the Book of Horse is the culmination of Michael Horse's intellectual response to large, often unseen forces surrounding the Osage people in this community, it is especially disappointing because it outlines general and often commercialized versions of indigenous-oriented philosophies. The book begins: "Honor father sky and mother earth. Look after everything. Life resides in all things, even the motionless stones" (Hogan 1990, 361). Considering the magnitude of loss in terms of human life both in the novel and in actual history, this general response lacks the depth of knowledge and energy one might have expected, and certainly lacks the insight and industry the Osage people themselves used to counter the murders in their communities.

Indeed, as with its use of metaphors, the novel heightens the melodramatic, highly politicized oppositions of good and evil by emphasizing the unequal distribution of power. While the oil companies have almost unlimited and unseen power over the Osage characters, few if any Osage people have the power to resist them, even those with enormous wealth through oil revenues. The novel closes with a prominent family abandoning their home and their community, beaten and impoverished, leaving readers with the impression that the Osage people in the town of Watona are utterly defeated. Yet in his historical study *The Underground Reservation* (1985), Terry Wilson writes that Superintendent J. George Wright and the Osage people, especially the tribal council, exercised considerable influence during the oil boom. For example, the council negotiated sublease agreements on behalf of the tribe, kept certain oil companies from cheating them, petitioned the United States Congress on the legal issue of competency, and contributed $20,000 and legal fees to the prosecution of William K. Hale, the historical oilman in the novel who schemed to rob and murder members of the Osage tribe.

By leaving out the ingenuity of the Osage people themselves in confronting the problems associated with the oil industry, Hogan heightens melodramatic intensity at the expense of actual Osage history. This tactic is most evident in Hogan's depiction of Ho-tah-moie, John Stink, who shunned the wealth from oil revenues. Wilson writes that according to a popular legend, John Stink died, was buried, but was seen later walking into town. This legend goes on to offer that John Stink was subsequently "shunned by his tribe, whose members stubbornly believed he was a ghost, ignoring the obvious explanation that he had recovered from a deathlike coma" (T. Wilson 1985, 169). Wilson tells us that this legend is "wholly false." In fact, while John Stink lived a quiet life away from the Osage community, and while he was offered numerous marriage proposals, he was certainly known to be alive and prospering, for the Osage tribal council helped to secure his large bank account against unscrupulous "guardians," and after his death, relatives became embroiled in an "unseemly" quest for his remaining fortune (170). Remarkably, Hogan (who must have read Wilson's book, for she included a verbatim letter from it in her novel) includes the fantastic but inaccurate representation of Ho-tah-moie's life rather than Wilson's historical version; that is, she offers the compelling spectacle of newspapers accounts rather than the mundane, more complicated story of his life.

In the novel's defense, Betty Louise Bell argues that rather than simply repeat the written history of the murders, Hogan "dared to rewrite history," creating a novel that is not only a testament to the power of the human imagination but also a reminder of the kind of devastation experienced by many indigenous peoples across the continent. Responding to criticisms about the novel's accuracy, she writes:

> These criticisms are founded on the grounds of experience: only an Osage can tell the story of the greedy destruction of the Osage, and a story, if founded on history, must rely completely on history as its muse. In *Mean Spirit*, Hogan courageously creates a pan-Indian community brought together by a shared history of sorrow and struggle and a belief in the sanctity of the land. (Bell 1994, 5)

Yet, at least in Warrior's criticisms of the novel, the fact that Hogan is a member of the Chickasaw tribe has much less to do with his problems with the book than its omission of important aspects of Osage history and spirituality. (Terry Wilson, whom Warrior praises, is Potawatomi). The desire to generalize the Reign of Terror, which Bell lauds as an inclusive move, results in precisely the novel's willingness to ignore what for many people are the most important aspects of indigenous life: local culture and history, which are the basis of Warrior's own concept of "intellectual sovereignty" (Warrior 1995b). Bell further defends the novel's approach by arguing that Hogan need not rely on history, which Bell rightfully points out often mutes or ignores subaltern voices. She writes:

> Hogan has been criticized for her deviation from some historical *facts* in *Mean Spirit*. This assumes that there is a sole and accurate historical narrative to every event and that truth resides only in that narrative. In fact, to the advantage of all peoples once absent from History, the privileged voice of History has long been reduced to its narrative form and intent. It is just another way of telling a story. As a Native American woman, Hogan knows the dangers of complicity with history; as a writer, she insists on the primacy of the imagination. (Bell 1994, 5)

Bell's point is compelling, for indigenous literature such as James Welch's *Fools Crow* and Frances LaFlesche's *The Middle Five* provides powerful, indigenous-centered alternatives to conventional narratives about war on the frontier or the boarding-school experience for indigenous children. However, the opposition Bell sets up between history and imagination does not altogether engage the question of a writer's ethical responsibility to both of these sources of knowledge and insight, as well as to other sources of information such as the oral traditions of the Osage people themselves, which Warrior suggests have also been omitted.

As both a mystery and a melodrama, *Mean Spirit* offers a compelling, lucid account of these murders to contemporary readers, but the novel achieves this clarity of style and content at a cost. Hogan's narrative, twisting and turning as it is, nonetheless is conventional in its linearity, challenging readers less with style than with her version of Osage history. As Roland Barthes argues in his essay "Authors and Writers," if one wishes to make a political point, one does not employ language that calls attention to itself, for this ambiguity challenges the reader at the level of style, not content. (This is the role of Barthes's "author.") Instead, to support a "praxis" or a political point of view, the "writer" must necessarily view language as a conventional "instrument of communication, a vehicle of 'thought,'" not as stylistic innovation. Barthes adds:

> Even if the writer pays some attention to style, this concern is never ontological. The writer performs no essential technical action upon language; he employs an utterance common to all writers, a *koïnè* in which we can of course distinguish certain dialects (Marxist, for example, or Christian, or existentialist), but very rarely styles. (Barthes 1972, 147)

Hogan's novel enjoys substantial popularity in part because, unlike the works of Young Bear, Vizenor, Erdrich, or Silko, it does not challenge readers' expectations for a conventional narrative. Yet at the same time, neither does the novel challenge certain widely held, colonialist views of indigenous peoples: that indigenous peoples are passive, unwilling, or unable to self-govern as sovereign peoples; that indigenous people cannot handle money well, perhaps because they are not materialistic; that indigenous peoples are part of a "vanishing race," leaving town defeated, or moving to the hills without a trace. While the novel asks readers to engage this important moment of political history, its compelling tactics as fiction move it away from a claim of historical representation, which ironically is an important reason for the novel's significance in the first place.

■ The Self-Conscious Use of Indigenous Oral Traditions

To different degrees of success, Erdrich's *The Beet Queen* and Hogan's *Mean Spirit* set aside the demands of representation for the political purpose of critiquing beliefs and institutions that are (or were) destructive to both indigenous and nonindigenous peoples. While these novels take enormous risks with their absence of critical history and specific indigenous traditions, they also avoid the problems of negotiating between the concepts of space and place were they to employ cultural stories or practices. Yet in avoiding specific indigenous traditions and history, these novels also relinquish the possibility of using these traditions to establish (as Fanon argues about African traditions) indigenous patterns of thought that may resist national American narratives that erase the future of indigenous peoples—for example, the narrative of the Vanishing Race arising from Henry Lewis Morgan's theory of social evolution. Offering yet another alternative to the use of indigenous traditions are novels by two authors who published them some sixty-five years apart: Mourning Dove's *Cogewea*, and Ray Young Bear's *Black Eagle Child* and *Remnants of the First Earth*. These novels employ oral traditions to suggest indigenous patterns of thought, and also, as I shall discuss in later chapters, to offer indigenous patterns of written literature. Thus in these works, the oral traditions are not movable signs of indigenous authenticity, but are integral to the philosophy and structure of the works. Furthermore, unlike Silko's *Ceremony*, these works are highly self-conscious about their use of oral traditions, explaining in rather stark terms their own negotiations between space and place. While these novels do not, of course, completely escape the ethical dilemmas of employing indigenous traditions in contemporary works of fiction, they nonetheless distance readers from the ethnographic goal of representation or mimesis through the uncritical use of sacred oral stories.

Cogewea directly confronts the ethical dilemmas of disclosing sacred oral traditions as an elderly grandmother, the Stemteemä, weighs the potential losses and gains of using sacred stories to influence her granddaughter Cogewea's marriage plans. At a critical point in this novel, Cogewea must choose between the indigenous world of the Stemteemä and that of the white eastern suitor Alfred Densmore. To thwart Cogewea's potential marriage to Densmore, the Stemteemä breaks with her responsibility to secrecy and discloses three stories: the Dead Man's Vision, the Second Coming of the Shoyahpee, and the Story of Green Blanket Feet. The Stemteemä is especially torn about the prospect of telling the story of the Dead Man's Vision, for she was entrusted with the safekeeping of this prophesy of the coming of the "pale-faced nation" (Mourning Dove 1981, 125). The Stemteemä says:

> This story I am telling you is true. It was given to me by my father who favored me among his many children. I was his youngest child from his youngest wife, who was cherished among his twelve wives. He told me the tales that were sacred to his tribe; honored me with them, trusted me. Treasured by my forefathers, I value them. I know that they would want them kept only to their own people if they were here. But they are gone and for me the sunset of the last evening is approaching and I must not carry with me this history. (Mourning Dove 1981, 122)

Similarly, the Stemteemä negotiates the widening of the place of "race" when she tells the story of the Second Coming of the Shoyahpee to Mary and Jim, both of whom are mixed blood. She says: "If you were not of my kind, I would not talk. Although the white blood has made fairer your skin, I like you and I trust you" (217). In both instances, the elderly Stemteemä makes her decision based upon her relationship with her granddaughter, and upon the ability of stories to have not only an epistemological or teaching function but also an ontological function, capable of becoming lived realities.

Mourning Dove must have understood the ethical dilemma of buying and selling tribal stories, especially after her experiences acquiring stories for her collection *Coyote Stories* (1990), some of which later appear in *Cogewea*. Under the persuasive influence of Lucullus Virgil McWhorter, founder of the

American Archeologist, Mourning Dove assembled this collection of stories, but discovered that some tribal people were not especially forthcoming with their knowledge. Dexter Fisher explains: "In her letters to McWhorter, she repeatedly complains that the Indians are suspicious of her and will not share any legends if they think they are to be published" (Fisher 1981, viii). Other tribal peoples, however, were willing to provide stories to Mourning Dove for a price, even though such a method, while perhaps acceptable to field workers in the social sciences at the time, placed Mourning Dove in direct opposition to her people's belief that oral stories were not to be written down. She writes in a letter (quoted by Fisher):

> There are some that are getting suspicious of my wanting folklores and if the Indians find out that their stories will reach print I am sure it will be hard for me to get any more legends without paying hard cash for them. (Fisher 1981, viii)

Fisher argues that Mourning Dove must have found it very difficult to resist McWhorter's vision of her as the only hope of preserving the oral traditions of the Okanogans, for she had "little education and no expectation that her deep desire to write should be recognized, let alone appreciated and enthusiastically encouraged" (ix). Given that Mourning Dove was an impoverished migrant worker who carried her typewriter from camp to camp; given that publication of her work depended on expectations of publishers whose views of indigenous peoples were likely influenced by destructive idologies and popular opinion; and given that McWhorter must have appeared to be her only hope of success at writing—her choice to disclose tribal stories in print was for her practically inevitable.

Though Mourning Dove makes the questionable decision to insert stories from the Okanogan oral tradition into *Cogewea*, at the same time the novel resists, to a degree, this disclosure of tribal secrets. For instance, while the Stemteemä expresses discomfort at telling the stories placed in her trust, even to her mixed-blood granddaughters, her dilemma perhaps communicates to readers the importance of privacy issues that surround the telling of such stories, and that are almost always overlooked by researchers wishing to unfold the inner life of indigenous peoples. Furthermore, the novel also resists the intrusive gaze of outsiders by calling into question the veracity of stories collected by social scientists (including perhaps McWhorter himself), citing examples where tribal peoples gave them the wrong information as a kind of joke. In the chapter "Lo! The Poor 'Breed,'" Cogewea becomes angry while reading Therese Broderick's 1909 novel *The Brand* because the book misrepresents life on the ranch where she lives, especially in its depiction of Indian life. She comments, for instance, about the translation of names given to the writer of *The Brand*:

> The jocose part of the romance is that it contains a few tribal phrases, supposedly the names of birds and animals. These have been conferred on some of the characters, or pet saddle horses; which, if properly translated, would shock the public immeasurably. The 'production' would be discarded by all respectable readers. (Mourning Dove 1981, 93)

The novel further combines fiction and reality when Jim points out that when the author of *The Brand* visited the ranch, he and his friends "locoed that there gal to a finish; and while she was a dashin' the information down there in her little tablet, we was a thinkin' up more lies to tell her" (94). Cogewea concludes to Densmore, "You now understand why I contend that the whites can not authentically chronicle our habits and customs. They can hardly get at the truth" (94).

Cogewea self-consciously offers readers some distance, and perhaps wariness, about the authenticity and appropriateness of oral traditions in the novel, but in the end the inclusion of these stories in her novel nonetheless constitutes, for many contemporary readers, an uncomfortable breach of tribal ethics. When teaching these novels, for example, Paula Gunn Allen (1990) writes that she feels considerable apprehension discussing with her students stories that members of Mourning Dove's community would likely not have wished to have published. Although Allen does not point out the references to specific oral traditions in *Cogewea*, she must be referring to the stories the Stemteemä reluctantly shares with Cogewea, Mary, and Jim. Given Mourning Dove's poverty and lack of education, given that her critics are addressing this question from much more advantageous positions, and given that the book itself critiques the use of oral traditions, contemporary readers may forgive her apparent compromise of tribal ethics. Yet as Mourning Dove's letters indicate, and as the book itself suggests, even in the early years of the twentieth century the tribal community had very definite beliefs about the proper contexts for their sacred traditions.

More recently, Ray A. Young Bear has also employed tribal traditions in a highly self-conscious way, but unlike Mourning Dove, he exercises more care about the possibility of disclosing tribal secrets. In the afterword to his *Black Eagle Child*, a book that also relies on tribal traditions for both its subject matter and its stylistic innovations, Young Bear explains why he chooses not to disclose certain information about his tribe and his community, namely because he is heeding the warnings of his grandmother, who advises against the unfettered use of tribal traditions. Young Bear writes:

> With early word-collectors (or informants) and their personal disasters as examples, my grandmother also forewarned commentary was destructive when untethered, for it had the capacity to either inflict or self-inflict harm. As much as has been permissible, I have attempted to hold on to this tenet. (Young Bear 1992a, 256)

Turning away from this tradition of anthropological "informants," Young Bear is careful about tribal information he discloses, not only in his fiction and poetry but also in interviews when discussing certain aspects of his work. When asked, for instance, about the significance of salamanders in his poetry, he replied: "Well, that one I better leave alone. It is a powerful image. It symbolizes something that can be discussed, but for safety reasons, I refrain" (Young Bear 1992b, 25). Young Bear's stated audience is primarily his "own tribal members" (23), but because he is an indigenous writer publishing primarily in English and desiring a wide readership, he must constantly go through the "delicate ritual of what can and cannot be shared" (Young Bear 1992a, 254). Writing to this divided audience, Young Bear sometimes writes in ways that in fact exclude outside readers, such as his symbolic use of salamanders in his work. Young Bear says, "It's a complicated system of trying to determine who is going to be reading my work. But I've discovered that I've been somewhat successful in terms of trying to reach various audiences who will pick up my book" (Young Bear 1992b, 23).

Like *Cogewea*, *Black Eagle Child* and Young Bear's later novel *Remnants of the First Earth* foreground ethical problems with the use of sacred tribal traditions outside their appropriate context. In *Black Eagle Child*, for instance, the character Edgar Bear Child recalls a childhood encounter with "pretty Elizabeth Marie," who left the community so she would "not die like her three sisters." Edgar tells us that "Her father had jeopardized her future at Black Eagle Child by selling sacred items, information, and songs to museums in Washington, D. C., and Germany. All the daughters except Elizabeth perished under mysterious circumstances" (Young Bear 1992a, 17). In *Remnants of the First Earth*, Young Bear once more addresses this specific example of infidelity, mentioning again Francis Marie (Elizabeth Marie's father), who sold a sacred mat to European collectors, and whose daughters subsequently "committed a string of mystifying suicides" (Young Bear 1996, 125). Furthermore, the novel asserts, as a result of Francis Marie's breech of trust, the community suffers from "vengeful rains—and the historic flood of the Iowa River" (120). Yet while *Remnants* strongly indicts the actions of Francis Marie, the novel appears to be much more forgiving in its discussion of another "informant," Jake Sacred Hammer, who not only unabashedly sold information about the community to outsiders but also provided personal tours of the Black Eagle Child Settlement, and even maps to sacred sites. The narrator tells us:

> When he wasn't cavorting with non-Indian visitors, he led them as they flitted from house to house on the Settlement, flaunting their leather shoulder bags that contained notebooks, pencils, and agreements for payment in return for information on the social and religious structures of the clans. What they wanted was known, but according to tribal precept it wasn't shared on a whim to strangers nor was it for sale. (Young Bear 1996, 119)

Edgar and his uncle William Listener understand that Jake Sacred Hammer was not the first to disclose secret tribal information; such information had been recorded by different tribal members for some time, and "somewhere . . .

were tens of thousands of pages collected at three cents a page in the late 1880s that had yet to be translated into English" (120). Even so, Jake Sacred Hammer broke a sacred trust to the community, where certain kinds of information are not commodities to be sold to profit individuals.

Yet while Jake was willing to give guided tours, contribute "voluminous information on the tribe's religious infrastructure to academicians from Illinois, Washington, D.C., and Belgium" (Young Bear 1996, 115), and generally offend members of the community by selling tribal information, there were limits even to his transgressions. While reading older stories about the tribe's secrets, Edgar realizes that the informants made changes in their versions of the stories to avoid revealing too much. He writes:

> Naturally, since my Grandmother had recited some in my youth, I could tell where changes had been made to hide the mysteries lurking within the words themselves. Even Jake was tribal law-abiding enough to reveal only the basic and not the whole. But no one knew that. Not even the expert teams of linguistically trained ethnologists. (Young Bear 1996, 124).

As in *Cogewea*, community members sometimes offered outsiders the illusion that they were acquiring tribal secrets, and even informants like Jake Sacred Hammer would not, finally, reveal certain truths. When Sacred Hammer passes away, he is careful to put aside money and traditional burial clothes for his funeral, which he receives even though he is something of a pariah in the community. In fact, not only does the clan elder William Listener say the important words that will help him pass over, but he also, with the help of a tribal attorney, stops the attempts of a nonindigenous newspaper photographer to intrude on the private services, even though his intrusion seems oddly appropriate. Bear Child observes the irony, commenting that "this was a white-intermingling pattern Jake had already established" (126). Thus Young Bear's novel, while making very clear that information (including photographs) involving tribal secrets are not to be disclosed, also offers a measure of compassion from William Listener, described by Edgar as "the closest any human could ever get to the Well-Known Twin-Brother, the Creator" (128).

Finally, in his novels Young Bear describes an uncompromising position about unethical disclosures of certain tribal information; yet at the same time, he also explores why tribal members transgress this ethical imperative, and gauges the community's reaction to such transgressions. Furthermore, Young Bear's approach, and to some extent Mourning Dove's as well, suggests that readers should look to indigenous writers not as sources of arcane indigenous knowledge or readable ethnology for the purposes of authentic representation, but as artists and gatekeepers who understand what can and cannot be shared. This kind of knowledge and sensitivity does not come easily: Ray Young Bear has lived his entire life on the Meskwaki Settlement, and yet he continues to engage in the "delicate ritual of weighing what can and cannot be shared" (Young Bear 1992a, 254). Other writers, such as Louise Erdrich, Leslie Silko, Gerald Vizenor, and (less successfully) Mourning Dove, also include oral traditions—not as a leitmotif or a device, but as a way to structure the contours and trajectory of their novels, suggesting the possibility of an indigenous tradition of literature outside conventions of American fiction. For this reason, I do not believe, as Allen argues, that employing the oral tradition is necessarily "to do violence to it." Rather, in the hands of knowledgeable, ethical indigenous writers—writers whose knowledge of their community allows them to know what may and may not be written—a tradition of indigenous literature arising from the traditions of indigenous people will continue to emerge.

CHAPTER FOUR

Writing a Friendship Dance: Orality in Mourning Dove's *Cogewea*

The first indigenous writer to attempt to use indigenous oral traditions to provide both substance and shape to the novel is Mourning Dove in *Cogewea, the Half-Blood: A Depiction of the Great Montana Cattle Range* (1927). Because of the novel's curious history as a collaboration between amateur ethnologist Lucullus V. McWhorter and Mourning Dove, both of whom apparently had quite different ideas about the nature of the project, *Cogewea* offers two distinct and perhaps mutually exclusive approaches to oral traditions. On the one hand, consonant with McWhorter's background in ethnography, detailed descriptions of indigenous artifacts and traditions (complete with McWhorter's footnotes) offer readers the promise of authenticity, an insider's representation of indigenous life. Often, however, when these detailed descriptions appear in the text, they are superfluous to either the narrative patterns or the thematic concerns of the novel. Thus, as David Treuer argues regarding Leslie Marmon Silko's

Ceremony, oral traditions in *Cogewea* sometimes serve a decorative rather than substantial function, appearing as signs of authenticity rather than as viable systems of indigenous beliefs. In contrast, oral traditions in *Cogewea* sometimes serve a much more vital function in the novel, offering characters in the novel ways to understand relationships among themselves, traditions, and the environment, and also serving as a pattern for the narrative structure of the novel itself. What is most interesting about McWhorter and Mourning Dove's uses of traditions is that they reflect and even recapitulate similar divisions for several characters in the novel about the relationship between past traditions and present circumstances, between oral and written traditions, and between the separate "races" of people in the novel.

Structurally, the "half-blood" in the person of Cogewea is the midpoint between these various divisions, the visible sign for the struggle for dominance between these two approaches to indigenous traditions. Much literature about indigenous peoples both before and after *Cogewea* posits the mixed blood in the compelling but overly simplistic paradigm as tragically "caught between two worlds," unable to find a home in either. Initially, *Cogewea* repeats this convention, for the narrator tells us: "Of mixed blood, was Cogewea; a 'breed'!—the socially ostracized of two races" (Mourning Dove 1981, 15). And later, under circumstances involving a competition for money, Cogewea is indeed ostracized—denied an identity as either white or indigenous when attempting to claim a prize for winning two horse races, one for whites and one for Indians. And yet at other times, the novel subverts this essentialist approach to identity: her grandmother, the Stemteemä, and her white suitor, Alfred Densmore, far from ostracizing her, actively seek to claim her against the wishes of the other. The Stemteemä tells stories from the Okanogan oral tradition to the "mixed-bloods" at the ranch—Cogewea, her sisters Mary and Julia, and Jim—to teach them that indigenous women have been treated poorly by certain (not all) nonindigenous men. Densmore, on the other hand, repeatedly urges Cogewea to forget the past, to deny the relevance of the Stemteemä's stories, and to affirm the "superiority" of her white lineage. After considerable deliberation, Cogewea chooses to ignore the Okanogan oral tradition and to elope with Densmore, a choice that ends disastrously. But in denying the oral tradition, Cogewea in fact relives the old stories, adding her name to the list of wronged indigenous women, affirming the truth and value of the stories. The novel, then, becomes an extension of the Okanogan oral tradition, creating a thematic bridge between the oral word and the written text.

These two different attitudes about the oral tradition embodied by Densmore and the Stemteemä are, in fact, discourses battling for a privileged position on the personal, communal, and aesthetic levels in the novel. Densmore's discourse embraces the ideology of science—in particular, the language of nineteenth-century anthropology, which posits that the oral tradition and indigenous life in general are essentially part of the past, with any cultural mixing with the present a sign of cultural debasement. The Stemteemä's discourse, in contrast, emerges from the Okanogan tradition and, as she presents it in the novel, is already "mixed," since the stories she tells are about moments of cultural intersections between indigenous and nonindigenous peoples. By including Cogewea within her private sphere of indigenous oral traditions, the Stemteemä denies Densmore's discourse of purity and impurity, showing instead the importance of conceiving of the oral tradition as relevant and indeed necessary to understanding a changing world. This chapter will explore the relationship of these two discourses to Cogewea, the community, and the novel. Although the languages of Densmore and the Stemteemä clash and sometimes blend, the oral tradition finally emerges as the discourse most valuable to the "mixed-blood" positions—individual, communal, and aesthetic—in the novel.

■ The Official "Race" Language

Unlike the other mixed bloods in the novel, Cogewea contemplates and asserts the difficulties of her life as a mixed blood. She says: "Yes, we are between two fires, the Red and the White. Our Caucasian brothers criticize us as a shiftless class, while the Indians disown us as abandoning our own race. We are maligned and traduced as no one but the despised breed can know" (Mourning Dove 1981, 41). Yet what is interesting is that Cogewea makes the claim for a limited space "between two fires" in language that shows an ability to easily cross different cultural boundaries, the result of growing up in two quite different cultural worlds. On the one hand, Cogewea experienced a traditional Okanogan upbringing under the tutelage of the Stemteemä; on the other hand, she underwent a formal education at the Carlisle Indian School in Pennsylvania. Thus Cogewea is able to speak the language of the Okanogan (she sometimes serves as a translator for her grandmother), the language of her formal education, and a third language—that of the Horse-shoe Bend Ranch, the area "between two fires" where the novel takes place. Her multilingual abilities are not lost on other people at the ranch, nor is she unaware of her linguistic dexterity. The mixed-blood foreman Jim LaGrinder tells her, "You'r bout the queerest I ever saw. Sometimes you talk nice and fine [the language of the ranch], then next time maybe yo go ramblin' just like some preacher woman or schoolmarm [the language of her formal education]. Can't always savey you." Cogewea replies: "That's what others tell me" (33). Indeed, at certain moments in the book, Cogewea consciously shifts to different voices when the need arises—using, for example, the language of her formal education to confront a bank clerk who considers her unable to handle her own financial affairs.

For the most part, Cogewea thus moves freely among these different types of discourse; indeed, she asserts her right to be part of them when she enters two different horse races—one exclusively for indigenous riders and the other only for whites—at a Fourth of July celebration in a nearby town. But participants in both races lash out at her for entering an arena to which they feel she does not belong. Thus rather than confirming her freedom to move among the different racial and linguistic groups, the races instead confirm her feelings that she is an ostracized mixed blood. The participants in the "Ladies Race" demand: "Why is this *squaw* permitted to ride? This is a *ladies* race!" (Mourning Dove 1981, 63). The riders in the "Squaw Race" echo this sentiment: "You have no right to be here! You are half-white! This race is for Indians and not for *breeds*!" (66). Cogewea reflects, "For her class—the maligned outcast half-blood—there seemed no welcome on the face of all God's creation. Denied social standing with either of the parent races, she felt that the world was crying out against her" (66). The situation is further exacerbated when she tries to collect the prize money for winning both races.

The race ("race") officials deny her the money for the "ladies" race, citing the altercation she had with another rider and the fact that she is a "squaw." The situation almost leads to Jim LaGrinder's arrest and even to gunplay, but Cogewea defuses tempers by thrusting the prize money she won for the Indian race at the judge. She asserts that if he is "disbursing *racial* prizes regardless of merit or justice," then the second-place riders deserve both. Furthermore, Cogewea eases Jim's temper by speaking to him "in their own tongue." In this moment of violent confrontation about her place (or lack of place) in these different groups, Cogewea uses the language of each of the groups to alleviate the violence; at the same time, however, she also uses her multilingual abilities to affirm the dominant political order of the separation of races ("races"), with the mixed blood as an outcast.

This same official "race" language is used not only by the judges at the Fourth of July celebration, but by the narrator of *Cogewea* as well. Throughout the novel, but especially at the war dances at the celebration, the narrator often describes the mixing of indigenous and nonindigenous cultures as a form of debasement, thus repeating the official obligations to separate indigenous people and whites into spheres of racial purity, with mixed-bloodedness a sign of impoverishment. Yet after the narrator's description of the war dance, a much less divisive language emerges in the description of the friendship dance—a language that stresses dialogue between racial, tribal, and gender differences. That is, unlike the language of purity and impurity, it embraces the mixed bloods Jim and Cogewea in the Okanogan dance circle, where relations between men and women are untangled and understood. Indeed, it is this language that offers an alternative to what Cogewea feels is the inexorable plight of the mixed blood.

The description of the war dance is remarkable for its enthusiasm for older indigenous cultures and its abhorrence of the mixture of indigenous and nonindigenous culture. It is doubtless an instance of what Dexter Fisher calls McWhorter's insertion of "historical facts about other tribes that are hardly relevant to the story" (Fisher 1981, xiv). McWhorter, who was Mourning Dove's friend and supporter, heavily edited Mourning Dove's initial draft of the book so that it would, in his mind, appeal more strongly to the general reading public and also arouse the sympathies of nonindigenous readers to change the conditions of indigenous life under the Bureau of Indian Affairs (xii). As a consequence, the novel contains scathing indictments of the Indian Bureau in language that is quite different in tone and diction from much of the rest of the book. For example, Cogewea describes the Indian Bureau as follows: "A nasty smear of Government escutcheon. . . . A stagnant cesspool swarming with political hatched vermin! Stenchful with the fumes of avarice and greed; selfishly indifferent to the Macedonian cry of its victims writhing under the lash wielded by the hand of Mammon!" (Mourning Dove 1981, 145). Louis Owens points out that such language contends with the language of Mourning Dove for a position of authority, "with Mourning Dove's easily winning out" (Owens 1992, 44). Thus even on a stylistic level, the two spheres of language collide and struggle to become, in Owens's words, the "internally persuasive discourse" for Cogewea (44).

McWhorter, in addition to conceiving of the novel as a form of social protest, was also interested in using it as a means of teaching about indigenous life. As Alanna Kathleen Brown points out, McWhorter was an "amateur ethnographer," and many of his intrusive comments about aspects of indigenous culture stem from his desire to explain or elaborate upon the Okanogan cultural elements in the book, such as the smoking of the pipe or the significance of the sweat lodge (Brown 1988, 10). Brown writes: "It must be remembered that so little was known about Indians in McWhorter's time that McWhorter felt compelled to explain and reinforce Mourning Dove's representation of Indian life" (Brown 1993, 280). But along with ethnological information, McWhorter also includes the ethnological philosophy of the late nineteen and early twentieth centuries, which conceives indigenous cultures as either pure or impure, with change in indigenous life as necessarily a debasement. For example, McWhorter (who was well versed in the traditions of the Nez Perce) focuses not on the local Pend d'Oreille dancers, but on a "visiting, stately Nez Perce" (Mourning Dove 1981, 74), whose presence provides McWhorter with an opportunity to expound on his knowledge of Nez Perce culture, and whose countenance presents a sharp contrast to younger, "mixed" dancers.[1] McWhorter writes: "See those young men! Their slouchy '*traipsing*' tells of contact with the meaningless 'waltz' and suggestive 'hugs and 'trots' of higher civilization—a vulgarity—a sacrilegious burlesque on the ancient and religiously instituted ceremony. Like other of his tribal cultures, the Indian's dance is suffering in modifications not always to be desired as morally beneficial" (75). The language of purity and impurity cannot accommodate the possibility that indigenous cultures, like any other culture, change over time in ways suited to their own needs. Thus, throughout the chapters devoted to the Fourth of July celebration, the narrator describes clothing, housing, dancing, storytelling—all as diminished by contact with nonindigenous peoples.

Much different in both style and substance is the description of the friendship dance. Here, the narrator makes no mention of diminishments of indigenous life but instead focuses on the purpose of the dance, which is to bring men and women together in ways that clarify their relationships to one another, whether friendship or love. La-siah, a Pend d'Oreille elder, says through an interpreter, "As you circle in this dance, the position of the hand and arm of the man will make known how his heart and mind runs out to the woman" (Mourning Dove 1981, 76). The friendship dance, then, emphasizes the importance of understanding the "language" (the hand positions) of a specific group to determine the nature of one's relationship to others. Furthermore, La-siah says: "This is a ceremony of friendly good will; where all distant tribes may meet in harmony; a peace to be regarded well. All may dance, but it must not be in mockery. It must be from the heart which should always be true" (76). Thus the dance brings people from many different backgrounds—including mixed bloods—inward toward a moment of social unity and clear understanding of personal relationships.

Significantly, the chief of the Pend d'Oreille chooses to dance with Cogewea, indicating a desire to include rather than to exclude the mixed bloods. After the dance, the Pend d'Oreille chief presents her with a gift of "one of [his] best horses," which Cogewea accepts according to tradition: "Cogewea's heart bounded with gladness but Indian etiquette forbade any outward demonstration of gratitude. It was for her to reciprocate in a subsequent friendship dance" (Mourning Dove 1981, 77). Likewise, Jim LaGrinder, the mixed-blood foreman of the Horseshoe Bend Ranch, also participates in the dance, giving the Stemteemä a blanket of "rare design" as a gift. The narrator tells us: "At that moment he ingratiated himself in the old heart, far more than he ever realized. That gift, received in stoic silence, was bread cast in the van of a fast gathering flood destined to break, dark and turbulent on the border shores of both their lives" (78). Both the Stemteemä and the chief of the Pend d'Oreille ceremoniously create a bridge between the older tradition and the younger mixed-blood dancers, drawing no hard distinctions between themselves and their changing relations—in contradistinction to the attitude of the narrator in the description of the war dance.

Indeed, the varying descriptions of the two dances present a microcosm of the central issues of the novel. The characters must negotiate their relationship to indigenous traditions, specifically the oral tradition, with the alternatives embodied by the two voices of the narrator. On the one hand, Densmore, Julia, and Cogewea (at least initially) see the oral tradition as fixed in the past, a view that reflects the attitude of the narrator of the war dance regarding pure and impure traditions. On the other hand, the Stemteemä and Mary (and later Jim) understand that a way of life is forever changing, and the oral tradition, like the dance, remains useful, even necessary, in pulling inward those who embody these changing conditions—namely, the mixed bloods who live on the ranch. Indeed, in the same way that the two voices of the narrator in "The Indian Dancers" mirror the tension between the voices of Densmore and the Stemteemä, these voices, in turn, mirror the tensions between McWhorter and Mourning Dove.

■ Claiming Cogewea

The novel sets up a balanced tension between the Stemteemä and Densmore, creating another kind of race where the victor claims Cogewea as a prize of the area "between two fires." The Stemteemä and Densmore arrive precisely at the same time, off the same train, on the same wagon, and at the bidding of Cogewea. Furthermore, both are outsiders to the ranch: Densmore does not take part, even nominally, in activities integral to the ranch; the Stemteemä also stands apart from the ranch, choosing to stay in her tipi rather than in the house with Mary and Julia. Most importantly, both are particularly adept at one type of discourse—in Densmore's case, the official "race" language of the judges, and in the Stemteemä's case, the language of the Okanogan culture. Although Cogewea understands and uses both discourses too, Densmore and the Stemteemä know them much more intimately and attempt to make theirs the "internally persuasive discourse" (in Owens's terms) for Cogewea.

When Densmore steps off the train at Polson, he (unlike the others at the station) notices Cogewea, Mary, and the Stemteemä standing together and feels disappointment that they are not "the painted and blanketed aborigine of history and romance." Seeing Silent Bob, who works at the Horseshoe Bend Ranch and who appears to agree more with his sense of what a westerner looks like, Densmore expresses to him "his vexation and disgust for the writers who had beguiled him to the 'wild and woolly'" (Mourning Dove 1981, 44). Later, at the ranch, he reflects: "Where were those picturesque Indians that he was promised to meet? Instead, he had been lured into a nest of half bloods, whom he had always understood to be the inferior degenerate of two races" (48). Indeed, like the race officials, Densmore regards blood, purity, and money as central to his conception of himself and his relationship to Cogewea. When he discovers that he is "half in love" with Cogewea, he is momentarily torn between his feelings for her and his desire not to lose his inheritance and social standing back east (81). He resolves to remember his genetic heritage, that he is a "scion of the ancient house of Densmore" (87) and that "such women" as Cogewea are "alright as objects of amusement and pleasure, but there it must halt" (81). Later, he even admits to Cogewea that he believes the white race to be superior (135), but this statement and other clues about the true nature of his character are lost on Cogewea, for she is unable to read his character with the insight of the Stemteemä.[2]

Initially, Densmore courts Cogewea as an "object of amusement," asking her to marry him in an indigenous ceremony, which he knows is binding within an indigenous culture but has no purchase in American courts. Densmore is anxious that this particular tradition be relevant for the present, and even goes so far as to attempt to please the Stemteemä by hunting and fishing for her to win her favor. But with all other traditions, especially the oral tradition, Densmore is adamant that they be relegated to the mythical past. His attitude is partly motivated by the official "race" language, which makes a hard distinction between pure and impure cultures, and partly by the desire that Cogewea might deny her indigenous half so that she will marry him. Densmore's desire to relegate indigenous culture to the past is evident when he expresses disbelief in the Stemteemä's story "The Dead Man's Vision," which tells of the prophecy and the event of the coming of Jesuit missionaries, who work for the good of the Okanogans, and the later arrival of other white men, who rapidly shrink the tribal land base. Densmore is incredulous, first because the story does not coincide with written history, which says that the Lewis and Clark expedition was the first arrival in that area, and second because he cannot fathom that any missionary would undertake such a voyage without proper compensation. (Mourning Dove 1981, 129–30) Densmore's attitude toward the oral tradition is especially evident when Cogewea confronts him with the stories she has heard from the Stemteemä that chronicle a history of deceit on the part of white men and indigenous women. Densmore says: "Cogewea, why do you so seriously and constantly remind me of a possible few questionable deals suffered by your people at the hands of the white man? There are bad individuals among all races, but the things of the past should be forgotten. People change and advance!" (231).

While Densmore advocates the language of division between past and present indigenous culture, the Stemteemä argues instead for the importance, and indeed the necessity, of using the past as a means to understand the present. In this regard, the languages of Densmore and the Stemteemä are analogous to those of the narrator in the descriptions of the two dances, one advocating a language of purity and impurity, and the other embracing the language of cultural exchange. Furthermore, although Densmore's forays into indigenous culture are a means to acquire wealth, the Stemteemä uses her knowledge of nonindigenous cultures for the benefit of others. For example, when Cogewea and her sisters were young girls living with the Stemteemä on the Columbia River, two men from town asked them if the ice was safe for them to fish. The girls, pretending not to speak English, failed to warn them that the ice was dangerously thin. The Stemteemä scolded them for endangering the men, and the young girls responded by asking why did she not tell them herself. The Stemteemä said: "I can speak when I have to do so. But what did you learn the language and books of the pale face for? They do no good unless you make use of them when needed." In broken English, the Stemteemä warned the young men, who "often visited her lodge after that" (Mourning Dove 1981, 119).

Although the grim history of relations between indigenous and non-indigenous people, especially as it appears in the oral tradition, causes the Stemteemä to distrust white people as a general rule, she does not close herself off to the possibility that there are important exceptions, such as the Jesuits from the "Dead Man's Tale." She also says that John Carter, her granddaughter Julia's husband and owner of the Horseshoe Bend Ranch, is "true and good" (Mourning Dove 1981, 217), and one assumes that she gives her blessing to the marriage between Mary and Frenchy, the wealthy, aristocratic Parisian who takes great pains to become part of the culture of the ranch, even learning the "language" of the ranch well enough to play an elaborate trick against his tormentor, Celluloid Bill. The Stemteemä therefore is opposed to Densmore—not because of race prejudice, but because she reads his intentions when she meets him, and places him in the oral tradition as another in a line of white men who treat indigenous women badly. The first time Densmore goes with Cogewea to speak directly with the Stemteemä, Cogewea brings up the indigenous marriage ceremony, which fascinates Densmore and which becomes the seed of his plan to take Cogewea by deceit. The narrator tells us:

> A covetous light had come into Densmore's eyes, which escaped the notice of Cogewea. But not so with Stemteemä, who sat opposite him. A close reader of character, it was not necessary that she comprehend any part of the conversation in determining the motives of her pale faced visitor. (Mourning Dove 1981, 101–2)

Later, when Cogewea and Densmore ask the Stemteemä to approve their marriage, the narrator says: "Covertly, she re-read the sordid character which others seemed not to understand" (247). Although her view of the world comes from the oral tradition, the Stemteemä in fact "reads" character much more accurately than others. She sees that unlike Frenchy and John Carter,

Densmore has become involved with Cogewea, indigenous culture, and the ranch not because he places value on them, but because he wishes to use them for personal gain.

Thus the Stemteemä conceives her relationship with Cogewea as an overlapping of cultural spheres; although she understands that she and Cogewea are different in many ways, she attempts to find ways to bring what is useful and relevant from her past to the present—that is, from the Okanogan culture to her mixed-blood granddaughter. Densmore, on the other hand, conceives his relationship to Cogewea, Okanogan culture, and the ranch as discursive sites that are fundamentally separate, even oppositional, certainly hierarchical, where his engagement is only a foray into the wild unknown for riches—an unknown he hopes eventually to leave.

The Stemteemä attempts to create a connection between the Okanogan traditions and that of her granddaughters, yet it is important to note that she leaves Okanogan discourse with misgivings (unlike Cogewea), especially when telling her stories to a nontraditional audience. For example, before relating the story of the Dead Man's Vision to Cogewea and Densmore, she says, "I know that they would want [the stories] kept only to their own people if they were here" (Mourning Dove 1981, 122). Later, when she tells Jim the story of the "Second Coming of the Shoyapee" (white men), she says:

> "If you were not of my own kind, I would not talk. Although the white blood has made fairer your skin, I like and I trust you. I will tell you this story of other snows. Troubles of long past should be buried, but I will speak."
> (Mourning Dove 1981, 217)

The Stemteemä feels that the Okanogan past is fast closing and perhaps should be left alone, yet she also knows that it must be enlarged if she is to keep her granddaughter from serious harm. For this reason, before she begins the story of Green Blanket Feet, she tells Mary, Julia, and Cogewea: "My grandchildren! I am now old and cannot stay with you many more snows. The story I am telling is true and I want you to keep it after I am gone" (165). Analogous to her reluctance to use English to speak, doing so only when she must, is the way in which she tells the young men to avoid the ice, or Densmore to leave (249); the Stemṭeemä tells stories to a nontraditional audience only when necessary, here precipitated by her love for Cogewea.

Yet for all her efforts, she ultimately fails to convince Cogewea of the value of the oral tradition, for Cogewea chooses to marry Densmore. After hearing the story of Green Blanket Feet, Cogewea responds: "The wisdom of the Stemteemä is of the past. She does not understand the waning of ancient ideas" (Mourning Dove 1981, 176). The narrator expresses very similar sentiments, and undoubtedly overstates the case in denying the ability of the "modern" to comprehend the Stemteemä. The narrator says:

> Thus the primitive and the modern are ever at variance; neither comprehending nor understanding the other. The Stemteemä knew many interesting tales of the past; legends finer than the myths of the Old World; but few of them known to the reading public and none of them understood. Whether portraying the simple deductive ideals of a primitive mind delving into the shadowy past, or constructive of the hopes of a future yet unborn, the philosophy is a sacred one. Ever suspicious of the whites and guardedly zealous in the secrecy of their ancient lore, seldom do the older tribesmen disclose ancient erudition, and when they do, their mysteries are not comprehended. (Mourning Dove 1981, 40)

But the difficulty in communicating the stories (even the translated story to Densmore) is not that they are incomprehensible, nor is the problem that they are false (the perspective of Densmore). The problem is that they do not become the "internally persuasive discourse" through which Cogewea understands the world. Instead, Cogewea accepts the language that separates the past from the present—that is, the language of the narrator in the above passage, the narrator in the description of the war dance, and the language of Alfred Densmore.

■ A Text Is Always a Text

Although the Stemteemä's stories fail to convince Cogewea of Densmore's corrupt nature, ironically the oral tradition nonetheless emerges as the dominant discourse of the novel, for the Stemteemä's stories provide a metanarrative of which the novel itself is a part. *Cogewea* repeats the basic plot of the Green Blanket Feet story and the Second Coming of the Shoyapee, not *in spite* of Cogewea's decision to marry Densmore, but *because* she chooses to follow him. In this regard, *Cogewea* is, in one sense, a novel much like Leslie Marmon Silko's *Ceremony*, which also uses a metanarrative from the oral tradition (drought, ceremony, and harmony) to define the parameters of a present-day story of Tayo, the returning war veteran. In *Cogewea*, the metanarrative consists of nonindigenous men taking indigenous women for wives, only to abandon them for wives they have elsewhere.

The oral tradition in *Cogewea* is similar to that of *Ceremony* in another important respect. In both, an effective oral tradition understands, engages, and negotiates on equal terms with elements from outside the culture. In *Ceremony*, the traditions known to Ku-oosh are insufficient to cure Tayo because the sources of Tayo's sickness range far outside Ku-oosh's knowledge of the non-Pueblo world. (Ku-oosh cannot, for example, imagine that one can kill an enemy without seeing him.) For this reason, Tayo turns to Betonie, a mixed-blood medicine man who understands the many ways that witchery ranges throughout the world. In *Cogewea* the oral tradition is also "mixed-blood," for each of the Stemteemä's stories is a meeting, an intersection between indigenous and nonindigenous peoples and beliefs. Thus, contrary to the narrator's description of the oral tradition, which portrays the oral tradition as pure and inaccessible, the stories of the Stemteemä are themselves evidence of the value of enlarging the oral tradition beyond a particular race or ethnicity to incorporate and make sense of nonindigenous elements, and thus to remain relevant to changing social conditions.

Because the novel mirrors the plot of the stories from the oral tradition, oral and written discourses join one another in the character of Cogewea. This is not to say that there are no fundamental, ontological differences between the two modes of discourse, but the novel shows that different traditions can "speak" to each other; that is, the oral tradition pulls the mixed-blood novel *Cogewea* inward toward an indigenous pattern of thought, similar to the way the Stemteemä embraces Cogewea and affirms her place in the tribe as an indigenous woman.

This relationship between the oral and written discourse is played out not only with the stories within the novel, but also with stories and written texts outside the novel as well. As Dexter Fisher tells us, Mourning Dove initially conceived *Cogewea* as based on the Okanogan Owl and Chipmunk story (Fisher 1981, xi–xii), a story that is never mentioned in the novel but is included in Mourning Dove's *Coyote Stories* (1990). In this Okanogan narrative, Chipmunk, or Kots-se-we-ah (Cogewea), is a carefree young girl who tries to elude Owl-woman, who devours children's hearts. Upon first seeing Chipmunk, Owl-woman tries to get her out of the berry bush by telling her a number of lies. Chipmunk momentarily escapes with the help of her grandmother, but Meadowlark tells Owl-woman where Chipmunk is hiding, and Owl-woman eats her heart. Fortunately, Meadowlark tells Chipmunk's grandmother how to restore Chipmunk to life, and the story ends happily. The parallels to the novel are evident. Through deception, Densmore wins Cogewea's heart, only to toss her aside later. Afterward, Cogewea returns to her former self with the help of the Stemteemä and, especially, Jim LaGrinder. It is perhaps because the novel is based on the Owl and Chipmunk story that Mourning Dove ends the novel happily, against McWhorter's vigorous arguments (Brown 1988, 12–13),[3] and contrary to the Stemteemä's stories, all of which end unhappily. Furthermore, Mourning Dove's use of the oral tradition in this direct way indicates her belief in the value and power of the oral tradition in her efforts as a writer.

While the novel is pulled toward the pattern of Okanogan oral traditions, it also is pulled toward the traditions of nonindigenous written discourse by both McWhorter and Mourning Dove herself. In his editing of the book, McWhorter not only included ethnographic information (and philosophy) in the novel, he also added epigraphs from writers such as Lord Byron, Badger Clarke, and especially Henry Wadsworth Longfellow. Using these intertextual references, McWhorter places the novel within the tradition of British and American letters rather than the Okanogan oral tradition. Mourning Dove, however, displays considerably more ambivalence to the written tradition—in particular, the written work she includes in *Cogewea*, Therese Broderick's 1909 *The Brand, A Tale of the Flathead Reservation*. In chapter ten of *Cogewea*, "Lo! The Poor 'Breed'," Cogewea reads Broderick's novel and castigates it for its misrepresentation of indigenous people, eventually throwing it into the stove. She argues that *The Brand*, "stigma of the blood," is false because it depicts a wealthy, educated, mixed-blood Henry West as one who denies his indigenous parentage because he is in love with a white easterner, Bess Fletcher. Cogewea says: "Show me the Red 'buck' who would *slave* for the most exclusive white 'princess' that lives. Such hash may go with the whites, but the Indian, both full bloods and the despised *breeds* know differently" (Mourning Dove 1981, 91).

Yet what is striking is the degree to which *The Brand* parallels the plot of *Cogewea*. In *The Brand*, Bess Fletcher moves to the Flathead Reservation with her brother. Instantly, Henry West falls in love with her but says nothing, in part because he feels beneath her—a situation not entirely different from that of Jim LaGrinder, who has similar feelings for Cogewea. In Broderick's novel, the villainous Indian agent Dave Davis pursues Bess Fletcher and persuades her to marry him, even though he, somewhat similarly to Alfred Densmore, has fatally wronged another woman in the East. In the end, Dave Davis is found out, and we are left with Henry West and Bess Fletcher together in love. In her reading of *The Brand*, Cogewea denies the relationship between "real" indigenous life and Broderick's novel; yet her own life mirrors key moments in that novel. Furthermore, although Cogewea rails against Broderick for suggesting that indigenous men would deny their parentage, Cogewea herself denies the relevance of the Stemteemä's stories and in effect reproduces the story that she so despises.

Thus the novel itself, like Cogewea, "speaks" the language of different spheres of discourse—the written tradition and the oral tradition—but feels pressure to choose its dominant mode. The choice for the novel is an affirmation of the oral tradition, for it repeats the metanarrative from the oral tradition in a written form. At the same time, however, the novel has a curious, ambivalent relationship to established literary traditions—both denying and embracing the forms of written discourse from which it cannot escape. Indeed, in this precise way, *Cogewea* is representative of the theoretical issues most pressing to many indigenous authors today, who find themselves between these different spheres of discourse while addressing questions of identity, community, continuity, and change. Mourning Dove's novel responds to these issues by showing that the oral tradition provides a theoretical and practical wellspring of language and philosophy, offering the potential for a written literature that reflects patterns of indigenous thought and oral literature.

CHAPTER FIVE

Bearheart: Gerald Vizenor's Compassionate Novel

L ike Mourning Dove's *Cogewea*, Gerald Vizenor's *Bearheart: The Heirship Chronicles* (1978, 1990)[1] combines two disparate narrative forms: an indigenous four-worlds narrative, and a linear reversal of the narrative of westward American expansion. Unlike *Cogewea*, however, these two narratives are not contentious—in fact, they become intertwined in the first chapters and ultimately combine to form the unified narrative for the novel. *Bearheart*, then, sets aside the binary, scientific desire for the purity or authenticity of indigenous forms, along with the subsequent belief that any mixing of traditions is a debasement. *Bearheart* instead revels in the intersection or crossroads between these forms; indeed, as a combination of these narrative forms, the novel itself becomes an embodiment of a vital hybrid or mixed-blood space. To illustrate this hybrid space, Vizenor frequently turns to trickster stories from the Anishinabe oral traditions, the crossroads character who allegorically enacts a dynamic tension between conventional and unconventional behaviors, beliefs, and forms—who ultimately offers fluid yet stable, self-conscious yet powerful narratives of culture, identity, and political resistance.[2]

In the novel, the character who most clearly occupies this borderland is Proude Cedarfair, the leader of a group of thirteen mostly mixed-blood pilgrims traveling from the headwaters of the Mississippi in Minnesota to the pueblos of the Southwest. Proude and his wife, Rosina, have managed to save their homeland, a stand of sacred cedar trees, from the engines of progress and from tribal avarice by leaving the trees, and hope they will remain overlooked. As they travel to the Southwest, Proude and Rosina welcome other pilgrims to their party, most of whom lack their altruism and compassion, and who allegorically fall into two distinct types. On the one hand, certain characters are extremely dedicated to their cherished beliefs about "race," culture, and identity—even assigning a morality to these beliefs or "terminal creeds," as Vizenor frequently refers to them. On the other hand, other characters have little or no concern for social questions, much like the amoral tricksters from oral traditions who care only for their immediate desires. Mediating between these two alternatives is what Vizenor terms "the compassionate trickster" in the form of Proude, his protégé Inawa Binwide, and to some extent Rosina.

In the introduction to his early collection *anishinabe adisokan: Tales of the People* (1970), Vizenor first refers to his concept of the trickster as "compassionate," because of the trickster's qualities as a helper and sometimes a healer. These stories initially appeared in the late 1800s in *The Progress*, a newspaper on the White Earth Reservation, and were originally edited and published by Theodore Hudon Beaulieu, a relation of Vizenor's. Revised further and annotated by Vizenor, *anishinabe adisokan* contains stories about culture and history, including trickster stories that demonstrate how the trickster helps human beings understand and live in the world. For instance, in one of the stories in *anishinabe adisokan*, the infant trickster tells his grandmother: "My name is manabozho and I shall do many things for the comfort of you and your people" (95). Manabozho's notable feats include obtaining fire for his grandmother, exacting revenge for the perceived murder of his mother, and defeating an evil gambler. Sometimes gaining inspiration from his dreams, the trickster provides instructions on how to build a birch-bark canoe, how to

use herbs for healing, and how to make beaver pelts into blankets. Furthermore, the trickster in fact saves the Anishinabe people from destruction, for,
the stories tell us, his defeat of the evil gambler determined "the destiny of
manabozho and the salvation of the *anishinabe* people" (149).

While his compassionate qualities are predominant in these seven trickster stories, the stories in *anishinabe adisokan* also show that the trickster can
be vengeful, and at times even cruel. Manabozho, for instance, threatens his
grandmother's life when she withholds information about his parentage; he
also (unjustly) kills a whale and later desires to kill the *manito*, "the spirit
of the *anishinabe*" (Vizenor 1990, glossary). Writing later of the trickster in
The People Named the Chippewa, Vizenor writes: "More than a magnanimous
teacher and transformer, the trickster is capable of violence, deceptions, and
cruelties: the realities of human imperfections" (Vizenor 1984, 4). In part
because of the trickster's unpredictable qualities, Paul Radin, in his collection
The Trickster: A Study in American Indian Mythology, claims that the trickster
is essentially amoral: "He possesses no values, moral or social, is at the mercy
of his appetites, and yet through his actions all values come into being" (Radin
1972, xxiii).

Similarly, Carl Jung, whose essay "On the Psychology of the Trickster
Figure" is included in Radin's volume, argues that the trickster does not
correspond to human laws and reason: "In his clearest manifestation, he is
a faithful copy of an absolutely undifferentiated human consciousness, cor-
responding to a psyche that has hardly left the animal level" (Jung 1972, 200).
As an expression of the unconscious, Jung argues, the trickster is a parallel
to the shadow in the human psyche—that is, the source of the often unac-
knowledged and sometimes irrational desires and emotions that manifest
themselves in dreams and/or in unexpected words or actions. Jung further
argues that, as a communal phenomenon, this collective unconscious takes
form (becomes "personified and incarnated") as a trickster in societies where
the "people get together in masses and submerge the individual" (206). As
part of Jung's overall vision of the human psyche, then, the trickster corresponds to the infantile, even "evil" aspect of the psyche that exists in dualistic
tension with "higher consciousness," both of which constitute an "energic
system" that is "dependent upon the tension of opposites" (209).

Like Jung, Vizenor proposes a dualistic, energic system to explain trick-sters and their function in societies; but unlike Jung, Vizenor does not place the trickster on one side of the equation as the antithesis to civilization. Nor does he agree with Radin's conception of the trickster as essentially amoral, writing in *Earthdivers* that his own version of the trickster is "not the trickster in the word constructions of anthropologist Paul Radin" (Vizenor 1981, xii). Instead, Vizenor writes, the trickster mediates between two differing forces, "the one who cares to balance the world between terminal creeds and humor with unusual manners and ecstatic strategies" (xii). As such, Vizenor argues that the trickster, rather than being a figure of amorality, actively creates a balance between stasis and change, the conventional and the unconventional, the Apollonian and Dionysian. Indeed, negotiating the space between the moral certainty of "terminal creeds" and the abrogation of responsibility in pure chance, the trickster is in fact a moralizing force in certain societies and in literature. Theoretically, Vizenor's trickster is more closely associated with the African trickster figure Esu-Elegbara, described by Henry Louis Gates Jr. in his *Signifying Monkey*. Gates argues that Esu-Elegbara is an ultimate mediator, providing a medium of exchange between the gods and man—both the "guardian of the crossroads" and also the "master of that elusive, mystical barrier that separates the divine world from the profane" (Gates 1988, 6). Jung himself suggests similar properties for the trickster, likening the trickster to Mercurius, who possesses a "dual nature, half animal, half divine" (Jung 1972, 195), although Jung focuses in his essay primarily on the "primitive" aspects of the trickster figure in indigenous oral traditions. Both Vizenor and Gates, however, foreground the trickster's power to negotiate between differing sides in putative opposition, demonstrating the trickster's conceptual usefulness as an interpreter, and therefore as a source for theories and practice of literature.

In both his fiction and cultural criticism, Vizenor asserts the continuing value and even necessity of the trickster tradition, not only for its teaching about indigenous philosophies but also for current theoretical discussions about language and literature. Consequently, in his essay "Trickster Discourse," he objects to Jung's position that the trickster "gradually breaks up under the impact of civilization" (Jung 1972, 202), arguing instead that the trickster is "a revenant holotrope in new and recurrent narratives" (Vizenor 1989, 205). Vizenor's most sensitive critic, Kimberly M. Blaeser, likewise emphasizes that Jung undermines the trickster figure's application to contemporary indigenous people. In her *Gerald Vizenor: Writing in the Oral Tradition*, Blaeser writes:

> Jung, too, succinctly museumizes the trickster stories of the Winnebago and denies both their satiric sophistication and any claim to contemporary applicability by characterizing the myths as a "remnant" and distinguishing between the contemporary tribal people for whom the mythic "still 'functions' provided they have not been spoiled by civilization" and the "thoughtful observer" who can presumably theorize more knowledgeably and disinterestedly about this "remnant" of culture. (Blaeser 1996, 141)

Jung argues that the trickster evolved from a lower level of consciousness, and thus his dualistic (energic) system between civilization (the animus) and the trickster (the shadow) is necessarily hierarchical. In the early stages of their development, "before the birth of the myth," Jung reasons, American Indians were "groping . . . in mental darkness" (Jung 1972, 202). Only when they had attained a "higher level of consciousness" could they picture or objectify the "lower and inferior state" in the form of the trickster figure (202). Ultimately, for Jung, the history of human consciousness is a narrative of evolution in which healing and liberation occur when the higher plane of consciousness brings light to the mental darkness in *agnoia*, or the unconscious.

Vizenor's concept of the compassionate trickster resists theories that create hierarchies between the conscious and the unconscious, encouraging positive manifestations of the unconscious in creativity, play, and self-criticism. Vizenor further demonstrates that such categorizations frequently result in binary exclusions, where the conscious mind—and its attendant signs, reason and intelligence—become defined as the absence of indeterminacy, contradiction, and creativity. As a result, reason becomes relegated to the simple repetition of existing ideas and language, the hardening of convention, and the valorization of the comforting but static visions of common sense and uncomplicated clarity. Vizenor calls such comforting beliefs "terminal creeds," signifying how beliefs and belief systems become ends in themselves (terminal), lacking the vital capacity to change, adapt, and self-criticize. In contrast, compassionate tricksterism—in the form of the novel itself or the character Proude Cedarfair—deconstructs such oppositions, reminds us that the conscious and unconscious exist as necessarily part of each other, and foregrounds the power of the liminal space between such oppositions as common sense and creativity, genre and innovation, indigenous and nonindigenous. Indeed, *Bearheart*, like many of Vizenor's works, asserts that the liminal, trickster space of crossing over—often in the form of the "mixed blood"—is neither powerless nor tragic, but potentially quite strong and liberating.

■ Two Metanarratives

Just as *Bearheart* reflects Vizenor's concept of compassionate tricksterism through its allegory of characters, so too does the novel reflect this dynamic through its use of two forms of narrative: an episodic travel narrative and a somewhat generic version of the four-worlds prophecy of certain tribes in the Southwest.[3] Although *Bearheart* is a more open-ended book than Leslie Marmon Silko's *Ceremony* (published one year before *Bearheart*), it is actually structurally similar because it combines a linear narrative with an indigenous story form, with both narratives merging at the end. Vizenor's conception of the linear narrative is different, however, because he offers it primarily as a critique of American progressivism. When asked whether the novel is a pilgrimage in the tradition of Dante, Chaucer, and Bunyan, Vizenor replies, "My first consideration was a conversion of the themes of discovery, western expansion, and manifest destiny" (Vizenor and Lee 1999, 96). By pointing specifically to Manifest Destiny, Vizenor thus challenges one of the most willfully blind terminal creeds in the history of the Americas, a concept that not only justified the greed for Mexican and Indian land and California gold, but actually regarded such destructive concepts as being natural, inevitable, and even ordained by God. John L. O'Sullivan, the originator of the term, wrote in 1845 that it was the nation's "manifest destiny to overspread and to possess the whole of the continent which Providence has given us for the development of the great experiment of liberty and federated self-government entrusted to us" (O'Sullivan 1845). A concept that even now continues to be taught uncritically in American schools, Manifest Destiny is an attempt to provide an quasi-religious alibi for the basest of human instincts, and, like so many stories about American history, it masks, wittingly and not, an underlying horror that Americans wish to ignore or forget. *Bearheart*, then, takes this concept and reverses its teleological movement, rejecting outright the presumed moral valence of providential progress and its attendant devastating effects.

As the pilgrims journey southward, they continue to witness the results of providential progress, as they themselves move backward in time toward the precolonial, indigenous city of Mesa Verde ("walking backward," as the Hopi clowns tell them). The movement of the pilgrims enacts a reversal of the phylogeny of America that has taken the ethos of greed to its logical end, namely, the loss of natural resources and the devaluation of humanity in the pursuit of personal gain. The narrator tells us: "Economic power had become the religion of the nation; when it failed, people turned to their own violence and bizarre terminal creeds for comfort and meaning" (Vizenor 1990, 23). When, for example, the pilgrims enter the town of Big Walker in an automobile (a rarity because few cars have fuel), the people in the town fight each other for no other reason than to have a chance to ride. Eventually, the excessive weight from the passengers causes sparks to fly underneath the car, igniting the gas in the tank and killing many of them. This irrational desire to ride in a car illustrates, in macabre microcosm, how an entire society continues to embrace consumption as an ethos even while it takes them to their death. At other times, the novel foregrounds the coincidences of their reversal of the narrative of westward expansion, even to the point of absurdity. For example, while traveling down the Mississippi River, the pilgrims encounter hungry and angry "whitestudents" from a nearby college who are anxious to sink their boat and eat their dogs. To ward off enemies as did his great-great-grandfather, the explorer Giacomo Constantino Beltrami, "Bigfoot" Saint Plumero takes the form of a compassionate trickster, distracting the students from their ill humor by opening a red umbrella and dancing around the boat in precisely the same way that Beltrami did many years before to avoid confrontation with indigenous people (72). In fact, Bigfoot not only uses the same method as Beltrami, he also uses the very same umbrella (purchased at "an estate sale in the cities" [72]) at exactly the same spot to distract the hostiles in the area.

Along with this linear reversal of westward expansion, the novel also employs the indigenous narrative of the emergence of human beings through four worlds, thus combining, in the manner of a compassionate trickster, narratives from both native and non-native traditions. In the opening chapter, "Heirship Chronicles," the narrator describes the first two of these worlds as filled with creation and magic, when the earth turtle emerged from the waters and the animals spoke to humans. The third world, however, loses its life-affirming qualities and reflects the deathly conditions the pilgrims find during their journey: "The third world turns evil with contempt for living and fear of death. Solemn figures are slashed open on the faces of tribal dream drums" (Vizenor 1990, 5). Only the philosophy of the compassionate trickster can overcome the end result of terminal creeds that have ravaged the continent: "In the fourth world evil spirits are outwitted in the secret language of animals and birds. Bears and crows choose the new singers" (5).

The narrative of the emergence through four worlds occurs in several ways in the novel. For example, in the prefatory section entitled "The Letter to the Reader," *Bearheart* playfully suggests that the fourth world is the retirement of an old bureaucrat working at the Bureau of Indian Affairs as a keeper of records. He writes: "We are finished with the third world now, and we wait here in the darkness, less than one month from federal retirement" (Vizenor 1990, vii). In fact, the personal history of this bureaucratic author of *The Heirship Chronicles* foreshadows both the narrative structure and thematic concerns in his work. For example, although the youthful American Indian Movement (AIM) activist Songidee Migwan treats him with contempt, the old bureaucrat has undergone considerable hardship in his life (his own version of the third world), having been taken as a child to boarding school and punished in progressively worse ways as he tries to escape. As a youth, he attempted to escape four times, suggesting the fourth world emergence that his life is about to take in the form of retirement. This sequence also adumbrates the four generations of Proude Cedarfairs, as well as the journey of Proude and Inawa through the third world to transcendence in the fourth at the close of the novel. Furthermore, it is after his fourth escape that the old bureaucrat learns the vital role of the compassionate trickster dealing with the evil of the third world. He tells us that he and his animal helpers "learned to outwit the government in darkness" (viii) as a means of remaining "untamed" and surviving without "assimilation" and "tribal death."

As the author of the novel proper (*The Heirship Chronicles*), the old BIA official uses similar imagery to begin and end the narrative. In the Minnesota cedars, the fourth Proude "dreams in sudden moods and soars through stone windows on the solstice sunrise" (Vizenor 1990, 5), adumbrating the stone windows and soaring transcendence both Proude and his protégé Inawa Biwide find at Chaco Canyon. Furthermore, the BIA author parallels the four-worlds narrative with four incarnations of Proude Cedarfairs. The first Proude is a compassionate trickster who outwits evil "in the secret language of animals and birds," frightening encroaching loggers by growling like a bear and laughing at them as they leave. But the methods of the compassionate trickster are lost on his son, the second Proude, who learns, through his service in World War I, the ways of warfare. The second Proude becomes an activist and uses tactics he learned while in the American military, rather than humor, to defend the cedars against corrupt tribal officials. Eventually, the second Proude is shot to death by tribal policemen while he is on his way to fight with the members of the American Indian Movement at Wounded Knee. With the third Proude, the pendulum swings back toward compassion and humor. He was raised by women who "taught him to seek peace and avoid conflict" so that he "abhorred violence more than evil and corruption" (Vizenor 1990, 14–15). He dies prematurely from a lightning strike while bathing in the river, but his legacy continues with the fourth Proude, who sacrifices his own peaceful existence in the sacred cedars so that they might be saved.

The four Proude Cedarfairs are able to halt the narrative of Manifest Destiny by denying the minions of progress ownership of the cedar forest: the loggers, corrupt tribal officials, the two bicycle-riding federal employees, and finally Jordan Coward. Each, in turn, loses out to the ecstatic strategies of the Proude Cedarfairs, even though they begin their quest completely resolute in the terminal belief that they have claim to the woods. In the case of the loggers and Jordan Coward, an elected tribal president, the Proude Cedarfairs employ humor, fear, and trickery to ensure the survival of the trees. With the two federal employees, the fourth Proude first learns about their "insecurities" before later becoming a "clown"—"a compassionate trickster for the afternoon, a bear from the cedar" (Vizenor 1990, 20). Then, as a compassionate trickster, the fourth Proude uses bluntness and humor to create a union between these two very different federal employees. The Federal Man is physically weak but has an intuitive connection with the cedar forests— perhaps through his father, who ironically lost his reservation summer cabin when the tribal government took it back. The Federal Woman, in contrast, is physically strong, but refuses to acknowledge anything except the letter of the executive order to cut down the trees. She disdains human contact and becomes angry with Proude for emphasizing "sexual differences" (29). By mere suggestion, the fourth Proude prods the Federal Man and Federal Woman into a sexual liaison that connects the hard-edged Federal Woman to the fecund, life-giving properties of the cedar forests; she then neglects to mention in her report that the trees even exist.

■ **Bearheart as a Moral Novel**

Introduced early in the novel, the Federal Man and Federal Woman foreshadow two general types of characters whom Rosina and Proude meet throughout their travels: those who adhere to terminal creeds, and those who challenge the bounds of convention, often through their sexual desires and practices. In the tradition of indigenous oral stories, especially those in Vizenor's *anishinabe adisokan*, the characters often suggest, almost allegorically, an affiliation with these general ideas of the conventional and the unconventional (although not allegorical to the extent of those characters in, for instance, *Pilgrim's Progress*).[4] Perhaps because the novel follows in this indigenous oral tradition, the characters in *Bearheart* lack developed psychologies in the tradition of modern realist fiction; it is unclear, for instance, why most of the pilgrims choose to follow Proude southward, except that they seem to recognize his shamanistic power. Kimberly Blaeser suggests that "while most of the American Indian novels in print are still clearly plot-centered, Vizenor's writing is more idea-centered" (Blaeser 1996, 202). Where desires are explained (Lilith Mae Farmer's love of her dogs, Bigfoot Plumero's love of his statue and later his desire for Rosina), or when desires are shown (Little Big Mouse's desire to possess the victims of pollution)—in these cases such desires are highly unconventional and always result in violence. On the other side, those who adhere too closely to terminal creeds or conventions either perish in violence (Belladonna Winter-Catcher) or do not complete the trip to the Southwest (Justice Pardone Cozener and Doctor Wilde Coxwain). In the final pages of the novel, the only survivors are those who manage to negotiate between these two extremes: Proude and his wife Rosina, and two other pilgrims, Inawa Binwidi and Pio Wissakodewinini, who arrive damaged, both being blinded for their efforts, unable to realize the final vision of transcendence that ends the journey.

In fact, for all its violence and its stylistic innovation, *Bearheart* is finally a moral novel, holding up the ethos of compassionate tricksterism as the only viable response to the dual forces of terminal beliefs and chaos—both of which create, and later predominate in, this futuristic vision of a world that is no longer in balance. In an early essay about *Bearheart*, Maureen Keady writes: "As strange as events of *Bearheart* may be, Vizenor's novel is really a teaching tale about truth and choice, about those who are willing to sacrifice their 'Terminal Creeds' for real meaning, and those who will not" (Keady 1985, 62).[5] More recently, Vizenor says in an interview, "The pilgrims who died on the journey lost the games because of their own greed, intensities, cultural reductions, traditional simulations, terminal creeds, absolutist views, and because of their temptations to court authority" (Vizenor and Lee 1999, 109). In episode after episode, Proude and his fellow pilgrims encounter a third world that is filled with violence and death, and it is essential that they be highly adept at negotiating with evil through humor, avoidance, and in the case of Proude, shamanistic power from the spirit of the bear. Despite Proude's presence, however, they are not always successful, for Proude and Rosina lose almost as many pilgrims as they pick up along the way. Consequently, the novel becomes a kind of moral crucible, in effect burning away those characters that are unable or unwilling to maintain the difficult balancing act of the compassionate trickster.

Belladonna Darwin-Winter Catcher is perhaps the clearest example of a character who cannot complete the pilgrimage because of her terminal beliefs. As Maureen Keady writes: "The cookie that kills her is, in effect, the poison of her own false-pride and superiority" (Keady 1985, 64). At the walled community of Orion, the "famous hunters" and "horse breeders" perform a kind of social purification by killing visitors who adhere too closely to their dogmatic beliefs. Their motivation for such drastic acts, the novel suggests, is that hunters in Orion make a game of exposing the spiritual death of passing pilgrims. A woman from Orion tells Bishop Parasimo, "People are the living dead with the unquestioned church in them" (Vizenor 1990, 192). Like the trophies the hunters and horse breeders kept in former days, the Orion community maintains a large leather-bound book containing the signatures and "one line thoughts" of all those who have failed to pass their test. During a banquet, Belladonna speaks for the pilgrims and chooses to discuss tribal values, but she relies upon clichéd, binary distinctions between her indigenous values and those of the hunters and breeders. Because Belladonna uses blood as a signal marker of her identity as an indigenous person, her task is theoretically hampered from the outset—because, as we learn from the previous chapter (and as her name suggests) she herself is a mixed blood.[6] The inhabitants of Orion have little difficulty dismantling her claims— suggesting, for instance, that she relies on an "invented" concept of Indians, that she presumes to speak for all native people, and that she does not speak from "real experience and critical substance" (196). Although frustrated and angry, Belladonna is quickly brought back to good humor with false praise and admiration, indicating, one breeder says, that Belladonna's (or anyone's) terminal beliefs are closely associated with narcissism.[7]

Yet, because the community of Orion has little compassion for those who hold terminal creeds, it too has its own peculiar kind of narcissism. Indeed, Orion is cut off from the rest of the world by its imposing red walls, metaphorically emphasizing the genetic (blood) makeup of the community. The writing on the wall to the entrance reads (in part): "Within the red walls live several families who were descendents of famous hunters and western bucking horse breeders. Like good horses, we are proud people who keep to ourselves and our own breed" (Vizenor 1990, 189). As Bishop Omax Parasimo observes, Orion appears to contain elements of the creed it rejects: "Your wall is more terminal than the church" (193). Although the community of Orion, like Proude, abjures terminal creeds, it lacks Proude's tolerance and compassion, and thus at least the possibility of any positive engagement with the world. Through their incessant questioning, the people of Orion keep themselves in a constant state of uncertainty to avoid any possibility of possessing terminal creeds. Their approach, however, places them within the well-known postmodernist dilemma of having, on the one hand, the salutary function of exposing the presumed "naturalness" of terminal creeds, but on the other hand, the difficulty of having any positive ground upon which to engage the world in meaningful ways. As Linda Hutcheon writes regarding a similar dilemma for postmodernism and feminism, "There has been an understandable suspicion of the deconstructing and undermining impulse of postmodernism at a historic moment when construction and support seem more important agendas for women" (Hutcheon 1989, 20). In its depiction of Orion, *Bearheart* critiques certain forms of postmodernism, suggesting that its narcissism extends to both those holding terminal creeds and those who have nothing more to offer than the never-ending deconstruction of the world.

While exposing the dangers of terminal creeds, the novel equally critiques the amorality of narcissistic tricksters as well—in particular, the trickster figures Bigfoot Plumero and especially Matchi Makwa. Having little regard for others in the novel, Matchi Makwa most resembles Paul Radin's formulation of the trickster who possesses "no values, moral or social" and who is "at the mercy of his appetites." Indeed, as with many tricksters from indigenous oral traditions, his appetite for sex results in his death. When he and other pilgrims attempt to free witches hanging from a ceiling in a restaurant in Oklahoma, Matchi Makwa and the witch are so overcome with their sexual desires that they immediately copulate on a restaurant table, where the restaurant owner finds and kills them. Matchi Makwa appears particularly disdainful of his structural opposite Belladonna Darwin-Winter Catcher, the purveyor of terminal creeds. When Belladonna lovingly quotes the translated words of Ten Bears, the Comanche chief, Matchi Makwa responds, "Superserious crap" (Vizenor 1990, 113). And later, when Belladonna bemoans the fate of the cancerous cripples, Matchi Makwa calls her musings "Squaw rubbish."

The reason Matchi Makwa makes such outlandish statements, the narrator tells us, is that he "seeks most opportunities for public attention, flourishing on the disadvantage of others" (145). Proude also makes it clear that although Matchi Makwa's mother married a mountain bear, Matchi Makwa himself "never speaks with bears." Indeed, because Matchi Makwa uses language that separates rather than heals ("Our women were poisoned part white"), Proude refers to Matchi Makwa's use of language as "terminal" (59). Only on the occasion of meeting the cancer victims does Matchi Makwa express sympathy for others, and even here the novel suggests that he does so involuntarily: "Their incomplete bodies lived whole through phantoms and *tchibai* dreams. Matchi Makwa twitched and limped from the silent suggestion of phantoms claiming his sympathetic limbs" (145).

Unlike Matchi Makwa, Bigfoot Plumero often expresses compassion for others, but his compassion takes on unusual and even grotesque forms, making him capable of loving a statue as well as exacting brutal revenge when the statue is taken from him. For example, before he encounters Proude, Bigfoot cared for Belladonna after she was raped by three men, having carried her home from the courthouse in Big Walker and possibly saving her life. In his travels with the pilgrims, Bigfoot drives through Big Walker so that Belladonna can accompany them southward. At the same time, like certain trickster figures from indigenous traditions, Bigfoot is both a creator and destroyer, capable of great good and great harm. For instance, because of his deep love for a large-footed bronze statue, Bigfoot viciously kills the anthropologist Orrel Hanson, who stole the statue from Bigfoot and planned to sell it to a dealer—a murder that is as carefully planned as it is cruel. Bigfoot also kills Sir Cecil Staples, the evil gambler whom Proude Cedarfair defeats and incapacitates through preternatural means in an ancient game of chance. Because Sir Cecil is no longer able to mesmerize others with his chromium eyes, Bigfoot's act of righteousness is gratuitous and simply repeats the cruelty Sir Cecil wrought upon weaker people in the world. Finally, although Bigfoot is one of the few characters who negotiates the third world and completes the journey to the Southwest with Proude and Rosina, ultimately he—like Matchi Makwa—dies because of his uncontrolled sexual passion, forcing himself upon Rosina while Proude and Inawa transcend to the fourth world.

While Matchi Makwa and Bigfoot Plumero constantly demand attention from others, Proude Cedarfair is almost always reserved, even distant, rarely offering more than a few (sometimes enigmatic) words of wisdom about their circumstances. Yet without question, Proude is the center of the group, attracting and uniting this incredible diversity of characters, just as he brings together the Federal Woman and Federal Man in the opening chapters of the novel. Similar to Professor Gates's description of Esu-Elegbara, Proude is a copula among diverse characters in the novel—a complex and "classic figure of mediation and of the unity of opposed forces" (Vizenor 1990, 6). As a compassionate trickster, Proude looks beyond his own personal desires, taking "care to balance the world between terminal creeds and humor," exerting his considerable powers at significant moments in the novel. In the episode with Sir Cecil, for instance, Lilith Mae Farrier attempts to win precious gasoline for the pilgrims but loses because, according to Sir Cecil, she "was possessed for one toss of the dish but then lost her good power through her own selfish need for praise and credit" (129). Because Proude lacks Lilith Mae's narcissism, and also because he possesses preternatural powers, he easily defeats the evil gambler, ridding the world of a severe imbalance of good and evil. (Lilith Mae is so consumed with narcissistic fears about her body after death that she immolates herself and her dogs with gasoline.) Later in the novel, Proude likewise exhibits the qualities of a compassionate trickster when, following the deaths of Belladonna Darwin-Winter Catcher, Matchi Makwa, and Bishop Parasimo, he ceremonially takes care of their remains, acting as a kind of bridge between this world and the next. With Belladonna, Proude must also see that her unborn children receive sacred names so that they too may enter the next world.

Rosina likewise acts on behalf of others with a compassion that often recognizes their deepest spiritual needs. For instance, Rosina lovingly embraces Sister Willabelle, whose scars from a childhood trauma initially repel her. Toward the close of the novel, Rosina comforts Pio Wissakodewinini, who became blind at the close of the journey because she/he opened Proude's medicine bag and gazed upon the powerful cedar figures. It is also telling that during the word contest to determine Sir Cecil's gambling opponent, the pilgrims mostly choose words that reflect themselves and their own narcissistic desires. Matchi Makwa, for instance, lists obscenities; Bigfoot Plumero lists the names of presidents (a comment on his sexual organ), Belladonna the names of historical indigenous leaders, and so on. In contrast, Rosina and Proude choose the names of people they met along the journey, indicating that their thoughts are generally about the welfare of others. Furthermore, their altruistic compassion is distinct from other examples of compassion based once again upon narcissism, which manifests in the hunters and breeders at Orion, who feign concern for the pilgrims, especially Belladonna, and also in Little Big Mouse, whose compassion for the mutilated cancer victims is actually an expression of her desire to possess them. In this episode, Little Big Mouse admires the wings of the scolioma moths because they remind her of her childhood with her mother and her dreams of flying. The moths recognize Little Big Mouse's narcissism, telling her, "You are perfect and now you want our imagination and visions for your own" (Vizenor 1990, 149).

Proude's compassion for his traveling companions, however, does not prevent him from finally leaving them to ascend to the fourth world, suggesting that he either accedes to his own version of narcissism (his transcendence ultimately helps no one but himself and Inawa), or that he understands that his powers are insufficient to affect the social conditions of the third world. The novel indicates that Proude's goal of transcendence works against his connection with others, particularly Rosina, who maintains a strong connection to her family and the pilgrims around her. It is Rosina, for instance, not Proude, who expresses concern for their daughters living in the cities, and it is Rosina who sends Proude back to the lightning hills in hopes that Bishop Parasimo might still be alive. The narrator tells us that Rosina's "life was personal. She did not see herself in the abstract as a series of changing ideologies" (Vizenor 1990, 39). As a consequence of Proude's preoccupation with transcendence, the novel implies—particularly with the Hopi clown's sharp reference to Proude's "rude prize"—that Rosina acquiesces to Bigfoot's sexual overtures, an act that indicates the severity of the break between Proude and Rosina and ultimately results in Bigfoot's death. While Proude is able to influence nature, speak to animals, and see into the future, his powers are limited within the overarching and pervasive sense of evil in the third world. Despite his compassion for other pilgrims, for instance, seven of the thirteen pilgrims die, mostly through extreme violence. In their most desperate circumstances, when imprisoned at Santa Fe, New Mexico, Proude appears as helpless as the rest, when the group saves itself only by working for their own preternatural vision with the help of Bigfoot's "precious vision vine leaves" (232).

■ The Postmodern Politics of *Bearheart*

Whether Proude's transcendence is an act of narcissism, or whether it is recognition of immovable social circumstances (or some combination of both), the transcendent conclusion of *Bearheart* is likely predetermined by the narrative structure of four-worlds emergence set up early in the novel. Nonetheless, the conclusion to this four-worlds trajectory offers little or no hope for the people Proude and Inawa leave behind: unlike the cedar forests that Proude leaves earlier in the novel, the rest of the world does not benefit from Proude's departure. But just as the novel has two narrative trajectories, so too does it have two quite different endings. The first is the transcendence of Proude and Inawa; the other is the possibility of resistance to the destruction and violence of the third world residing in the fireside voices of Diné singers near White Horse (New Mexico), whom the remaining four pilgrims encounter after a brief stay at Walatowa (Jemez). The narrator tells us: "Evil had been turned under with the sunrise and their sacred voices. The good power of the dawn was attracted toward their rituals. . . . The men laughed and laughed knowing the power of their voices had restored good humor to the suffering tribes" (Vizenor 1990, 243). The novel offers the power of indigenous ceremonialism as a kind of cure to the tremendous ills of the third world, referencing N. Scott Momaday's *House Made of Dawn*, a novel that makes similar assertions about the power of the oral tradition to keep evil at arm's length. In the second half of Momaday's novel, the protagonist, Abel, cannot resist his desire to exact revenge upon a corrupt (evil) policeman in Los Angeles for accosting him and his friend Ben Benally. As a consequence, the policeman almost kills Abel, beating him severely and leaving him for dead. In this terrible condition, Abel remembers the teachings of his Pueblo and finally seems to understand the proper way of dealing with evil—namely, through the ceremonial dawn-running at Walatowa that begins and ends the novel. These runners are charged with dividing the world at dawn between good and evil: "They were whole and indispensable in what they did; everything in creation referred to them. Because of them, perspective, proportion, design in the universe. Meaning because of them" (Momaday 1968, 104). Abel ultimately returns home and joins the dawn runners, helping the Pueblo and himself by properly dealing with evil, even if he stumbles and loses pace with the other runners because of his damaged body.

House Made of Dawn examines in extraordinarily sensitive ways indigenous philosophies of good and evil, and includes the Navajo, Kiowa, and Pueblo oral traditions as part of its narrative. But its narrative methods—for example, flashbacks and psychological fragmentation—reflect the conventions of the written modernist tradition rather than an indigenous oral tradition. (It is for this reason that I have not included either Momaday's works or James Welch's in this study.) In contrast, like *Ceremony* and to a lesser degree *Cogewea*, *Bearheart* completes a narrative substantially based upon native oral traditions—in this case, a generalized version of the Hopi, Diné, and Pueblo creation narratives. As Vizenor says in an interview, such four-worlds narratives are specific to indigenous communities:

> But actually, the number four in the way of the words depends on the time,
> place, and native creation story. Bearheart, the old man, envisions the fourth
> world, a season of creation and transmutation, and a world of shamanistic
> journeys and visionary survivance. (Vizenor 1999, 98)

On the one hand, the movement toward this generalized tradition with the Diné singers provides a kind of grounding in the practical ceremonial life of indigenous people; on the other hand, the move to transcendence is, at least for those in the third world (as well as readers of the text), decidedly unknowable, almost completely outside the conventional, comprehensible universe. Therefore, just as the novel mediates between terminal creeds and chaos, so too does the ending mediate, as a kind of compassionate trickster, between the physical and spiritual worlds as well as between textual (modernist) and oral traditions (four worlds).

In avoiding a conventional narrative of closure, *Bearheart* also avoids the philosophical problems of terminal creeds. The novel remains open-ended, with several strands of the narrative unresolved, providing both complicity and critique of closure, and perhaps modernism in general. In other words, the novel foregrounds the fictional nature of closure, and instead asserts its own ontological status as a fictional text. That is, the novel shows that it is not an objective reflection of reality, nor the product of an omniscient narrator or even one that especially inspires much confidence. Rather, through form, technique, and narrative structure, *Bearheart* foregrounds the textualness of his fiction, and indeed any fiction, and thus critiques as a kind of "terminal creed" the world-building omniscience that must resolve tensions in the novel.

Because Vizenor's fiction often moves deftly among a variety of discourses, writers such as Alan Velie and Craig Womack consider Vizenor's work to be an example of postmodernist fiction. In his essay "The Trickster Novel," for instance, Velie argues that *Bearheart* (and postmodernist novels in general) has the salutary effect of unsettling "mainstream culture and ideology," particularly realistic fiction, which has "the air of total authenticity" (Velie 1989, 130). Velie rightly suggests that realistic fiction often offers the illusion of authenticity, not because it reflects reality more accurately, but because it accurately reflects the conventional codes of novelistic discourse—language, genre, character development, and so on. That is, realistic fiction provides readers with what they expect. The novels *seem* or *feel* real, whereas fiction such as *Bearheart* disrupts the conventional flow of reading, reminding readers to question and critique the conventional worlds—and not just fictional worlds—they inhabit. As Blaeser writes, "By unmasking all rules, revealing their true nature as fragile social constructs, [Vizenor] encourages readers to relinquish their moral props and to reevaluate things on their own merits" (Blaeser 1996, 185).

While Craig Womack agrees that Vizenor's aesthetic has the effect of deconstructing fixed concepts in language and culture, he challenges the value of this approach on two fronts. First, he argues that this postmodernist approach leaves no stable ground upon which to claim an identity or to fix a political movement. Second, Womack asserts that the poststructuralist language of Vizenor's aesthetic limits his audience "to a handful of academics, effectively cutting himself off from Native people" (Womack 1997, 99). To ensure that literature has the ability, in Jane Tompkins words (1989), to do "cultural work," Womack argues that Vizenor should balance his postmodernist preoccupations with "free play" against the "fixed meanings" within the reality of indigenous social and political concerns (Womack 1997, 98). Yet as Louis Owens points out, Vizenor's trickster figure anticipates this specific criticism by "containing" both sides of the apparent Hegelian dialectic: the stasis of "terminal creeds" and the "infinite proliferation of possibility . . . so common to postmodern literature and theory" (Owens 1992, 234). Focusing on the question of indigenous identity, Owens argues that Vizenor's works offer a provisional identity within the dynamic open-endedness of narratives. He writes, "Through language, stories that assert orders rather than order upon the chaos of experience, a coherent, adaptive, and syncretic human identity is possible without the 'terminal' state of stasis" (235). We can apply this concept of "syncretic human identity" to the compassionate tricksters in the novel, as well as the novel itself, for it provides two kinds of narratives that correspond to the two sides of the "dialectic."[8] In this way, *Bearheart* responds to Womack's call for Vizenor and his critics to "mediate theory with tribal worldviews" so that his work will have sufficient grounding to be applicable to tribal life (Womack 1997, 100).

Furthermore, *Bearheart* also portrays, often graphically, contemporary realities of human violence and depravity, as well as more general political concerns about fuel shortages, indigenous land rights, and materialist philosophies replacing the value of human relationships. Through its use of postmodern metafictional techniques and its genre (futuristic fiction), the novel distances readers from this violence; nevertheless, readers often have extremely strong reactions to the graphic events in the novel. Louis Owens, for instance, relates his experience with three female Native students who reported him to the dean of his college because they were upset with the novel's "wild humor" (Owens 1990, 248). In an interview, Vizenor likewise relates his interaction with a class of college students who were angry with the violence in the book, especially the violence toward indigenous women.

Vizenor says: "My first response was to say, 'What, then, is not true in this novel? The students could not think of anything untrue in *Bearheart*. So the descriptive scenes of violence were what troubled them, not that the scenes were not true" (Vizenor 1990, 110).[9] Furthermore, because *Bearheart* includes graphic scenes of death, it seems to me that the novel insists that we respond emotionally to it, but with a measure of distance that also insists that we recognize that these circumstances—like fictions themselves—are potentially of our own making if we continue to subscribe to terminal creeds. Thus, by combining the techniques of realism and metafiction, *Bearheart* mediates between two distinct approaches to constructing fictional worlds, and thus performs a parallel function to its protagonist, Proude Cedarfair.

Womack's second criticism focuses on Vizenor's frequent references to contemporary theorists such as Jacques Derrida and Roland Barthes when describing the attributes of the compassionate trickster. Contemporary theory provides Vizenor with convenient shorthand to describe the ways that indigenous trickster figures embody the conventional and the unconventional, the sacred and the profane—a constant dynamic that prevents indigenous traditions from hardening into dogma. In addition, Vizenor (like Derrida) frequently employs neologisms—for example, *postindian, socioacupuncture,* and *paraeconomics*—that have the effect of breaking down conceptual (sometimes unconscious) preconceptions of indigenous people. Indeed, these conceptions are frequently reinforced by the apparent clarity of such terms as *Indian, treaty rights,* or *sovereignty,* each of which contains complex and sometimes contradictory meanings, even within tribal communities.[10] Consequently, what appears to be clarity in writing and other communication that employ these terms may actually be the illusion of clarity—a kind of mask of resignation to the unconquerable elusiveness of language. At the same time, however, neologisms (and literary theory in general) sometimes have the effect, as Womack points out, of limiting the readership of Vizenor's essays to persons in the field of indigenous studies, perhaps rendering Vizenor's work incapable of adding a political voice in support of tribal "sovereignty." Although there is no way to tell how literature of any kind affects federal Indian policy, Womack is probably correct that Vizenor's theoretical works are not often read by public officials, indigenous or otherwise. Yet this statement is also probably true with regard to all literary studies, including indigenous essays and fiction—even works that do not especially challenge the readership with either its form or content.

Furthermore, *Beartheart* itself questions the value of self-referential language, especially in the chapter "Word Wars on the Word Wards," where government employees play endless word games upon old government documents and recorded conversations. With the help of linguistic machinery that analyzes language for attributes such as heat content, the government employees at the Word Hospital are primarily interested in rendering language clear (no contradictions) and present (synchronic). They tell the pilgrims that "what we want out of our lives is more clearness and meaning to our words" (Vizenor 1990, 164). Later, they say that "we are still working out models and paradigms and experiments on our language to learn where we are and where we will be, all at the same time that we consider the moment at which we meet and speak" (165). The Word Hospital, then, operates upon the belief or theory that language is a medium for the exchange of communication, attempting to set aside the irreducible complexity of language for the illusion of clarity. Moreover, because the government employees can only use language to determine the meanings of language, their task is an ever-receding horizon, an Escher print of two hands drawing one another. Nevertheless, the Word Hospital receives funding because the government believes that there is a political connection between clear language and conventional institutions. Their reasoning: a breakdown in the meaning of words means a breakdown in law and order, institutions, families, and communications.[11] Yet, as the novel shows, such dreams of a clear and comprehensive social order or social narratives, such as Manifest Destiny, through conventional language can only seem to exist by ignoring or even erasing certain unpleasant complexities, such as the existence of indigenous peoples.

After hearing the terminal philosophy of the workers at the Word Hospital, the tricksters Bigfoot Plumero and Matchi Makwa (as one might expect) immediately respond with nonsensical but humorous language—the kind of language that exists to communicate an emotion, not the clear communication of thought. The employees at the Word Hospital have difficulty with this kind of language, just as they had difficulties with the pilgrims' unspoken communication with animals and Bishop Parasimo's communications with his hands. The Word Hospital employees must reduce communication to understand it on their terms, indicating the degree to which their theory of language is inflexible and inadequate (terminal), unable to comprehend the full range of human communication. They can only understand emotion, for instance, by using machines to color-code the varying degrees of language, rather than understanding it through the maze of human experience. The narrator tells us: "The machines were humanized while the humans were mechanized" (Vizenor 1990, 167). Despite this dismal vision of the future of language, the novel also offers the possibility of a much different kind of language that is emerging in this post-technological third world. The chapter begins with an almost nostalgic tone about a new or resurgent ethos of human communication and interaction that occurs among the many disenfranchised travelers along the interstate. "Oral traditions were honored," the narrator tells us. "Myths became the center of meaning again" (162). In the absence of an industrial society, the pilgrims now gather around a fire in an idyllic setting, where "Proude told stories about his father and grandfather and the sovereign nation." In the ruins of the third world, the novel offers the nostalgic but hopeful return to a communal, changing indigenous oral tradition.

Finally, throughout his writing career, Vizenor has certainly written highly theoretical works, most notably his *Fugitive Poses: Native American Indian Scenes of Absence and Presence.* But Vizenor has also written a number of quite conventional works, such as his autobiography *Interior Landscapes,* and his articles for the *Minneapolis Tribune* collected in *Crossbloods: Bone Courts, Bingo, and Other Reports.* Although Vizenor may be "cutting himself off from Native people" by employing the language of theory, he also addresses issues such as education, treaty rights, water rights, and the American Indian Movement in straightforward language. Both forms of writing—the theoretical and the practical—offer audiences variations of the same melody: that fear of uncertainty and the subsequent desire for clarity often drives people to embrace terminal creeds, often without regard for the human costs, whether in terms of complex personal issues such as indigenous identities or complex social issues such as indigenous history or culture. It is within his novel *Bearheart,* however, that Vizenor creates worlds where tricksters travel with terminal believers, where narratives of conquest merge with narratives of transcendence, and where theoretical and practical considerations merge into compassionate narratives of caution and possibility.

CHAPTER SIX

Muted Traditions and Dialogic Affirmation in Louise Erdrich's *Love Medicine*

I n the previous chapters, I argue that authors such as Leslie Marmon Silko, Mourning Dove, and Gerald Vizenor use indigenous oral traditions as a means of creating new forms and patterns of indigenous literature. The philosophies of this new tradition, as we have seen, are significantly different from philosophies (such as those of the social sciences) that see indigenous life through the categories of pure, mixed, or assimilated, impeding their ability to envision indigenous cultures as constantly changing, not only in relation to Euro-American cultures, but in relation to other indigenous cultures as well. The oral tradition shows us, moreover, that a philosophy of change does not equate to relativism, for the oral tradition is both a stabilizing and destabilizing force in the creation of individual and communal identity. Consistent with this view of the oral tradition, Louise Erdrich's *Love Medicine* enacts a dynamic tension of an indigenous community that simultaneously moves both inward toward its traditions, and outward toward fragmentation and loss. Unlike the use of tradition in the works of Silko, Mourning Dove, and Vizenor, however, the traditions in *Love Medicine* are muted and less distinct, as are the characters in the novel that represent these traditions—Eli, Fleur, and Moses. Nevertheless, despite their subtlety, the traditions in *Love Medicine* remain a powerful force, not only in the lives of the characters and the community, but also in the creation of the novel as well.

An early example in the novel of this dynamic tension is the relationship between the brothers Eli and Nector Kashpaw, who are separated from one another at a very young age when boarding-school officials take Nector from his home to teach him the ways of non-Indian people. Their mother, Rushes Bear (according to their granddaughter Albertine), understands the stakes of losing her sons to the government educational system; she knows that the experience will change her sons in profound, possibly immutable ways. Consequently, she hides Eli in the "root cellar dug beneath the floor" so that she might gain "a son on either side of the line" (Erdrich 1993, 19). Because of her decision, the novel tells us, "Nector came home from boarding school knowing white reading and writing, while Eli knew the woods" (19). On one "side of the line," Nector leads a varied life, working as an actor, when he is filmed dying and falling off a horse; as a model for a famous painting "The Plunge of the Brave," which hangs in the state capitol building; and as the chairman of the tribe. Eli, on the other side of the "line," lives in the woods, alone except for the brief time June stays with him.

In other words, as their lives progress, Nector becomes more visible to the world, while Eli remains less visible, in a sense never leaving the "root cellar under the floor." Only in the chapter "Crown of Thorns" do we get a brief glimpse of Eli's thoughts. Thinking back to when June lived with him when she was a little girl, he remembers buying her bath-oil beads, which she mistook for candy and ate. He reflects: "Then, when she'd started crying out of disappointment and shame, bubbles had popped from her lips and nose" (Erdrich 1993, 215). He laughs, but as he watches her ex-husband Gordie walk away, he is jarred by the juxtaposition of the memory of her innocence and the reality of the harshness of her later life. We learn through other characters that Eli practices many of the older traditions, including (Marie tells us) singing traditional songs:

> Eli would sing his songs. Wild unholy songs. Cree songs that made you
> lonely. Hunting songs to attract deer or women. He wasn't shy when he sang
> them. I had to keep to my mending. (Erdrich 1993, 92)

Within the oral tradition, Eli has confidence, strength, and power, but it is
a quiet strength. Indeed, aside from these moments and his reflections on
June, we know very little about how Eli perceives the world. Nector says he is
"shy and doesn't like to talk" (61), and Marie says that when he came to visit
he "rarely spoke" (92). Yet he remains a crucial figure in the novel, not only
as a formative influence on June, who figures largely in the novel, but as a
reminder of the abiding traditions just under the surface of the novel.

On the other side of the line, Nector moves outward from the home, ever
more visible; yet in the twilight of his life, he loses his ability to integrate his
thoughts into a stable center of identity. Albertine says, "Now, these many
years later, hard to tell why or how, my Great-uncle Eli was still sharp, while
Grandpa's mind had left us, gone wary and wild" (Erdrich 1993, 19). Albertine
goes on to say:

> Elusive, pregnant with history, his thoughts finned off and vanished. The
> same color as water. Grandpa shook his head, remembering dates with no
> events with them, names without faces, things that happened out of place
> and time. Or at least it seemed that way to me. (Erdrich 1993, 19)

Nector, having spent his life dealing with the outside world, becomes fragmented, while Eli, the novel suggests, remains intact by staying closer to the
center of his culture. And yet, although Nector's life ends in a much less positive way than Eli's, the novel is careful to show that we cannot make absolute
judgments about either character. On the one hand, Eli lives closer to the
traditions of the community, and although he raises June, he nevertheless
lives alone in his old age, separate from the community. On the other hand,
while Nector's life ends in fragmentation, he is invaluable as a leader in the
community. Albertine says, "Somehow he'd gotten a school built, a factory
too, and he'd kept the land from losing its special Indian status under the

policy called termination" (19), a governmental policy which would have ef-fectively destroyed the indigenous community altogether.

In fact, the novel suggests that rather than seeing the brothers as opposing one another (in a binary way), we should instead see them as being intricately a part of the other, suggesting the ever-present possibility of dialogue, in the Bakhtinian sense, complementing one another.[1] Indeed, it is possible to see Eli and Nector as two halves that come together in the figure of Nanapush, especially in *Tracks*, where Nanapush is both a wellspring of tradition (osten-sibly the trickster tradition) and a bureaucrat, holding office as a tribal chair at the bidding of Father Damien.[2] In *Love Medicine*, after Nector returns home from boarding school, he and Eli work well together to earn money, combin-ing their knowledge from both sides of the line. Because Eli stays home from boarding school (the novel suggests), he is the better hunter; and because Nector is familiar with the other side of the "line," he is the better salesman. In other words, the brothers recognize their strengths and pool them for the benefit of both. Nector says, "I get the price from the Sisters, who cook for the priests, and then I come home and split the money in half" (Erdrich 1993, 61). Nonetheless, probably as a result of the boarding-school officials moving in and separating them, they grow to have different interests. Nector goes on to say, "Eli usually takes his bottle off into the woods, while I go into town, to the fiddle dance, and spark the girls" (61).

This relationship between Eli and Nector—and many others like it—illustrates a central tension in *Love Medicine* between the inward-moving forces that consolidate culture, and the external forces that fragment culture.[3] This tension is significant not only for Eli and Nector, but also for many other pairs of characters in the novel, and even for the novel itself. On one side of the line, those who most clearly carry the traditions—Eli, Fleur, and Moses—are muted, below the surface (to use a recurring image in the novel), as are the traditions themselves (such as the true love medicine). In placing these characters, and especially the traditions, in the background, Erdrich reflects the realities of life in certain indigenous communities that have experienced fragmentation from the other side of the line through years of destructive interaction with nonindigenous peoples—including the fragmentation of the land base through the Allotment Act (to which Albertine refers as she drives home). Yet in these fragmented communities, and in the characters who embody this fragmentation—Nector, Henry, and possibly King—there nonetheless remains the possibility for a reconnection to a strong center of culture. David Mitchell argues that "the task of many Native American novels (and Erdrich's *Love Medicine* is a prime example of this strategy) is to examine ways in which characters either succeed or fail to re-build the ideological bridges that can lead them back to their pasts" (Mitchell 1991, 163). In her article "Where I Ought to Be: A Writer's Sense of Place," Erdrich argues that the task of American Indian writers is to "tell the stories of the contemporary survivors while protecting and celebrating the core cultures left in the wake of the catastrophe" (Erdrich 1985, 23). *Love Medicine* not only tells the story of "contemporary survivors" and the "core cultures," it also shows the delicate, sometimes painful relationship between these two "sides of the line." Thus, in affirming the "core cultures," *Love Medicine* is more than a revisiting of the modernist, aesthetic, Yeatsian vision of the center that does not hold. The portrayal of this tension in *Love Medicine* is messier, for the novel presents both "sides" (Nector and Eli, for example) without romanticizing or demonizing either. That is, the novel shows that moral claims about either Eli or Nector are essentially reductive, forgetting the necessity (and cost) of Nector's engaging the outside world on its terms, and the isolation (like Moses's island) of Eli's core culture.

Like Eli and Nector, Lulu and Marie also demonstrate this central tension in the novel; yet unlike the relationship between Eli and Nector, which grows distant over time, the relationship between Lulu and Marie moves in a different direction: from antagonism (binary) to friendship (dialogic).4 Their relationship represents two sides of the Indian community, and in this sense is very similar to Eli and Nector's. On the one hand, Lulu's lineage goes back to her mother, Fleur Pillager, a repository of Anishinabe tradition in the novel, and possibly, as is suggested in *Tracks*, to the water monster Missepeshu. On the other hand, Marie's relations, the Lazarres, are a source of shame for her, for they are a pitiful crew, existing for the most part on the fringes of tribal life. In other words, while Fleur's background suggests a center of Anishinabe culture (much like Eli's background), Marie's relations display a sense of fragmentation, similar to Nector's later life. Initially, these two strong women regard each other with considerable animosity, for the trajectories of their lives often intersect in their love for the same man, Nector Kashpaw, resulting in competition and jealousy. Yet even when their love for Nector puts them most at odds, and despite their substantially different backgrounds, they are in some ways quite similar.

For instance, their households are almost mirror images of each other, for Marie and Lulu are at the center of households of considerable diversity. Lulu's home consists of several boys who, if their appearances are any indication, are from several different liaisons:

> There were eight of them. Some of them even had her maiden name. The three oldest were Nanapushes. The next oldest were Morrisseys who took the name Lamartine, and then there were assorted younger Lamartines who didn't look like one another, either. Red hair and blond abounded; there was some brown. The black hair on the seven-year-old at least matched his mother's. (Erdrich 1993, 109)

In spite of its diversity, Lulu runs the household with astounding efficiency, as Beverly Lamartine observes when he visits her (119–20). Marie, too, has a remarkably diverse household, for she took in a number of children following two tragedies in her and Nector's life. Nector says:

> In one year, two [of their] children died, a boy and a girl baby. There was a long spell of quiet, awful quiet, before the babies showed up everywhere again. They were all over in the house once they started. In the bottoms of cupboards, in the dresser, in trundles. Lift a blanket and a bundle would howl beneath it. I lost track of which were ours and which Marie had taken in. (Erdrich 1993, 126)

Consequently, even in their home lives, both Marie and Lulu enact the same thematic tension that exists between different characters and on different levels in the novel. At the same time, however, it is clear from the descriptions of their households that Lulu and Marie are not equally successful in maintaining a balance between themselves and this diversity. One important reason, perhaps, is that Lulu is more centered within herself and traditions; she is better able to maintain a healthy balance between herself and her diverse sons. Marie's household, on the other hand, is more fragmented and out of control, partly because her diverse household is the result of great personal loss, and possibly because she lacks a strong personal identity, for so much of her concept of herself is bound up in Nector's position in the community.

Within this dynamic of sameness and difference, the plot of the relationship between Marie and Lulu moves from antagonism to dialogue—literally. Even after Nector dies and Lulu and Marie are grandmothers, he remains a powerful, binding force between them through the figure of Lyman (raised by Lulu, yet the son of Marie's husband Nector), who owns the factory where they both work, side by side. When Lyman hires Lulu and Marie to teach beading at his factory, he hopes that he may be able to "phase them out" slowly over time. Instead, they develop a relationship that astounds him. Lyman says:

> Their positions, at the beading table, which overlooked the entire workplace, had to be precisely measured. They each needed territory to control.
>
> Their friendship, if that's what you'd call it, was hard to figure. Set free by Nector's death, they couldn't get enough of their own differences. They argued unceasingly about the past, and didn't agree on the present either. Whenever I was caught, they drew me in as a referee, and so I tried to avoid them, walked quickly past their table, which always seemed to be in motion, set awhirl by history's complications. (Erdrich 1993, 311)

No longer stubbornly silent in their antagonism, Marie and Lulu now engage each other, dialogically interpreting community history, each with her own stories about history, each with her own equal, sovereign space. Thus the plot of their relationship moves from adversarial (binary) to coequal and speaking (dialogic), indicating a healthy exchange between two sides of the community—namely, Lulu's traditional past and Marie's questionable relations. *Love Medicine*, then, is in large measure a presentation of the value, power, and even beauty of these moments of balance and dialogic exchange between the "core culture" and "contemporary survivors."

Perhaps no relationship indicates this general plot from opposition to affirmation than Lipsha's relationship to his mother, June. Lipsha desperately desires a sense of affirmation that has "staying power," that is, the ability to love over a long time until one or the other "died or went crazy" (Erdrich 1993, 234). Initially, Lipsha has an adversarial, binary relationship to June, refusing to acknowledge his mother because he is told (probably by Marie) that June tried to drown him. He tells Albertine that "even if she came back right now, this minute, and got down on her knees and said, 'Son, I'm sorry for what I done to you,' I would not relent" (39). Yet after listening (reluctantly) to the story of his mother from his grandmother Lulu Lamartine, Lipsha eventually does accept June once he begins to understand the difficult circumstances of her life. June seemed to know that those in the orbit of her life—Gordie and King—could not count on her for stability; thus she gives Lipsha to Marie, who cared for June when she was, according to Marie, staying alive "by eating pine sap in the woods" (85). Lipsha says:

> How weakly I remembered her. If it made any sense at all, she was part of the great loneliness being carried up the driving current. I tell you, there was good in what she did for me, I know now. The son that she acknowledged suffered more than Lipsha Morrissey did. The thought of June grabbed my heart so, but I was lucky she turned me over to Grandma Kashpaw. (Erdrich 1993, 367)

Although Lipsha remembers June "weakly," he understands that she was carried along in a current of loneliness, away from any sense of belonging or identity. Thus, by untangling the contradictory stories of his past and of June, Lipsha (re)connects with his larger family: his father Gerry Nanapush, his grandmother Lulu, and his great-grandmother Fleur Pillager, whom he initially fears and avoids, but with whom he is now unavoidably connected. As James McKenzie writes, "Lipsha, the man who completes his mother's journey home, the one with the 'powers' and the 'touch' is, as Gerry's son, if not an avatar at least a contemporary transformation of the great Chippewa spirit hero Nanabozho" (McKenzie 1986, 60). It is a tenuous connection but an all-important one, for once Lipsha establishes the relationship, he is able to say: "I decided I belonged, whether King thought I did. I was a real kid now, or halfway real" (Erdrich 1993, 348), with the other half to be established in his meeting with his father, Gerry. Furthermore, by affirming June, Lipsha brings the novel back full circle, in a sense bringing June home once again.

■ Untenable Binaries

The general plot of *Love Medicine* is a movement from opposition to affirmation—from the death of June to Lipsha's embrace of her in the final pages. Indeed, as Lissa Schneider argues, "With the exception of Nector, the many first person narrators describe a movement toward forgiveness and transformation through the act of sharing their stories with one another, a movement that influences the entire community" (Schneider 1992, 11). While the relationships between Eli and Nector, Lulu and Marie also follow this optimistic pattern, others are far less successful. Three pairs of brothers in the novel—King and Lipsha, Beverly and Henry, Lyman and Henry Junior—remain separate, unable to create a bridge between themselves and their siblings. For example, King, who has been away in the military, has an antagonistic relationship to his half-brother Lipsha, who remains at home and who has, apparently due to his lineage of medicine people, the ability to heal with a touch. No such connections compel King to return home, including a relationship with his father, Gordie; at the same time, he also fails to make a life for himself off the reservation in Minneapolis. As a consequence, King lacks a sense of connection either to his home on the reservation or to his new home in the city, finally ending up in a windowless, impoverished apartment, symbolic of how much he has separated from his community and his own family. Indeed, even his connection with reality becomes tenuous: Lynette confides to Lipsha that King never left the West Coast while he was in the military; yet King nevertheless regales Lipsha with stories of his heroics in Vietnam, even pathetically acting out the parts of his fictional exploits when no one is watching.

Unlike King, Beverly has much more success in Minneapolis, yet he too comes to live a fantasy life, constructing an unreal image of his life with his and Lulu's son, Henry Junior. Initially, a wallet-sized picture of Henry proves to be an effective tool in helping Beverly sell math-enrichment books, for Beverly impresses upon potential customers the power of the math program to make them a part of the American Dream, just as it had done for his own son in the picture. Yet, ironically, Beverly eventually begins to believe his own sales pitch, considering the possibility of going to the reservation to claim his son and take him back to the city. When he tries to make the fantasy a reality, he quickly realizes how distant he has become to his home community having left the reservation after Lulu chooses his brother Henry as her husband. Although he congratulates "himself for years after on getting free of her slack, ambitionless, but mindlessly powerful female clutches" (Erdrich 1993, 115). The truth, however, is that Beverly is in fact quite jealous of his brother, and has suppressed those feelings as he makes his life in Minneapolis. These feelings, combined with the view of his parents "who considered those who thought of themselves as Indian quite backward," cause Beverly to separate himself from the community, creating a life in the city so different from that on the reservation that the idea of moving back is clearly out of the question. He muses about selling math-enrichment books on the reservation, but he intuitively grasps the fundamental truth that the American dream (his dream of himself) that sells in Minneapolis has no place in this indigenous community. "No one on the reservation would buy them, he knew, and the thought panicked him" (121). In short, both King and Beverly choose the outside world, surviving there only by sacrificing some crucial aspect of their lives.

In contrast to Beverly and King, Nector does not embrace the outside world, nor does he accept fantastic representations of his life. Yet at the same time, Nector is not especially compelled by the "core culture" of his brother Eli. Instead, Nector moves between both, floating along inexorably toward old age and fragmentation. Looking back on the early phases of his life, Nector points to his reading of literature and his jobs in film and painting to derive this basic lesson of staying afloat. In South Dakota, Nector is filmed dying and falling from a horse, and in Kansas, he poses for a painting, "The Plunge of the Brave," which shows him jumping naked off a cliff to his death in a river. Nector is keenly aware of the implications of these representations; he knows that films and the painting are popular because they play on the general view that Indians are vanishing from existence. Nector concludes: "The only interesting Indian is dead, or dying by falling backwards off a horse" (Erdrich 1993, 124). Nector decides that instead of accepting this portrayal of Indians, he will overcome them. He says:

> I remembered that picture, and I knew that Nector Kashpaw would fool the pitiful rich woman that painted him and survive the raging water. I'd hold my breath when I hit and let the current pull me toward the surface, around jagged rocks. I wouldn't fight it, and in that way I'd get to shore. (Erdrich 1993, 124)

In his reading of *Moby Dick* (a book which he liked so much that he stole a copy from school), Nector finds kinship in Ishmael, who "survived the great white monster like I got myself out of the rich lady's picture" (125). Nector goes on to say: "He let the water bounce his coffin to the top. In my life so far I'd gone easy and come out on top, like him. But the river wasn't done with me yet" (125).

By floating with the current rather than playing an active part in his own life, Nector refuses to accept those conceptions of his life that offer only his demise. Yet in denying these images of death, deciding instead to "float" to stay alive, Nector becomes a passive observer in life, never actively affirming either the traditions or the people around him. Once Nector decides to float along the river, his life rushes forward in a swift current, in some ways drawing him closer to the community as a father and as a tribal chair; yet at the same time, his passivity inexorably leads to fragmentation in his old age. He says:

> So much of time went by in that flash it surprises me yet. What they call a lot of water under the bridge. Maybe it was rapids, a swirl that carried me so swift that I could not look to either side but had to keep my eyes trained on what was coming. Seventeen years of married life and come-and-go children. (Erdrich 1993, 127)

Even the most notable moments in Nector's life usually occur as a result of actions not his own, eroding his sense of self a little each time. For instance, Nector became the tribal chair of his tribe, not because he sought it, but because it simply happened to him. He says: "I never even ran for the office. Someone put my name down on the ballots, and that night I accepted the job I became somebody less, almost instantly" (127). Other instances of his extreme passivity include his description of his sexual encounter with Marie when she leaves the church as a "saint" (64–66), and his burning of Lulu's house (144). Without a center of identity that would anchor him against fragmentation and that would give him direction for personal action, he becomes "somebody less," until he eventually loses his identity altogether.

Besides presenting examples of both balance and antagonism between "core cultures" and "contemporary survivors," *Love Medicine* also presents two characters—Henry Junior and June—who cannot find a balance and refuse to accept a fragmented existence like that of King, Beverly, and Nector in his old age. Seeing no other alternative, they tragically choose to end their lives. Henry Junior, for instance, comes home shattered from his war experiences, both in body and in spirit. His brother Lyman actually considers Henry to be a kind of father, but even he fails to bring Henry back despite his efforts to relive their carefree travels before the war—a shared experience for which the red convertible is an icon. Likewise, June's life outside the community is a series of failed jobs and plans; yet the community offers little better than the pain of an unhealthy relationship with Gordie. As Aurelia says: "She walked out of there because . . . what did she have to come home to after all? Nothing!" (Erdrich 1993, 413). In the eggs June eats in a bar in an oil boomtown, she sees only fundamentally binary alternatives now that she has drifted so far from the community—the cracked surface of her life in the oil boomtown, and the "pure and naked" skin underneath—either fragmentation or purity, with no dialogue possible between the two. Thus she likens herself to the egg, insisting that what she is wearing is not a turtleneck but a "shell," and later thinks, "underneath it all her body was pure and naked—only the skins were stiff and old" (2, 4).

In fact, in her death, June once again reenacts the central tension in the book, here figured as the tension between those traditions below the surface of the water, like the water monster Missepeshu, and the realties of everyday life, existing above the surface of the water. This image of water foreshadows many instances of tension in the novel between life above the water and those elements below the surface—elements such as the older traditions, the past, or even a willingness to immerse oneself in love for another. For instance, when Nector tries to remember past events, the book likens his efforts to fishing for thoughts, trying to hook something substantial to the past to bring it to the surface (Erdrich 1993, 19). Elsewhere, when Nector returns to Marie after he almost leaves her for Lulu, Marie welcomes him across the wax floor "which gleamed like a fine lake" (166), reaching out and pulling him in with her. This tension occurs even in the imagery of the first chapter, which offers several examples of Christian references to describe the last day of June's life, suggesting a mythological connection to Christ and Easter. Yet this imagery exists in tension with the indigenous traditions in the book; indeed, as we learn later, the more significant imagery has to do with the impossible desire to find a lost innocence in the womb of the past—what Lipsha calls "them vast unreasonable waves" (367). The narrator tells us that after leading a hard and unfulfilling life, June now desires to be "pure and naked" (4), remembering a time of innocence when she was "walking back from a fiddle dance or a friend's house to Uncle Eli's warm, man-smelling kitchen" (6). These nostalgic reminiscences and the overcast day, "like going underwater," foreshadow her descent into the freezing snow where she "walked over it like water and came home" (2, 7).

■ Fragmented Voices and Muted Traditions

In her essay "Fragments of Ojibwe Stories: Narrative Strategies in Louise Erdrich's *Love Medicine*," Lydia A. Schultz makes a compelling argument that writers such as Gene Lyons and Robert Silberman, who see a lack of unity in the novel, read it through a modernist perspective (Schultz 1993, 411; Lyons 1985; Silberman 1989). In other words, because Lyons and Silberman read the novel as exemplary of the breakdown of a larger metanarrative, according to Schultz, they argue that the novel lacks a unifying plot or unity through, in Silberman's words, "a sustaining central consciousness or protagonist"

(Silberman 1989, 104). For Schultz, these writers fail to understand that Erdrich writes from a perspective that already sees the "essential unity of all things" (Schultz 1993, 513), and that this unity is expressed in the novel through the oral tradition.⁵ For example, Schultz shows that Erdrich weaves the oral tradition through the use of the trickster tradition in Anishinabe culture in the persons of Gerry and Lulu.⁶ Schultz further shows that the stories or the voices of the characters repeat different stories to give an indirect path to the truth. She writes: "These repetitions pick up on the Ojibwe tradition of telling a tale in a variety of ways instead of giving direct answers to questions" (514). Schultz's most daring statement is that "June helps restore a sense of unity to these people's lives" (515). Schultz goes on to say, "Even though she may have failed in her physical attempt to return home, by the end of the novel she has achieved a metaphorical homecoming when thoughts of her bring together the community she sought" (515–16).

Schultz's essay convincingly shows how the oral tradition works to bring different perspectives to bear on the question of truth; yet her view that the community comes together at the end of the novel is perhaps too optimistic. The novel nods toward the importance of affirmation when Lipsha accepts June as his mother, but overall the community remains divided, poised between the two alternatives of fragmentation and the possibility of unity through an evolving tradition. This philosophical tension is precisely the manner in which certain theories of the oral tradition conceive of stability and change.⁷ In her writings on the oral tradition, Leslie Marmon Silko emphasizes that a storytelling culture constantly moves toward integrating its individual elements—points of view, old and new stories—into a complex, changing community. It does so not only in spite of conflicting points of view, but also *because of* these different points of view, for they provide valuable correction and supplemental information. Silko says, "There is always, *always*, the dynamics of bringing things together, of interrelating things. It is an imperative in Pueblo oral literature, it seems to me, and it occurs structurally in narrative and in fiction" (Silko 1986a, 64). She writes:

> The stories are always bringing us together, keeping this whole together, keeping this family together, keeping this clan together. "Don't go away,

don't isolate yourself, but come here, because we have all had these experiences together"—this is what the people are saying to you when they tell you these other stories. (Silko 1986a, 59)

In this conception of the oral tradition, and of the creation of meaning in general, conflict is not inherently negative, and in fact can be seen as having positive influences, if it is conceived within the context of a dialogic philosophy that accepts truth as provisional rather than absolute.

Love Medicine enacts this thematic tension in the oral tradition between the centripetal movement inward toward a unifying Indian culture, and outward toward fragmentation. On one side of the line, the different chapters in the novel, representing the voices of different narrators, do not all add up to a single unity. These voices are—much like Nector in his later life—fragmented, conflicted. On the other side of the line, those who most clearly carry the traditions that normally unify a tribal community—Fleur and Moses—are much like Eli: muted, below the surface (to use a dominant image in the novel), as are the traditions themselves, such as the traditional love medicine. Thus the novel itself, like many characters within it, remains poised between two alternatives: the ever-present possibility of fragmentation, and the subtle yet powerful and unifying forces of tradition.

Love Medicine suggests the possibility of fragmentation not only thematically, with characters like Nector, Beverly, and King, but also stylistically, with different characters "telling" the stories of their lives, most of time in their own "voice" using highly subjective first-person narration. Lipsha, for example, says: "I really never done much with my life, I suppose. I never had a television" (Erdrich 1993, 230). Each voice is dated to a specific moment in history and is not necessarily in chronological order, thus disturbing any sense of clear continuity. Furthermore, when different characters think of specific incidents, they do not always agree with the "facts," thereby eliminating the possibility of an unquestioned authority (author) about what happens in the novel, presenting instead conflicting information from a conflicted community. As Debra C. Holt writes: "Ultimately, the reader must fill in the gaps, connect people to events and to each other. Because we see the people from multiple viewpoints, we can reach no final truth. Value judgments, so

easily arrived at in the Western tradition, have no place here" (Holt 1991, 151).
For instance, when Henry Junior drowns in the river, even Lyman, who was
there, did not see precisely how he died, for Henry Junior seemed to fade into
darkness (Erdrich 1993, 193). Others in the community have different explanations, which they take for truth. Lipsha believes Marie's contention that she
saw Henry Junior's death in the reflection of a toaster oven: "Sure enough,
the time came we heard how Lyman and Henry went out of control in their
car, ending up in the river. Lyman swam to the top, but Henry never made
it" (240). Other events where characters have conflicting views are whether
or not Gerry killed the highway patrolman, the circumstances of Marie and
Nector's meeting down the hill from the church (they both have different
version of this event), and the circumstances of Henry Sr.'s and June's deaths.
As Hertha D. Wong points out, "Often such narratives are told in isolation,
each person nurturing his or her own private interpretation of events" (Wong
1995, 176).

By using first person narration, writers emphasize the particular voice
of the speaker—its nuances and individual sensibilities. David Mitchell
writes: "There are a few instances of moral judgment being passed down
in this work, for Erdrich treats each character as an individual worthy of
respect and understanding. Thus while the reader listens and tellers re-
hash events that are told and interpreted several times over the course of
the novel, we quickly understand the blurred nature of perception that
highlights each character's tale with the limitations of experience and
understanding" (Mitchell 1991, 164). For instance, Henry Sr.'s death is the
subject of controversy between Marie and Lulu, and their interpretations of
his death arise from their own personal histories and sensibilities. Henry
died late one night after drinking heavily, driving his car up the railroad
tracks after uttering these enigmatic words at the bar: "She comes barreling
through and you'll never see me again" (Erdrich 1993, 107). After considering for a time that "she" was Lulu, the people in the bar finally decided
that "she" meant the train, and therefore that Henry committed suicide.
Marie shares this view because she thinks the worst of Lulu. For most of
her life, Marie has been preoccupied with gaining respectability and leaving behind her roots as a Lazarre, relying heavily on Nector's position as a

tribal chairman as a symbol of her success. When she reads Nector's note saying he is leaving her for Lulu, Marie thinks of Lulu's reputation and concludes that Lulu's husband Henry killed himself by driving his car up the railroad tracks because he was overwhelmed by Lulu's affairs (161–62). Lulu, on the other hand, interprets Henry's death in a way that fits her own view of life. When she was a small girl, she discovered a dead body (who, we learn in *Tracks*, is the father of Marie) close to her playhouse in the woods, an experience that in some ways defined her life afterward. She explored the death body, feeding it and even taking off its clothes; in this way, the novel suggests, she came to terms with death by making it very ordinary. For Lulu, as for Nector after his encounter with the arts, death is no longer a mystery; it no longer holds an allure, as it does for June and Henry Junior. She concludes: "Everyone who knows me will say I am a happy person. I go through life as a breeze. I try to greet the world without a grudge" (281). For this reason, it is perhaps incomprehensible to her that Henry might have committed suicide. Instead, she leaves it as a mystery: "He stalled in the middle of a soybean field, or maybe the train did not blow its warning whistle. There's really no way to tell" (278). Indeed, as Hertha D. Wong says about all the voices: "Throughout the work these narrators and their unique voices, perspectives, and uses of language convey surprising revelations about other characters as well as themselves. Their stories, like their lives, are intimately related" (Wong 1995, 175).

Perhaps the greatest source of conflicting interpretation within this community is the ongoing discussion of June's life and death. Virtually every speaking voice in the novel refers to her either directly, through family relations, or through a repetition of the themes and imagery that characterize her life and death. At the same time, however, the references do not add up to a complete picture of June. In discussing her death, various members of her family offer different reasons why she tried to walk home in a blizzard when she knew the signs for bad weather; they suggest, for example, that she was drunk, or that she was dropped off to die. Even Albertine, who comes closest to understanding June, admits her own loss of understanding: "I saw it laid out clear, as I sat there at my table, how down to the limit that kind of life would have gotten June. But what I did I know, in fact, about the thing that happened?" (Erdrich 1993, 9). And yet, although the family lacks a clear understanding of June's death, June nevertheless remains an important presence in their lives.

While the novel stylistically uses subjective voices to show a fragmented community, on "the other side of the line" the traditional characters, such as Moses and Fleur, and traditional elements, such as the true love medicine, remain below the surface of the novel, replaying on another level the tension between Nector and Eli. Moses, for example, is set back from the main activity of the community; indeed, he lives on an island, both geographically and metaphorically, his only prolonged contact his love affair with Lulu (from this union Lulu gives birth to Gerry Nanapush, Lipsha's father). When Lulu first appears to him, he believes himself to be, in fact, invisible, and becomes alarmed that she is able to see him. Moses also carries an older tradition, sometimes "speaking in the old language, using words that few remember, lost to people who live in town or dress in clothes" (Erdrich 1993, 81). An even more telling example of submerged traditions is the character of Fleur Pillager, who remarkably never actually appears in any of the narratives, but who remains an almost mythological figure whose power resonates throughout the novel. Marie tells us: "The Pillager was living back there with no lights, she was living with the spirits. Back where the woods were logged off and brush had twisted together, impassable, she kept house and cared for Nanapush" (101). When Marie gives birth to Lyman, she has considerable difficulty, causing Rushes Bear to send for Fleur. Although Fleur midwifes this difficult birth, she remains just outside the scene, appearing only as a dream, or as a ghostly hand helping Marie.

Elsewhere, at a thematically crucial juncture in the novel, Marie sends Lipsha for love medicine so that she can get Nector back from Lulu. Lipsha knows that he should go to Fleur, "Old Lady Pillager," but he decides to create his own "love medicine" because he is afraid of her. Lipsha says: "I know the best thing was to go ask a specialist like Old Lady Pillager, who lives up in a tangle of bush and never shows herself. She was known for putting the twisted mouth on people, seizing up their hearts. Old Lady Pillager was serious business, and I have always thought it best to stay clear of that whenever I could" (Erdrich 1993, 241). Because of Lipsha's fear, the traditional love medicine, like Fleur, remains distant from the novel. Indeed, it is extraordinary in *Love Medicine* that the depth of tradition in the novel is never reached, never surfaced, much like the water monster Missepeshu, whom no one has seen for ages but who seems poised to return home.

■ Affirming Love Medicine

Because the novel expresses both elements of the "core culture" and fragmentation, the novel is neither a hopeless expression of loss, like D'Arcy McNickle's *The Surrounded*, nor is it an example of the kind of unified wholeness that ends novels such as Leslie Marmon Silko's *Ceremony*. It is, rather, a novel with elements from both sides of the "line"; indeed, it is possible to see *Love Medicine* (and the more recent *Bingo Palace*) as a novel in tension between two other works by Erdrich: her novels *Tracks* and *The Beet Queen*. On the one hand, *Tracks* contains much stronger elements of tribal traditions, having been set earlier in Chippewa history, although it too contains divisions between two sides of the line—the subjective voices of Nanapush and Pauline—a division involving Nector that results in the loss of Fleur's allotment. *Beet Queen*, on the other hand, has far fewer aspects of Chippewa culture, focusing instead on mixed-blood characters living in a small town off the reservation who have a very tenuous relationship to their "core culture." Consequently, in terms of characters, style, themes, and even within Erdrich's series of works, *Love Medicine* exemplifies the important theme of tension between centrifugal and centripetal forces.

In her well-known review of *The Beet Queen*, Leslie Marmon Silko argues that Erdrich's novel is, in both style and content, isolated from any linguistic or human community. Silko writes that Erdrich's prose is "academic" and "post-modern," with the words freed from the "tiresome interference of any historical, political, and cultural connections the words may have had in the past" (Silko 1986b, 179)—connections, not incidentally, that Silko stresses are fundamental to her own work. In terms of content, Silko points out that *The Beet Queen*, besides ignoring the racism that must exist in these North Dakota communities, "never ventures near the reservation." Silko observes: "The reservation is where, for most of the novel, Erdrich keeps Russell, Celestine's half-brother, a full-blooded Chippewa. What Russell does, who Russell visits and how Russell feels about moving back and forth between the white town and the Indian reservation are a mystery" (183). Silko's observations are certainly accurate; the novel portrays a community and people cut off from the heart of the reservation, similar to the characters Beverly or King in *Love Medicine*. But seen in the context of Erdrich's works and the themes of those works, *The Beet Queen* is entirely appropriate in its portrayal of Indians on the edge of reservation life, its presentation of a world much different from the more culturally grounded *Tracks*, with *Love Medicine* displaying the tensions between both "sides of the line." Indeed, as a text on the fragmented "side of the line," the self-referential, postmodern quality of the writing in *The Beet Queen* is a mark of Erdrich's gift for creating appropriate language for the project, rather than an indication of her inability to write culturally-based fiction.

Furthermore, it is precisely this self-referential nature in *Love Medicine* that asks us to consider our own abilities to affirm those conflicted people and cultures that inhabit our worlds. Indeed, the novel itself is a household of diversity, much like Marie's or Lulu's, which is held together by an author's affirmation of the varying voices of the novel. *Love Medicine* is a much different novel than Silko's *Ceremony*, in which the oral tradition neatly dovetails into the present story of the protagonist's life, giving Tayo direction and identity in a time of confusion and fragmentation. Yet I would argue that it is a difference in degree, not in kind. That is, both novels show the importance and value of a traditional center, of a unitary language that offers a changing place or site that brings the community, or at least families, back inward toward a sense of an individual identity in relation to a familial or communal identity. Furthermore, both novels depend upon the use of stories to establish this provisional center, with characters affirming one another by working through the stories of their lives and their communities. Therefore *Love Medicine*, like *Ceremony*, is a philosophical and stylistic work of art that calls for a return to the value of the oral tradition, and it is itself a call for an affirmation of those traditions that may be muted or silenced. But it is a call known only if one first hears the indeterminate, sometimes conflicting "voice" of the novel.

CHAPTER SEVEN

Perpetual Metamorphosis: Transformational Journeys in Ray Young Bear's *Black Eagle Child*

"Because of the differences of the bilingual/bicultural worlds I live in, it sometimes seems as if what is actually published turns out to be a minute and insignificant fraction of one's perpetual metamorphosis."

—*Ray A. Young Bear, "Epilogue,"* Block Eagle Child

In the *Wretched of the Earth*, Frantz Fanon argues that African oral traditions in contemporary literature offer a potent source for awakening the consciousness of a colonized people to a sense of unity and purpose. While such an approach to literature is fraught (as we have seen) with theoretical and ethical difficulties, Fanon nonetheless contends that such a literature is crucial to colonized people who have become complacent within the system of a colonized society. "Instead of according the people's lethargy an honored place in his esteem," Fanon writes, "he turns himself into an awakener of the people, hence comes a fighting literature, a revolutionary literature, a national literature" (Fanon 1963, 222–23). This new revolutionary literature, Fanon tells us, does not occur immediately, but follows a series of three evolutions or phases in the writings of colonized people. During the first phase, Fanon explains, colonized writers desire to produce a literature that mimics the conventional forms, genres, and sentiments from European literary traditions. Examples include early indigenous writers, such as William Apess, Samson Occum, and Charles Eastman, and the Cherokee playwright Lynn Riggs. In the second phase, Fanon observes, colonized writers become "disturbed" by an increased recollection of their indigenous pasts, yet they continue to publish in the forms and genres of European literature, a "borrowed estheticism and a conception of the world which was discovered under other skies (Fanon 1963, 222). Because these writers are no longer a part of their communities, Fanon argues, they offer in their writings only nostalgia, the "bygone days of childhood," or employ oral traditions only within the context of European literary traditions.

Indigenous literature of the twentieth century might well be defined by Fanon's second phase, for novels often include oral traditions or indigenous ceremonialism within the "borrowed estheticism" of realist or representative fiction and generic forms such as the mystery and the melodrama. In such cases, as David Treuer writes, "Tribal myth, devoid of context and continuity, serves only to thicken the prose-stew, like the flour my mother adds to her delicious gravies; it had to do with consistency, not taste" (Treuer 2002, 60). This use of indigenous traditions, regardless of how carefully or accurately they appear in works of fiction, usually offers only signs of authenticity, or perhaps examples of interesting exotica, rather than systems or even narratives informed by indigenous thought, esthetics, or politics. Moreover, as skillful or profound as this fiction might be, it rarely voices an effective critique of the forces of colonialism, because it uses indigenous culture as a reflection of its own beauty or authenticity rather than as an expression of a political or national pattern of thought. For example, N. Scott Momaday's Pulitzer Prize–winning novel *House Made of Dawn* is replete with references to indigenous traditions, in particular its use of Pueblo dawn running as an essential ceremony to counteract the pervasive powers of evil. Unlike Leslie Silko's *Ceremony*, however, *House Made of Dawn* offers this approach to evil, at least within the context of the novel, primarily in the service of its desire for aesthetic modernist unity, similar to Eliot's "fragments I have shored against my ruins" (Eliot 1971, 50). As Fanon observes, whether a colonized people have a beautiful culture or no culture at all makes little difference to a colonizing power. Fanon writes, "You will never make colonialism blush for shame by spreading out little-known cultural treasures under its eyes" (Fanon 1963, 223).

Fanon argues that the third phase of fighting literature attempts to change the social and political conditions of colonized communities, shaking and then crystallizing indigenous people into an awareness of the realities of colonialism and the possibilities of freedom. He writes:

> The example of Algeria is significant. . . . From 1952–53 on, the storytellers
> . . . completely overturned their traditional methods of storytelling and the
> contents of their tales. Their public, which was formerly scattered, became
> compact. . . . Colonialism made no mistake when from 1955 on it proceeded
> to arrest these storytellers systematically. (Fanon 1963, 240–41)

Furthermore, Fanon tells us, when indigenous artisans modify older traditions in the interest of contemporary nationalist goals, colonizing powers attempt to keep traditions static and irrelevant, so that it is actually "the colonists who become the defenders of native style" and who "rush to help the traditions" when indigenous artists attempt to modify them (242). Within indigenous studies in America, this kind of "help" to defend unchanged, authentic tradition—a defense often connected to supply and demand—usually involves representing indigenous cultures by means of artifacts in museums, or through detailed, elaborate textual descriptions usually in the form of anthropological studies. Rather than help indigenous peoples, these efforts offer the alibi of preserving authentic culture without the more complicated, and certainly more ethical, task of securing the rights and freedoms of indigenous people themselves. Moreover, the idea of authenticity acts as a kind of sentinel for the colonizer, and at times for the colonized, safely marking indigenous traditions as part of America's mythic past—as unfortunate causalities of the larger and inevitable American metanarrative of progress from savagery to civilization, rather than as sources of knowledge and strength for viable nations within the United States.

In the tradition of Fanon's third phase of literature, indigenous writers such as Leslie Marmon Silko, Mourning Dove, Gerald Vizenor, Louise Erdrich, and Ray Young Bear look to indigenous traditions for narrative patterns that resist cultural imprints of indigenous peoples reflecting, for example, binary images of the Noble/Ignoble Savage, or the self-justifying narrative of the Vanishing Race. As vital forms for contemporary fiction, oral traditions do not appear in the novels of these writers only as signs of authenticity, nor as evidence that these novels accurately represent indigenous culture, nor even as a demonstration of the beauty of indigenous culture. Instead, oral traditions offer patterns that shape the narratives of contemporary fiction and thus shake, as Fanon suggests, the expectations of a reading public. Additionally, Young Bear's novel *Black Eagle Child*, perhaps more than any other novel by an indigenous writer in America, further coincides with Fanon's third phase of literature because it relies upon oral traditions to shape a trajectory that moves the tribal nation toward a pre-colonial, indigenous form of governance.

■ Permutations of a Master Journey

Describing his literature of combat, Fanon writes, "The storyteller replies to the expectant people by successive approximations, and makes his way, apparently alone but helped by his public, toward the seeking out of new patterns, that is to say national patterns" (Fanon 1963, 241). *Black Eagle Child* locates this pattern in one of the oldest traditions in the community, a peyote sacrament that finds its origins in the long-ago figure of Dark Circling Cloud. In this story, Dark Circling Cloud travels far from the community during a hunt and decides to sleep by a river where others are afraid to go. There, otherworldly beings provide him with the gifts of the Star Medicine and attendant ceremonial songs, which he then brings home to the members of his tribal community. In a sense, Dark Circling Cloud undergoes a transformative or metamorphic journey, having gained a new awareness of his relationship to the stars. He thus provides the means for a ceremonial journey for other members of his community, who can now experience a spiritual, metamorphic journey with the use of the Star Medicine and sacred songs within the haven of Well-Off Man Church.

This metamorphic journey or trope adumbrates the lives of the characters in the novel, including Edgar Bearchild, Junior Pipestar, Claude Youthman, and Ted Facepaint, all of whom experience different versions or riffs of this foundational narrative. As a consequence, the novel provides neither a unified plot nor a central protagonist; instead, the novel builds upon the circular, metamorphic narrative by episodic, "successive approximations," with different characters repeating the journey of Dark Circling Cloud, each with important variations. These differences show the potential rewards and dangers when attempting a metamorphic journey. In some cases, characters return home, like Dark Circling Cloud, with knowledge that helps the community find its way; other characters return to find that their knowledge, while useful, is unwelcome; others return home damaged; and some do not return at all. For the community as a whole, the same metamorphic pattern informs a journey that began with an unwise choice from a non-hereditary leader, a Bearchild patriarch, who "accepted education on behalf the tribe" (Young Bear 1992a, 86), disrupting both the lives of the children who were taken away to boarding school and also tradition of hereditary names that "gave order and stability / to the defiant but immiscible clans / of Black Eagle Child" (86). For each permutation of the master narrative, for both individuals and community, success is not determined by American progress; indeed, progress at the expense of one's relationship to others is a failure in the novel. Instead, success in the novel is determined by whether the characters and the community are able to complete their journeys and return home.

The trajectory Edgar's life offers an example of a successful metamorphic journey. Edgar never returns to the Well-Off Man Church after his first visit, but the experience remains a central figuration in his life, adumbrating his later "journey of words" when he leaves his community to learn the skills of being a writer. From Ted, Edgar learns that the members of the Church share the Red Hat Medicine, "an imported medicine from a distant desert owned by members of the Well-Off Man Church" (Young Bear 1992a, 7–8). Ted confides that "if this plant, which is a form of mushroom, is ingested and the mind is free of bad thoughts, it produces a pleasant intoxicating effect" (8). Although Edgar is quite apprehensive about participating in the ceremony (he in fact swallows only half of the Star Medicine given him), he does participate in the psychic and perhaps spiritual journey that offers knowledge and insight into his own relationship with his family, his friends, and even his place in the cosmos. For example, Edgar learns that his grandmother Nokomis has been involved with the church for a very long time; he learns that his name, Ka ka to, is an ancient Bear clan name; and he learns the origins of the Well-Off Man Church through a recitation of the oral story about Dark Circling Cloud and the Three-Stars-in-a-Row. In addition, Edgar learns that he is prophetic, sensing trouble for his friends even before they try to enter the Well-Off Man Church. He further understands that these friends abandoned both him and Ted, not only because the two lacked money, but also because they held strong prejudices about Edgar's absent father. And perhaps most important, Edgar gains a profound sense of humility about his own insignificance in relation to "the Star that is God." Edgar writes: "Me, a powerless speck of dust; He, a powerful giver of medicine" (39). By participating in Star Journey—the Principle Belief of the tribe—Edgar moves away from his conventional views of himself, metamorphically enhancing his awareness of his relationships with people and traditions in the community, and with the larger universe.

Furthermore, Edgar's individual "journey of words" mirrors the Star Journey of the entire group of participants at the Well-Off Man Church. The ceremony enables members to break out of their usual reticence: Edgar observes that the "prayers from individuals who were normally quiet in public became vocal—and personal" (Young Bear 1992a, 29). Also, the youthful Bearchild initially describes the members of the church through the multifarious influence of popular culture, likening different members of the church to such figures as Al Capone, Elvis Presley, and Ali Baba. Later, however, the ceremony brings everyone together in a journey that establishes, in fact demands, unity among the members of the church. At the height of the ceremony, for instance, Edgar tells us that their minds are together in the arc of the journey: "Our collective perspectives became concentric" (36). Moreover, once the boys begin the journey, they are then essential parts of this spiritual unity. While they get approval to go outside for a time, Jason Writing Stick eventually retrieves them, saying: "You must finish the Star Journey with the rest of us. This goes for your friend and guest. Any diversion from fear or disrespect will keep the Three-Stars-in-a-Row from visiting us" (32). Thus the ceremony of the Well-Off Man Church serves at least two important functions: it provides insight for individual members of the community—breaking them free, at least for a time, from their conventional lives—and it also consolidates diverse parts of the community into the form of a metamorphic journey.

As the journeys with the traditional Star Medicine were in former times, Edgar's personal metamorphic "journey of words" and indeed all such journeys, involves tremendous risk and danger. Ted explains to Edgar that the original star medicine—"Grandfather Red Hat," or the red-topped mushroom—grew during severe lightning storms around the Black Eagle Child Settlement. These mushrooms are capable of producing spiritual visions, but they are also capable of causing great harm, perhaps even causing one to lose "sanity and health" (Young Bear 1992a, 85). Similarly, almost every journey in the novel—personal, intellectual, and spiritual—carries a tremendous risk. For instance, the book describes several characters who leave the community and never return home (Nokomis calls them "breakaways"), or who return home damaged from their experiences (66). Examples of "breakaways" include Jason Writing Stick, whom Edgar pities (until he is forced by Writing Stick to carry the ceremonial water) (33); the Outsiders, "the wanderlusts whose caravan stopped for supplies long ago and decided to stay" (87); even Junior Pipestar, who initially left his Canadian home community with absolutely no intention of returning. The Black Eagle Child Settlement also has its own breakaways, such as Elizabeth Marie, who left the Settlement so she would not "die like her three sisters and mother" after her father abused the community's trust (17). There are also members of the community who have been damaged by their experiences in the outside world—for instance, young men who died in the war in Vietnam, or who have returned physically or emotionally damaged and unable to live peacefully at home. Edgar tells us: "And with those who safely returned some were emotionally crippled with a nightmarish montage of handkerchief drownings, ass grenades, and digits as targets in exchange for gin, a pass out, and care" (111). Finally, the novel suggests that the community as a whole is also taking a metamorphic journey, perhaps moving so far from its traditions that it might not be able to return to its previous governance and clan structures.

Both Edgar and Ted experience this danger when they undertake their own journeys, traveling far from the Black Eagle Child Settlement and eventually returning home, only to have a difficult time placing themselves back into the rhythms of their community. In terms of American success, Edgar achieves a certain measure, having received a fellowship and some notoriety for his poetry. Yet this success also threatens to separate him from his relationship to Ted and perhaps to his community. Rather than simply accept American ideas of success (assimilation) or reject his own writing in an attempt to be accepted at Black Eagle Child (nativism), Edgar instead envisions a different approach that includes both his community and his writing. This approach takes the form of Edgar's cocoon, within which he reconnects to his personal and tribal history through an unusual form of metamorphic rebirth. He writes: "The long arduous task of pasting paper to every inch of my body had already begun, and all that remained was for me to wait for it to set like a cocoon. I figured metamorphosis was my only salvation (Young Bear 1992a, 147). Edgar's immersion in his literal cocoon of paper and his figurative cocoon of writing has separated him from normal life in the community and from his childhood friends. Indeed, Ted tells him directly that he has "created a paper wall from tribal responsibilities" and their friendship (135).

Within his paper cocoon, Edgar affirms his place in the community by remembering specific moments in his past, which he calls "four places," that not only continue to have profound influences on his present life, but also provide him with an identity with roots in the very origins of the settlement. Edgar begins by relating the origins of the Black Eagle Child settlement through its initial purchase in 1856 by Ma mwi wa ni ke, "the young O ki ma, Sacred Chief" (150). In the first place of his life, Edgar remembers an encounter with his grandfather, Ke twe o se, who in turn was the grandson of Ma mwi wa ni ke, suggesting a crucial link to hereditary leadership in accord with its pre-colonial system of government. In the next three places of his life, Edgar recalls moments when he witnessed transitions or metamorphoses of his relatives from this world to the next. For example, in the second place of his life, Edgar remembers seeing his uncles help his grandfather make a final journey that became a metamorphosis from man to bird. Edgar recalls:

> I later realized it was only Grandfather's low voice, giving constant instructions. In soft respectful voices the young men were responding and informing each other what they were doing, where they were. The metamorphosis of arm to wing and mouth to beak . . ." (Young Bear 1992a, 151)

Similarly, in the third place of his life, young Edgar roams from his home, sees a "fiery-red sunset," bordered by a "thin, horizontal fragment of blue sky," followed by the starry night sky. This background of celestial transition inspires him to think about the transition of his grandfather on the path where he stands; this sunset also inspires a vision of him "flying beyond the branchtops of the forest," where he sees a meteor he believes to be sent for his benefit, mirroring his own "journey of words." In the fourth place of his life, young Edgar experiences the loss of his grandfather, who is then replaced by another man with the task of helping to guide him through life. An elder woman tells him: "Here is your grandfather now. . . . He will take the place of your grandfather" (154). The concept of transitions from one world to the next—life to death, day to night, ground to sky, even the transition from one elder relation to another—permeates the latter places of his life, indicating in his young life the power and possibilities of metamorphic transformations.

By tracing his roots to the earliest memories of the tribe and grounding himself in its history and its traditions, Edgar is able to envision within his cocoon a crucial center of identity as he moves forward in his "journey of words"—a journey that takes him far from home, but from which he always manages to return home. The trajectory of his educational journey likewise has its roots in his past when he, a child, leaves the comfortable orbit of his family to explore the Black Eagle Child Settlement. For instance, one of the memories he recalls in the cocoon involves the warnings of his family: "Do not desire to go anywhere. This is where we live. Should you traverse about, if you are seen, somebody will surely say things about you" (Young Bear 1992a, 157). Despite the warnings, young Edgar seems predisposed to journey outward and uses every opportunity (the need for him to fetch water, for instance) to explore the world around him. In this way, he learns a little about Jim Percy, who possesses the "knowledge and gift of communicating to the deities who controlled our destinies" (162), and also catches his first glimpse of the Well-Off Man Church when he sees Jim Percy emerge from a white canvas tipi where the ceremony occurred. Furthermore, Edgar learns in his youth that he can explore other worlds through the use of words alone, for in the winter, his grandmother would tell them stories in which Edgar "would be taken in mind and spirit to another world" (162). Her stories gave him an understanding of the mythic history of the settlement, and also an intimate knowledge of "the unseen but ubiquitous presence of powers who maintained a permanent control and effect upon our lives" (163). In all cases, Edgar's personal history provides a foundation to which he can return, and also a precedent for metamorphic journeys outside of his tribal world.

While Edgar receives scholarships, travel money, and speaking fees from his skill in writing, Ted's life is an example of the dangers of metamorphic journeys, for he returns from his travels impoverished and lacking direction. In terms of American success, and indeed according to the standards of Black Eagle Child, Ted is probably considered a failure. He stops by Edgar's house only to ask for food, and now spends "his days with the group cursed to a 'hundred years of suicides,' commiserating with them" (Young Bear 1992a, 147). Ted's "overpowering sense of being directionless" (248) is particularly telling, for it suggests that he lacks a coherent narrative to frame the trajectory of his life. Unlike Edgar, whose vocation coincides well with his hereditary role as mediator, Ted is unable to find a vocation outside the community that coincides with his. Edgar tells us that the Facepaints were "Painters of Magic and Protective Symbols for the soldier clans and their subdivisions," and that they "were known for accurately depicting visions on faces and ornaments" (85). Ted demonstrates his abilities when he mimics the voices of an elder and a wino knocking on the door at Edgar's college apartment. Edgar says: "They sounded so real. I half expected to be transported to another dimension when I opened the door" (114).

Like Edgar's "four places" of his life, Ted's journey home engenders a meeting between the past and present. At the beginning of the ceremony at the Well-Off Man Church, Ted's grandfather reaffirms the origins of the church to renew its relevance for the present. He says: "There exists a past which is holy and more / close to us than ourselves. In gatherings / such as we have tonight, we would be remiss / in not remembering it, acknowledging it / as something new for the young minds here. / For us, the aged, we must never let it grow / old, for it is as much a religious history / as it is tribal" (Young Bear 1992a, 20–21). The elder Facepaint emphasizes that even very old stories, such as the story of Dark Circling Cloud, must not only be retold, they should also remain powerfully relevant regardless of the age of either the story or the listener. For Ted, the stories of the Well-Off Man Church do, in fact, remain part of his life until he leaves for college. Even while he is getting "mizzed" with Edgar and Charlotte, Ted reverently recalls details about the Well-Off Man Church and its relation to the thunderstorm that descends upon them (Young Bear 1992a, 85).

After Ted returns home, his past asserts itself into his life in two very different ways. As an intemperate youth, Ted clashes with the belligerent Hi-na family, inadvertently causing one of the family members to have a miscarriage, and others to have permanent disfigurements. His actions eventually result in his own death, for the family "planned their impassioned revenge" for twenty-one years, sending him to the hospital with puncture wounds from a screwdriver (Young Bear 1992a, 246). On his deathbed, Ted also understands that perhaps his disrespect for the Well-Off Man Church may also have influenced the trajectory of his life, for the reason he and Edgar decided to attend the Well-Off Man Church was that their friends left them for a party. His mistake becomes clear to him when the salamanders approach to recite a "familiar story":

> There were once two young men
> who wanted desperately 'to do something'
> they unwisely chose to visit us with their needs.
> In spite of the words offered by their grandfather
> they ate and drank the Star-Medicine together
> and laughed at our expense. In looking back
> we see the carelessness you have exhibited
> toward your faith. (Young Bear 1992a, 249)

While Ted eventually dies because of his harmful decisions in his youth, he also benefits from his tribal past, finally returning home through the traditions of the community, completing the arc of his life. This trajectory repeats the structure of the Well-Off Man Church, and indeed signifies upon the idea of "Well Off," for ultimately success is not whether Ted has material wealth but is instead whether he completes the traditional journey home. Just as Edgar's grandfather changes, with the help of Edgar's uncles, from man to bird as he enters the next life, so too does Ted enter the next life with the help of Rose Grassleggings, who brushes cedar smoke on him with a fan that "had been blessed with the Ancient Fire of his Grandfathers" (250). In the last moments of his life, Ted's immobilized arm takes the form of a repaired wing, and he "leaned forward, and took flight, / keeping altitude at treetop level" (251).

While Ted and Edgar have different kinds of success with their metamorphic journeys, Junior Pipestar, an Ontario native from Canada, has the most arduous journey of all, yet he returns to his home world perhaps most completely. The difficulty of his journey stems primarily from his grandfather's unwise affair with an evil sorcerer's daughter. This sorcerer was so powerful and angry that he destroyed an entire village in revenge: "Fifty-two beloved kin and twenty-one / bystanders died in the winter of 1915" (Young Bear 1992a, 69) The evil sorcerer continued to hound Junior's family, now numbering only fifteen, turning himself into a rat and searching for them with a "supernatural beacon" that became known as the "Blue Light" (68). Fear of the Blue Decree is one obstacle to Junior's return home to Pinelodge Lake in Canada; ignorance of his personal and tribal traditions is another. Unlike Edgar and Ted, Junior is an entire generation removed from his indigenous home. Furthermore, when his grandfather tells Junior, "A part of you belongs to the medicine man's daughter," meaning that Junior is a descendent of the evil rat sorcerer, Junior's mother understandably denies this part of his family history (69). In addition, although his Ontario language and the Black Eagle Child language are similar, Junior feels cut off from this important aspect of his tradition: "Not knowing your people's / language, in the harshest consequence, meant excommunication with God" (67). In spite of the enormous obstacles before him, Junior returns alone to the Pinelodge Lake village, overcoming fear and cultural loss to embrace his family's past. Although Junior does not feel he has much choice in leaving the Black Eagle Child community (the "Buck Buck-Naked" story would probably not ever go away), and although, as the title of the chapter ("Junior Pipestar: The Destiny Factor") suggests, it may have been his fate to return, Junior nonetheless offers a sense of hope since even he, of all the characters in the book, is able to return home and reconstitute his life at Pinelodge. His novel offers a measure of hope, for after living at Pinelodge for fifteen years, Junior eventually gains an assistant, who, like him years before, becomes an apprentice to carry on the traditions.

Junior's return home is perhaps more successful than any other character's in the book, but part of the reason for his success is that he has no community that might question his motives or sincerity, the way that members of the Black Eagle Child community question Lorna Bearcap or Claude Youthman. Both Lorna and Claude are somewhat marginal figures even within the community, as Maureen Salzer points out—positions that undermine their efforts to critique and improve conditions there (Salzer 1995, 301). Lorna Bearcap, for instance, though educated and committed to the education of the young at Black Eagle Child, remains something of a spectacle. Edgar tells us: "And every week Lorna Bearcap made the news. Yesterday commodity surplus flour was poured over her lover and stepchild. With white powdery faces they could be seen running through the valley before crying in horror. This, the people speculated, was a result of the turmoil of being unenrolled" (Young Bear 1992a, 4–5). As the term "unenrolled" suggests, Lorna is further distanced from the community because she does not have official membership in the tribe. In the alphabet of identity that demarcates tribal members, Lorna's lack of tribal membership means she does not even rank with those given the "caustic nickname . . . EBNO, Enrolled But in Name Only" (95). Like Edgar, Lorna has gained a measure of success by American standards through her education, but, unlike Edgar, complicated family and personal histories prevents her from attaining the tribal version of success she seeks by completing her journey home.

Claude Youthman's connection with the community is even more ambiguous than Lorna's. On the one hand, his precise parentage remains a mystery, for he was abandoned when he was a small child—"the stories of his origins were purposely kept vague" (Young Bear 1992a, 225). Similar to Lorna, his familial place in the community is a source of considerable consternation for him. The novel tells us, "He could / not stand the prospect of one day / being questioned about his mother and father" (226). Yet on the other hand, he, like Ted, has a connection to the Well-Off Man Church, having been taken in and raised by Jim Percy, "a kind hearted leader / of the Star-Medicine Society"

(225). Throughout much of his life, Claude is highly introverted, creating his own personal cocoon-like life in the attic of Jim Percy's house, where he reads his crime and movie magazines. When he does venture out, he distances himself by assuming the guise of Ed Sullivan: "he would pucker his large lips and speak in a deep voice," for he "was his own ventriloquist and wooden dummy" (226).

Only a misunderstanding forces him violently out of his shell and onward on his metamorphic journey, when he throws cantaloupes at visiting state officials who he mistakenly believes made lewd suggestions to his wife. In the "cocoon" of his jail cell, serving time in prison for his acts, Claude experiences intense metamorphic change:

> Enclosed in the subhuman surroundings
> of a Kansas prison, Youthman completely
> reversed his outlook and philosophy.
> By scooping up triangular edges
> of his facial skin with a jagged piece
> of glass he sewed himself with carpet
> thread and curved needle to the iron bars.
> Satisfied the exterior mask would peel
> cleanly at the end of a backward run,
> he severed himself from the hunchbacked
> figure—and was born. From the musty
> compartments of his paranoia the black-
> and-yellow wings broke out, extended
> and dried out in the red prairie wind. (Young Bear 1992a, 227)

Within the confines of a cell and the "musty compartments of his paranoia," Youthman throws off his introversion, his mask of the television personality Ed Sullivan, and emerges with "black-and-yellow wings." Claude embraces the opportunity "to forever understand the English language," the reason for his imprisonment, and to acquire a degree in art history, "with an emphasis in Postimpressionism" (227). Like Lorna and Edgar, Claude attains considerable success by American standards in his education and accomplishments as a painter, but once again success for members of this community is the completion of the old transformative journey. Unfortunately, Claude discovers that despite his education and fame from an article in *Life* magazine, his insights into education and politics appear to matter little to people at Black Eagle Child. Although they were initially happy to speak with a celebrity, the narrator tells us that "they couldn't fathom his intellect"; moreover, rather than "listening and responding / to what he planned to do with health, education, and socioeconomics, they spoke / about family spats and burned food" (Young Bear 1992a, 232–33).

In her article "Ray Young Bear's Cantaloupe Terrorist: Storytelling as a Site of Resistance," Maureen Salzer emphasizes how marginal characters such as Claude Youthman and Lorna Bearcap undergo a metamorphic journey and use their newly acquired knowledge to subvert certain groups in the community. She writes: "A cast of petty criminals, alcoholics, sexual adventurers, and political radicals, while clearly marginal to [Young Bear's] Mesquakie community, act in ways that force the Indian community to reassess itself in relation to them and to the surrounding non-Indian cultures of Iowa" (Salzer 1995, 301). This cast of characters, Salzer argues, undermines the corrupt groups in the community, such as the school board, by using nonindigenous tactics, ideas, and information gleaned from their time in school or in prison, a method that Salzer finds consistent with Mary Louise Pratt's definition of "transculturalism." As described by Pratt, transculturalism is the manner in which subjugated peoples sometimes have the ability to "determine to varying extents what [from the dominant culture] they absorb into their own, and what they use it for" (Pratt 1992, 6). As an example, Salzer points to a historical moment in the Mesquakie Settlement when the community earned enough money to buy a parcel of land in Iowa. She writes: "The purchase exemplifies Pratt's idea of transculturation; the Mesquakie saw that their survival as sovereign people could depend on land ownership, and so they became landowners" (Salzer 1995, 302). In Young Bear's fictional world, Salzer argues, the characters most representative of transculturation are Youthman, Bearcap, and Bear Child—characters who can survive and work in the contact zones between the indigenous and nonindigenous communities.

The concept of transculturalism offers an important insight into the book, but it is worth noting that the concept is neither new nor foreign to the Black Eagle Child Settlement. In the context of the novel, at least, this concept has been well known to those in the Well-Off Man Church since its inception as a gift from Dark Circling Cloud. Gaining new and useful perspectives by means of a transcultural journey is inherent in the story of Dark Circling Cloud, and expressed, as Ted's grandfather tells them, each time the members of the Well-Off Man Church embark on their spiritual journey by means of the sacrament. Furthermore, besides the "cast of petty criminals, alcoholics, sexual adventurers, and political radicals," other characters who are much more central to the community also experience similar metamorphic journeys. For instance, when Edgar Bear Child first encounters the Well-Off Man Church, he is surprised that the cars parked nearby belong to "sober family types," and upon entering, he immediately experiences the normalcy of "plump women wearing floral-print aprons" who "were exchanging news and busying themselves / with pots, pans, and firewood" (Young Bear 1992a, 9). He is also somewhat surprised to learn that his grandmother Nokomis frequently helps with the feast at the Well-Off Man Church, "like she did with every religious group on the Settlement" (10). Thus while marginal figures such as Claude Youthman who experience transcultural journeys become visible, somewhat exotic obstructionists within the community, similar metamorphic journeys that also benefit members of the community have long existed within the unseen, quite normal walls of the Well-Off Man Church.

■ The Black Eagle Child Destiny

Desperate to move the community to complete its transformational arc and return to its traditions, Claude exposes and critiques corruption in the schools and tribal government in the community publication *The Black Eagle Child Quarterly*. Yet he finds that not only are his words unheeded, but he is also "ostracized for revealing ugly truths" (237). At this moment in Black Eagle Child's history, the community is highly suspicious of change, from both the few tribal members who profit from a monetary relationship with the federal government, and also from those tribal members who have seen how change has damaged the integrity of their traditions. Consequently, certain members of the community refuse to accept any change at all, especially changes in the ceremonies. Edgar writes: "There were critics on how proper ceremonies should be executed. Possessing various interpretations of the prayers, songs, and rituals was inevitable. But exactness was touted as the only form of communion" (60). Edgar goes on to write, "They, the clans, never gave each other credit for trying; it had to be the exact way or else it was a dismal failure" (61). Because of the undeniable effects of colonialism and cultural loss, the critics of change have experienced the damage sometimes caused by cultural metamorphosis. Therefore, they consolidate themselves ever tighter, arguing that any change represents a failure to adhere to authentic truth, freezing the community in a past that they themselves may have trouble remembering. Edgar tells us, "We each held [the elders] in such high esteem that we could never doubt their memories, even if they forgot our own names" (60–61).

Black Eagle Child shows that if history is any guide, the members of the Settlement are wise to be careful about the amount of change they admit to their world, especially with respect to the education of their youth. Yet, while their motives are understandable, these critics of change foreclose the possibility that certain kinds of change can in fact be useful, as they are in the Well-Off Man Church when members experience their conventional lives anew; or in the case of Edgar, Claude Youthman, or Lorna Bearcap, whose educational experiences outside the Settlement give them insights into the corrupt leadership at home; or in the possibility that the community will change and return to its traditional leadership structures. Furthermore, whether they recognize it or not, the community already participates each year in a metamorphic journey through its summer ceremonies. The narrator explains that during the winter months, the community becomes fragmented, for the many hardships often bring "bickering and verbal backstabbing" (Young Bear 1992a, 60). But the summer ceremonies once again bring unity from this fragmentation, for these ceremonies are a "binding reality" that "held everyone by their hearts, and their reenactment assured passage for another season" (60).

If the community is able to return to the old hereditary structures of tribal leadership, then, like the congregation at the Well-Off Man Church, it will have undergone a long metamorphosis from stability, to fragmentation, and then a return to stability in its older traditions of governance. In other words, because the Well-Off Man Church unifies, at least for a time, a wide variety of people who attend the ceremony, the church may be seen as a pattern, to use Fanon's term, for a possible future for the community as a whole. Just as the church members find unity in its metamorphic, ceremonial journey, so too might the community eventually find a similar unity in its return to a traditional form of government in hereditary leadership—returning once again to, as Claude Youthman says, "the old ways beginning from the bottom up" (Young Bear 1992a, 238).

This openness to some forms of change is especially evident in Edgar's grandmother Nokomis, who is at once strongly grounded in the traditions of the Settlement, but who is also willing to consider and even embrace outside beliefs when necessary. For instance, Edgar tells us that "Nokomis respected both [Christian and Mesquakie] beliefs, unlike [George] Whirlwind Boy," who believed, conservatively, that no connection exists or should exist between the two. Nonetheless, the narrator tells us, Nokomis not only respected the two beliefs, she "depended on both during World War II." She tells Edgar: "To believe in two, three, or even four is a far better means to pray. Combined, the religions brought your uncles back from the Germans and Japanese" (Young Bear 1992a, 63). It is the same kind of openness that characterizes the Well-Off Man Church, for despite its apparent obscurity in the community, the church is neither secretive nor exclusive. Edgar tells us: "I was aware people called them Those Who Partake. But boldly stenciled in English on a mailbox on Whisky Corners Road was the name they preferred: The Well-Off Man Church, a name which amused me" (7). The Well-Off Man Church is, like Nokomis, open to different religious perspectives, as is indicated by the painting of Jesus Christ in the ceremonial room. Furthermore, the church admits outsiders, such as Jason Writing Stick, who is from another tribe, and Edgar, who may be less of an outsider because they know his grandmother, but whose motives and commitment are questionable.

By establishing an undeniable presence, and remaining open without compromising its central traditions, the church is a visible reminder to the community (and to readers) of a deep and abiding power just under the surface of this often divided, even embattled tribal world. The tribal community at Black Eagle Child has itself embarked on a long metamorphic journey, which it may or may not complete. Although it might be difficult for Americans to imagine, success and failure for this community are not legitimated by American ideas of progress and wealth. Instead, the community has its own, quite distinct destiny that finds its pattern in the longstanding traditions of the tribe. Although most indications are that the community is spinning away from its center, the novel offers the possibility of centering the community once again through ceremonies, such as the Well-Off Man Church, or through the works of people like Claude Youthman, Lorna Bearcap, and Edgar Bearchild. The metamorphic wheel continues to turn for members of the community, for the structure of the fiction, and for the community itself—but in every case, the novel hopes, the direction of the journey is, finally, home.

Writing the Indigenous Nation

One underlying question in the novels I have discussed in this study, and indeed in indigenous studies in general, is the destiny of indigenous people, whether that destiny be in terms of "race," culture, geographic boundaries, economic development, or political empowerment. It is worth considering, finally, what these novels might suggest to us about the role of resistance narratives in the future of Native America. For the most part, indigenous writers and activists have emphasized the fundamental importance of sovereign geographic spaces to the future of indigenous groups, indicating their commitment to a measure of independence within America's own grand narratives of national unity. For most Americans, the educational systems teach that any question of dissembling the "united" in the United States was most clearly settled in the late nineteenth century with the American Civil War and later with subsequent campaigns against indigenous tribes in the West, most notably the massacre at Wounded Knee Creek in 1890. It was in this era that America achieved a sense of national completion with the "closing of the frontier" and the full realization of "manifest destiny," two highly visible terms that offered a kind of narrative denouement to the long struggle from savagery to civilization. This sense of national completion was further reinforced with various national pedagogies (to use Bhabha's inflection of the term, suggesting both ideology and national instruction), including holidays such as Thanksgiving (1863), nationalist songs such as "America the Beautiful" (1895), and observances such as the Pledge of Allegiance ("one nation, under God, indivisible") (1892). Americans, now more or less safe from the possibility of armed Indian resistance, confident that indigenous people would soon vanish into history, began reflecting upon previous generations of indigenous peoples nostalgically and romantically. Actual living Indians remained a "problem" and a "burden," subject to any number of attempts to vanish them still further—boarding schools, the Dawes Severalty Act (1887), and later the Indian Citizenship act (1927). But for most Americans from the late nineteenth century and throughout the next century, Indians were no longer independent peoples with a measured claim to their own forms of nationhood; instead, they were and are an essential and quite malleable character of the great story of America's inexorable movement upward.

The attempted erasure of indigenous nations thus came from two directions: one through assimilationist policies and practices and the other through more diffuse national pedagogies of an indivisible nation. Politically, indigenous nations overcame efforts to deprive them of their status as tribes and nations, in part due to the efforts of the assistant secretary of the Interior John Collier and his 1934 Indian Reorganization Act. In terms of more general national pedagogies, however, as Vine Deloria and Clifford Lytle argue in their *Nations Within: The Past and Present of American Indian Sovereignty*, most Americans would not think it possible that separate nations do in fact exist within the borders of the United States. They write: "when the idea of Indian tribes as nations is voiced, many Americans laugh at the pretension, convinced that Indians have some primitive delusion of grandeur that has certainly been erased by history" (1). In the vacuum of accurate information about indigenous history, the pedagogy of an indivisible American nation legitimates an erasure of indigenous nations, leading to untenable yet power-fully compelling narratives about the place of indigenous people in America. For instance, many Americans conclude that federal benefits, reservation lands, and legal exceptions are "gifts" from the United States, rather than rights of independent peoples who never completely relinquished them (legally termed "reserve rights"). This discourse of the gift has the further benefit of providing Americans not only a narrative of their innocence, but also, ironically, a testament to their benevolence and largesse. This same pedagogy of the indivisible nation also informs the narrative of American conquest, which suggests that western expansion was inevitable, justifiable, and complete. Furthermore, because conquest offers the narrative of glorious battle rather than the grim and largely bureaucratic and uneven advance of colonialism, it likewise provides a measure of innocence, for (the logic goes) "to the victor goes the spoils."

Of the over 500 hundred indigenous tribes, in fact very few were conquered through battle. Most tribal leaders understood that they could not defeat the Americans militarily and, rather than proclaiming that "it is a good day to die," as popular American narratives go, instead negotiated contractual treaty agreements, which varied, sometime considerably, among tribes, in hopes that they would ensure their continued existence as a people. By definition, treaty agreements connote an international dimension, and to the extent that indigenous leaders saw their tribes as distinct linguistically, culturally, and spiritually, these agreements should be understood as compacts between separate nations. Yet, in spite of the diversity of agreements and histories be-tween tribes and Americans, federal Indian policy such as allotment and the Indian Reorganization Act generally offered (and continues to offer) uniform approaches in their dealings with indigenous peoples. Such uniformity also appears in the cultural narratives of American conquest and benevolence, which appear to offer comprehensive clarity to the history of America, but which actually deny more complex but more accurate local narratives of indig-enous peoples. After 500 years of contact, the destiny of indigenous peoples is without question inextricably connected to the destiny of America—legally, politically, and globally. But these destinies are not necessarily the same; indeed, the national American pedagogy of the indivisible nation impedes those tribal nations that wish to affirm their own narrative destinies, many of which pre-date the existence of the United States.

Throughout most of the twentieth century, written indigenous literature has been a record of the degree to which indigenous characters succeed or fail within American metanarratives, not indigenous metanarratives. Yet even for the most ardent of indigenous assimilationists, the American narratives of an indivisible, benevolent nation prove to be tragically inadequate. At the turn of the century, for instance, Dakota writer Charles Eastman writes himself directly into the discourse of progressivism by offering what we might call a recapitulation narrative, an analogue to Ernst Haeckel's theory that ontogeny recapitulates phylogeny, in other words, that the growth of the individual organism recapitulates the organism's evolutionary growth. Eastman offers a personal narrative that ostensibly demonstrates that his journey from savagery to civilization recapitulates the social narrative of American progress. Specifically, his *From the Deep Woods to Civilization* chronicles his eventual claim to the two preeminent signs of civilization: American education and Christian religion. Eastman's fundamental commitment to the metanarrative of progress and Christianity never wavers in his autobiography. Indeed, in a first-person account of the aftermath of the Wounded Knee massacre near the Pine Ridge Reservation, Eastman appears to offer his reading audience some measure of absolution for the destruction of indigenous peoples. Elsewhere, Eastman offers a number of examples of how he accedes to his recapitulation narrative by moving away from his indigenous beginnings to become part of the "civilized" world, for instance, separating himself from his Indian brethren at Beloit so they won't hold him back; assuming the guise of a "Turk" to sell the appropriately named book *Knights of Labor*; using indigenous etiquette to collect sacred artifacts from indigenous groups; translating important Lakota names into English that was "easily pronounced by the white man" (Eastman 1916, 183).

In spite of how the recapitulation narrative ostensibly determines the trajectory of the book, this narrative structure is finally insufficient to contain Eastman's growing uneasiness with American civilization—its agency, not innocence, in the suffering of indigenous peoples, especially in his dealings with unscrupulous Indian agents and politicians. This disillusionment

contrasts with his experiences with indigenous peoples, who appear to embody the values of the highest Christian ideals—selflessness and disregard for
materialism. Thus the end of the book recalls its beginnings, where Eastman
defines the man or warrior as one who is trained "not to care for money or
possessions, but to be in the broadest sense a public servant" (Eastman 1916,
1). As the title of the book suggests, Eastman hopes to communicate a vision
of the future that is progressive yet non-materialistic, Christian yet infused
with some indigenous ideals—but none that include, Eastman makes very
clear, indigenous ways of life. He states in the penultimate paragraph of the
book that "there is no chance for our former simple life anymore" (Eastman
1916, 195). Yet in spite of his stated commitment to American pedagogies, a
shadow narrative emerges that returns to the beginning as a kind of circular
plot moving him towards indigenous traditions. Indeed, Eastman earlier suggested that such a move was a signal marker of indigenous thought: "What
is the great difference between these people and my own? I asked myself.
Is it not that the one keeps the old things and continually adds to them new
improvements, while the other is too well contented with the old, and will not
change his ways nor seek to improve them?" (64).

This shadow narrative of indigenous triumph throws into question the
terms of savagery and civilization, giving the book an almost chiasmic structure. It is a structure that parallels one of Eastman's memorable statements:
"Some persons imagine that we are still wild savages, living on the hunt or on
rations; but as a matter of fact, we Sioux are fully entrenched, for all practical
purposes, in the warfare of civilized life" (165). As Gale P. Coskan-Johnson
writes in her similar reading of Eastman's *Soul of the Indian*, Eastman "uses
the tragic figure of the noble savage overcome by progress that makes up
an essential aspect of the national story of the United States of America."
She adds: "Even though Eastman borrows the language of progressivism, he
deploys it in novel ways that transform its linear temporality and the assumptions underlying the civilized/primitive binary" (Coskan-Johnson 2006, 123).
The conclusion of his narrative emphasizes his powerful ambivalence about
America, where one group of people proclaims freedom at the expense of
another, where one group acquires enormous wealth and another is impoverished. Yet because he is a product and apologist of American pedagogies,

Eastman can never quite abandon the belief in "progress along social and spiritual lines" toward unity in the form of "universal brotherhood." This vast chasm between his experience as an American and American's pedagogy can only be expressed as an aporia in the final paragraph of his autobiography: "I am an Indian . . . I am an American."

While the American narrative of progress threatens to annihilate tribal life altogether, almost equally untenable is the status quo of an unjust America, where "savagery and cruelty and lust hold sway" (194). The shadow narrative that emerges from these two alternatives suggests a different destiny, not in the form of nativism which, as Eastman himself points out, offers little hope for the future, nor in projects like contemporary multiculturalism, which frames indigenous struggles as "preserving culture in the modern world" with visible signs of identity. Nor is this shadow narrative an example of Gloria Anzaldúa's borderlands, as Eric Peterson postulates, with its suggestions of social evolution. (Peterson 1992, 146).[1] Instead, the shadow narrative evokes a future for indigenous peoples that is both connected to but also distinct from that of other Americans, emerging from the particular histories and local narratives of the individual tribes themselves. Because Eastman fervently believes in the future of Christian civilization, he finally cannot claim this shadow narrative as his own, even though it haunts him to the last paragraphs of his autobiography.

The emergence of this shadow narrative follows certain features of Homi K. Bhabha's (1990) argument in *Nation and Narration* that narratives in the name of "the people" or "the nation" inevitably exhibit ambivalences about "the shreds and patches of cultural signification and the certainties of national pedagogy" (294). Bhabha writes: "It is an ambivalence that emerges from a growing awareness that, despite the certainty with which historians speak of the 'origins' of nation as sign of the 'modernity' of society, the cultural temporality of the nation inscribes a much more transitional reality" (1). The writing of a nation as narrative, for example, produces "double-times," the people as temporal practice and the nation as expression of myth beyond time. Much like the relationship between signifier and signified, the mapping of performance to pedagogy does not produce a complete sign of the nation, "out of many one" (the phrase Bhabha considers) or, to refer to my previous discussion, the nation indivisible. The nation as narration thus undermines the certainty and ideology of nationalism: "The liminal figure of the nation-space would ensure that no political ideologies could claim transcendence or metaphysical authority for themselves." For minority discourses, too, this conception offers a space of enunciation between the two discursive registers of nativism and nationalism. Bhabha quotes Fanon's critical stance toward the fetishization of fixed markers of culture ("stereotype and realism"), and focuses on Fanon's idea of a people as "the fluctuating movement that the people are *just* giving shape to" (303).

Because Eastman is committed to the American pedagogy of unity and progressivism, he is only able to acknowledge certain indigenous beliefs and practices from his past, not the emerging shadow narrative that offers the possibility of distinct destiny for indigenous peoples. In this "contest of stories," to quote Jana Sequoya Madagaleno's phrase, Eastman envisions success and failure for indigenous people as the degree to which they—as individuals and tribes—recapitulate the American narrative of progress, of which he is an exceptional example. Historically, indigenous literature has appropriated this general narrative form, from the beginnings of indigenous writing with Samson Occum and William Apess, through the twentieth century with writers such as D'Arcy McNickle, John Joseph Mathews, and James Welch. More generally, literature by non-tribal writers, and indeed almost all representations of indigenous people by non-tribal people in art, sculpture, movies, and television likewise follow this predominating narrative structure of indigenous success and, more frequently (and perhaps necessarily), indigenous failure.

For a few indigenous writers, as I hope this study has shown, this "contest of stories" has resulted in narrative approaches that offer much different destinies than those dependent upon American pedagogies for significance and legitimation. *Cogewea, Ceremony, Bearheart, Love Medicine,* and *Black Eagle Child* not only explicitly reject the American pedagogy of unity and progressivism; they also reverse the terms so that characters that accept the American pedagogies are in some sense failures rather than successes. Densmore in *Cogewea,* Rocky in *Ceremony,* Nector and Beverly in *Love Medicine*—all appear as characters that are damaged in large part because their versions of

American progressivism separate them from those they care about or should care about the most. In *Black Eagle Child,* characters such as Claude Youthman, Lorna Bearcap, and Edgar Bearchild, who find some measure of success by American standards, discover that their skills in education, art, or writing can be a hindrance when they return home to work in their indigenous community. Structurally, *Ceremony* and *Bearheart* offer a more general critique of American pedagogies of progress and unity. In *Ceremony,* the American narrative offers returning World War II veterans the Manichean choice of either extreme failure in the form of the stereotypical drunken Indian, or success at the cost of separation from the indigenous community. *Bearheart* provides a cultural critique at American progressivism by first, showing that its logical end is a depletion of natural resources and, next, by reversing the direction of the narrative so that the book returns to a four worlds vision of indigenous beginnings.

Similar to Bhabha's arguments about minority discourse, these novels question the American nation's claim of "transcendence or metaphysical authority," given the degree to which the flesh and blood events of history (the performance) unmask the myths, and given how the very existence of indigenous nations subverts the pedagogy of national unity. This continuing indigenous existence in the closing chapters of *Cogewea* and *Love Medicine* is somewhat tenuous, a moment of personal victory for the protagonists. As a rewriting of an indigenous oral story, *Cogewea* appears both as a confirmation of the truth of the oral story and as an assertion of a mixed blood territory. *Love Medicine* is less sanguine but nonetheless hopeful, offering a profound connection to an absent mother against the fragmenting history of a tribe. In a sense, both these novels suggest Fanon's "fluctuating movement that the people are *just* giving shape to," that is, a rejection of American pedagogies and an affirmation of a presence of indigenous people and their narratives. Going a step further, *Ceremony* and *Black Eagle Child* not only offer a "shape" of an indigenous presence; they also offer longstanding tribal, perhaps national, metanarratives. In doing so, however, these novels embody the same ambiguities that Bhabha identifies in other national narratives: namely, the slippage between performance and pedagogy. Both *Ceremony* and *Black Eagle Child* structure their novels on a tribal metanarrative, and in both novels, a central thematic question is whether characters are able to parallel the narrative of their own lives to that of the tribal nation.

Ceremony is perhaps the most complete example in indigenous literature of the marriage between the two discursive registers of the performed and the pedagogical. By the end of the novel, the trajectory of Tayo's life through his personal ceremony is an almost exact recapitulation of the tribal narrative of drought, ceremony, and balance. If the relationship between the performed and the pedagogical is an analogue to sign and signified, then Silko's novel allows for little slippage in narrative and language. Silko's commitment to these clear and repeated systems is evident in her critique of Louise Erdrich's *The Beet Queen*:

> Erdrich's prose is an outgrowth of academic, post-modern, so-called experimental influences. The idea is to "set language free," to allow words to interact like magic chemicals, in a word sorcerer's pristine laboratory, where a word and its possible relationships with other words may be seen "as they really are, in and of themselves" without the tiresome interference of any historical, political or cultural connections the words may have had in the past. (Silko 1986b, 179)

Of course, slippage does occur in Silko's novel. It must occur, Betonie tells Tayo, for even in ceremonies that are performed the same way each time, there is always a difference, "if only in the aging of the yellow gourd rattle or the shrinking of the skin around the eagle's claw, if only in the voices from generation to generation, singing the chants" (Silko 1977, 126). Betonie argues that this slippage between the performed and the pedagogical is essential if traditions are to grow, instead of becoming frozen in time like displays in a museum. Furthermore, as Bhabha (1990) observes, the liminal position allows a space of enunciation for minority discourse—in this case, the discourse/narrative of the mixed-blood protagonist. But *Ceremony* makes clear that this essential slippage is potentially quite dangerous: just as it almost destroys the protagonist, so too can this space of enunciation widen into the discourse of opposition and the fragmentation of the witchery.

Young Bear's *Black Eagle Child* offers a similar writing of the nation: several characters recapitulate to varying degrees the tribal/national pedagogy of the metamorphic, circular journey adumbrated in the ceremony at the Well-Off Man Church. Also, the description of religious language in *Black Eagle Child* is similar to Silko's vision of language, for the religious songs that the mythical Dark Circling Cloud gives to the community are so exact that even the substitution of a syllable will change the meaning of the songs entirely. *Black Eagle Child* differs, however, from *Ceremony* in important ways. Unlike *Ceremony*, where almost every event is highly mythologized (the protagonist himself is a figure from older traditions), the community in *Black Eagle Child* shows the mundane and sometimes humorous rifts between the performed and pedagogical: American holidays, old cars, popular music and television, and corrupt school-board members. Similarly, the novel offers American pedagogy not as a generalized, mythical presence, but as the literal boarding-school system, which initiates a crisis by fostering distrust in the community and by (presumably) educating children away from their hereditary leaders to those chosen by the American government:

> *Unfortunately, the deterioration of a strong*
> *Nation began the day white politicians asked*
> *the Bearchild patriarch for his own ideas*
> *on education and community welfare.*
> *It was then that the master plan was unfolded:*
> *he unknowingly accepted education on behalf*
> *of the tribe.* (Young Bear 1992a, 86)

From this event onward, the tribal community loses its way, moving toward a recapitulation of the American pedagogy of success based on money, rather than recapitulating the tribal/national pedagogy. The tension of the book becomes a contest of national pedagogies, suggesting the potential and indeed the necessity for the community to decide its own fate, despite the difficulties and despite the American pedagogy that frequently tells them that they do not have the cultural or mental capabilities to do so. When individuals choose to parallel their lives with the metamorphic structure of the Well-Off Man

Church, their successes are highly attenuated, never whole and complete as they are in *Ceremony*, indicating that the journey home will not be easy—but these individual acts nonetheless suggest an important direction for the community as a whole.

Against the pedagogy of the American nation, these novels envision a viable indigenous presence in America and, in some cases, affirm a quite different narrative destiny for indigenous peoples. Like Eastman's shadow narrative, these indigenous narratives rarely emerge as part of the academic or popular pedagogy about the formation and character of America, but they never quite disappear either, in spite of the insistence of Americans to mass produce images that situate Indians into the American pedagogy: helpful natives, ethnic sidekicks, and sports mascots. While the audience of resistance fiction, and indeed all indigenous literature, remains relatively small, and while fiction of any stripe has rarely motivated social change in America, these novels help to bring indigenous narrative possibilities from the shadows to the light, and contribute to a growing conversation among indigenous writers, activists, grass roots organizations, and academics, who steadfastly assert the rightful freedoms of indigenous tribal nations.

Notes

■ **INTRODUCTION. Indigenous Resistance Fiction**

1. In the original French version, *Les damnés de la terre*, Fanon (1991) uses the term *modèles*, e.g., "de modèles nationaux" (289). Constance Farrington's translation into English, *The Wretched of the Earth* (1963), uses the term *patterns*. I use Farrington's translation throughout the book.
2. Bhabha 1990, 147.
3. Ivor Indyk (1992) points out that while Mudrooroo critiques his fellow Aboriginal writers for relying on European forms, Mudrooroo's own works and theoretical approaches also borrow considerably from non-Aboriginal sources.
4. Eva Rask Knudsen (1992, 36) writes that Fogarty's "language, a blend of Aboriginal vernacular and distorted English, is a subversive act, a deliberate raid against paternalism designed to de-familiarize the poetic genre and destroy the

European desire for recognisable sequence." Knudsen also offers insightful criticism of Mudrooroo's construction of an essentialist Aboriginal identity.

5. Fanon 1963, 222.

6. Alfred provides a theory of government based upon the Haudenosaunee condolence ceremony. This important work utilizes the structure of the condolence ceremony—peace, power, and righteousness—to frame its major arguments, similar to the way Native novelists are employing oral traditions to re-constitute Native narrative structures. Alfred writes: "I have chosen condolence as the metaphorical framework for my own thoughts on the state of Native America and the crucial role of indigenous traditions in alleviating the grief and discontent that permeate our existence" (Alfred 1999, xi).

■ **CHAPTER ONE. Assimilation or Appropriation?**
The Idea of the Center in N. Scott Momaday's *Way to*
Rainy Mountain* and Leslie Marmon Silko's *Ceremony

1. Drawing from Roman Jakobson, McHale defines the *dominant* as a generalized "common denominator of the conventions" of modernism and postmodernism. McHale identifies the dominant for modernism as epistemology and for postmodernism as ontology (1987, 9).

2. See Henry Louis Gates Jr., 1988.

3. For an insightful critique of Tedlock's methods, see Anthony Mattina (1987).

4. See, for example, *The Dialogic Imagination* (1989), 272–73. The idea of centripetal movements in American Indian literature was first discussed by William Bevis in his essay "Homing In" (Bevis 1987). Conceptually, this chapter is indebted to the work of Professor Bevis, which was first suggested to me by the Blackfeet writer James Welch.

5. See Silko's use of the word "fragile" in *Ceremony* (1977, 35), and her discussion of her Aunt Susie as the last person to hand down a culture through orality in *Storyteller* (1981a, 5–6).

6. See, for instance, Hertha Dawn Wong (1992).

7. See Galen Buller (1980). Buller says that Momaday's idea of the self is in "the moral values a person holds, as exhibited particularly through that person's own recognition of the power of language, of the power of his affiliation with a sense

of place, and the importance of racial memory." Moreover, Buller argues that in "defining the American Indian, Momaday has also defined American Indian literature" (166).

8. For a discussion of the role of readers of texts in *The Way To Rainy Mountain*, see Kimberly Blaeser (1989).

■ CHAPTER TWO. "Authenticity" and Leslie Marmon Silko's *Ceremony*

1. Fitzgerald (1981). See especially the final chapter, "Starting Over."

2. Although contemporary uses of authenticity in literature, law, and politics connotes purity in origins or determinate borders of cultural identity, the origins and determinate borders of the term itself remain elusive (if you will, the authenticity of authenticity). In other words, as David Lowenthal (1999) points out, *authenticity* itself has a long and changing history of meaning, and continues to be a source of considerable dispute. Lowenthal writes that when European churches began collecting large numbers of religious relics, many having dubious origins, the church fathers often determined the authenticity of a relic not by an investigation of its physical genealogy, but by the relic's ability to perform miracles. In the Age of Enlightenment, as the technology for reproduction and thus forgeries increased to a large degree, authenticity came to mean that an artifact was "untampered," "natural," or "not artificial" (6). More recently, Lowenthal observes, the concept of authenticity has included the changing features of the artifact, such as the unavoidable aging process of a painting or a building. Lowenthal cites the Victorian writers John Ruskin and William Morris, who decried the wholesale restoration of Gothic churches and cathedrals, arguing that their organic integrity and authenticity was the "entire record of the changes they had endured" (7). Yet, as the recent attempt to restore the original colors of the Sistine Chapel or the cleaning of the Statue of David remind us, definitions of authenticity continue to waver between, in Lowenthal's words, the desire for an "original state" and acceptance of an artifact's "historical palimpsest" (7). Lowenthal thus places authenticity itself into a historical palimpsest so that it is perhaps possible to conceive of the term, as did Ruskin and Morris, without the burden of recreating (miraculously) an "original state" of an artifact or even a culture.

3. Shiner (1994) critiques the generally accepted opposition between aesthetic art and popular artisans, showing that the terms themselves do not have clear homologues in tribal thought, but are primarily useful in determining the monetary value of tribal creations.

4. For a thorough discussion of the Indian Arts and Crafts Act, see Laura Turney (1999). Turney discusses both the positive and negative consequences of the Arts and Crafts Act along with the trickster discourse of Jimmie Durham. See also Gail K. Sheffield (1997).

5. Coleman's thesis (2001) is that an Aboriginal perspective on authenticity is similar in many ways to European concepts of the insignia, particularly the British Coat of Arms, which depends, for instance, on genetics (family inheritance). Coleman makes a powerful case for the authenticity of works signed by an Aboriginal artist but in fact produced by his daughters. Yet her understandably political desire to remain within the binary of authenticity/inauthenticity is at odds with her arguments and findings of an Aboriginal concept of a "good" or "appropriate" use of cultural symbolisms.

6. David Treuer (2002) makes a similar claim regarding language in *Ceremony*, Momaday's *House Made of Dawn*, and Erdrich's *The Antelope Wife*. Treuer argues that because the use of indigenous languages in these novels is not especially relevant to the reading of the novel, they are "museum pieces," creating texts that function as "Native Informants" (55). Treuer further argues that the use of oral stories in *Ceremony* represents a "longing for culture" capable of transcending barriers, yet in the process of articulating this desire also creates the possibility that "the original ground and primary languages are forgotten" (61).

■ **CHAPTER THREE. The Ethical Use of Indigenous Traditions in Contemporary Literature**

1. See Mihesuah (2000); Fine-Dare (2002).

2. I agree with Walsh and Braley's general contention that Indianness in *The Beet Queen* is "nearly invisible but subtly present and latent" (1986, 16). For precisely this reason, however, I cannot concur with their contention that Dot necessarily

returns to her "Indian heritage" (15) at the close of the novel, nor that the works of Basil Johnston clearly parallel *The Beet Queen*, as Walsh and Braley suggest.

3. This concept of the reservation as a place of healing was suggested to me by Michael McDaniel in a graduate seminar.

■ CHAPTER FOUR. Writing a Friendship Dance: Orality in Mourning Dove's *Cogewea*

1. It is a safe assumption that McWhorter is responsible for this section. The visiting Nez Perce carries a club, which, McWhorter says in his notes to the novel, "is now in my possession, a present from the Nez Perce warrior of the dance. A thrilling personal narrative, dictated by its owner, is still in manuscript form" (Mourning Dove 1981, 289).

2. For example, when Cogewea asks about his religious faith, Densmore names several positions in various denominations, and concludes: "A sort of free prospector, I have panned wherever the colors showed most promising" (Mourning Dove 1981, 132). His statement reveals his mercenary character, as well as a connection to Cogewea's father, who abandoned her for the Alaska gold fields.

3. Brown (1988) writes: "McWhorter argued long and hard for a tragic ending and, in fact, appended all the beginning quotes to chapters as a thematic guide toward a presumed tragic finale" (13).

■ CHAPTER FIVE. *Bearheart:* Gerald Vizenor's Compassionate Novel

1. The novel first appeared as *Darkness in Saint Louis Bearheart* (1978) and was later revised and reissued as *Bearheart: The Heirship Chronicles* (1990). Vizenor said the reason for the name change was that the book is already known to most people as "Bearheart" (1999, 95). For a discussion of the differences between the two versions and the reappearance of characters in *Bearheart* in Vizenor's subsequent works, see Elisabeth Blair (1995).

2. As Roland Barthes, whom Vizenor frequently cites, tells us in *The Pleasure of the Text*: "Neither culture nor its destruction is erotic; it is the seam between them, the fault, the flaw, which becomes so" (1975, 7).

3. Wolfgang Hochbruck points out that some Native traditions consider the present world to be the fourth. He speculates that Vizenor might have had in mind the conditions of the contemporary reservations: "Within the context of *Bearheart*, however, the pilgrims' progress (of course, this is one of the intertexts) into the fourth world makes the one they leave the third, which is what tribal politicians have claimed on several occasions: that their reservations are actually part of the Third World" (1992, 275). A. Lavonne Brown Ruoff writes: "Vizenor's descriptions of the four worlds of Indian people combine the emergence and migration myths of Southwestern tribes with the flood myths of the Algonkin-speaking tribes" (1985, 71).

4. For a discussion of the possible relationship between *Bearheart* and Bunyan's allegorical *Pilgrim's Progress*, see Bernadette Rigel-Cellard (1997). See also Ruoff (1985), who writes: "Accompanying Cedarfair on his journey is a bizarre collection of followers that represent various figures from Indian mythology as well as human vices and virtues" (71).

5. Keady (1985) discusses those characters who fall victim to their narcissistic terminal creeds, especially Belladonna Darwin-Winter Catcher.

6. Her name is likewise a combination of two views of the world, Winter Catcher offering an indigenous vision of the world, Darwin suggesting the totalizing narrative of natural selection.

7. Paul Pasquaretta suggests that gambling stories in *Bearheart* demonstrate how the novel rejects cultural narcissism: "In Vizenor's *Bearheart*, gambling stories are also employed to advance particular attitudes, values and, most importantly, modes of expression. These may be regarded in terms of the things they oppose— terminal creeds and cultural narcissism" (1996, 30).

8. I hesitate to use Hegelian terminology with its connotations of upward progress, a concept the book itself critiques.

9. The novel similarly questions the idea of distance from our relations with oral traditions, providing an old indigenous story about a woman having sexual relations with dogs who later became hunters. Couched in the protective, distancing

epistemology of anthropology, sexual relations with animals is not especially troubling for many readers. Yet, when placed in contemporary circumstances, many of us readers are taken aback. Thus the novel implicitly questions our relation to older oral traditions.

10. In a section of his book entitled "Sovereignty: An Inappropriate Concept," Taiaiake Alfred (1999) points out that the concept of sovereignty has come to mean a limited amount of power for indigenous nations within the borders of the United States and Canada. For example, the word "sovereign" no longer means "freedom," but instead means a state of perpetual colonization.

11. Two writers who argue for such a connection between clear language and institutions are E. D. Hirsch (1988) and William Bennett (1992). Both are surprisingly confident, for example, in the ability of a single sentence to summarize the complexities of novels, and argue that such clarity is the substance of American culture. If all Americans had this level of "cultural literacy," they argue, the conversation about American policy would be much more informed. Such an approach, however, offers only the illusion of clarity, or if clear, then exists only with the exclusion of such complications as American Indian history.

■ CHAPTER SIX. Muted Traditions and Dialogic Affirmation in Louise Erdrich's *Love Medicine*

1. In his discussion of Dostoevsky, Bakhtin argues that the ability or willingness of a character to "hear" the subjectivity of another is the primary theme of his works. When Nector and Eli, as well as many other characters, affirm each other's subjectivity, they achieve a strong sense of connection and value. Bakhtin writes: "Thus the affirmation of someone else's consciousness—as an autonomous subject and not as an object—is the ethico-religious postulate determining the *content* of the novel (the catastrophe of a disunited consciousness). It is a principle of the author's worldview, and from that vantage point the author understands the world of his characters. Ivanov subsequently shows how this principle is refracted, solely and entirely on the thematic plane, in the content of the novel—a refraction which is, it turns out, predominantly negative: the heroes

suffer destruction because they cannot wholeheartedly affirm the other, 'thou art.' Affirmation (and nonaffirmation) of someone else's 'I' by the hero—this is the theme of Dostoevsky's work" (1984, 10).

2. For another reading of the Eli/Nector relationship, see Barbara L. Pittman, who argues that Nector and Eli represent two views of time. She writes: "The clearest dichotomy is between the Kashpaw twins, Eli and Nector, who represent the chronotope [space/time] of the tribal community versus the dominant chronotope of progress and individualism" (1995, 785).

3. This dynamic between centrifugal and centripetal forces in American Indian literature was first discussed academically by William Bevis in his essay "Native American Novels: Homing In." Bevis writes that, in contrast to European traditions of the novel, "most Native American novels are not 'eccentric,' centrifugal, diverging, expanding, but 'incentric,' centripetal, converging, contracting. The hero comes home" (1987, 582). In her essay "Continuity and Connection: Characters in Louis Erdrich's Fiction," Margie Towery briefly discusses Bevis's essay in relation to *Love Medicine* in terms of "homecoming" (1992, 109).

4. Kristan Sarvé-Gorham also points out that Marie and Lulu constitute a pair of twins, with Marie leaning "heavily toward Euro-American culture" (1995, 184) and Lulu maintaining "stronger ties to the old ways" (186). Sarvé-Gorham's argument is that together, Lulu and Marie provide a compromise between two "extremes" that allows them to confront a changing world. "And for each individual to find the balance between tradition and assimilation, between conflicting religious beliefs of animism and Christianity, becomes the dilemma of the descendants of these medicine women," Pauline and Fleur (189).

5. For a fuller account of how *Love Medicine* contains "macroscopic unifying aspects," see Hertha Wong (1995). Wong argues that the stories are linked in several thematic ways: through retellings of different events, water imagery, and humor.

6. For other discussions of the trickster motif, see William Gleason (1987, 60–64); Louis Owens (1992, 199–201); Margie Towery (1992, 105–8); and Barbara Pittman (1995, 781–83).

7. For instance, another theory of reading from the oral tradition includes Barbara L. Pittman's discussion of the trickster tradition. Pittman writes: "Thus all the characters and narrators, the author, and the reader perform an act of (trickster)

transformation in the text—they create community. Vizenor is attempting to free Native American narratives from the monologues of social science and the individualism of modernism" (1995, 782).

■ **CONCLUSION. Writing the Indigenous Nation**

1. Anzaldúa writes: "There is an exhilaration in being a participant in the further evolution of humankind, in being 'worked' on" (Anzaldúa 1987, unnumbered preface).

Works Cited

Alfred, Taiaiake. 1999. *Peace, Power, Righteousness: An Indigenous Manifesto*. Ontario: Oxford University Press.

Allen, Paula Gunn. 1986. *The Sacred Hoop: Recovering the Feminine in American Indian Traditions*. Boston: Beacon Press.

———. 1990. Special Problems in Teaching Leslie Marmon Silko's *Ceremony*. *American Indian Quarterly* 14, no. 1: 379–86.

Anderson, Eric. 2000. States of Being in the Dark: Removal and Survival in Linda Hogan's Mean Spirit. *Great Plains Quarterly* 20, no. 1 (Winter): 55–67.

Anzaldua, Gloria. 1987. *Borderlands/La Frontera: The New Mestiza*. San Francisco: Aunt Lute Books.

Bakhtin, M. M. 1981. *The Dialogic Imagination: Four Essays by M. M. Bakhtin*. Ed. Michael Holquist, trans. Caryl Emerson and Michael Holquist. Austin: University of Texas Press.

————. 1984. *Problems of Dostoevsky's Poetics*. Ed. and trans. Caryl Emerson. Minneapolis: University of Minneapolis Press.

Barthes, Roland. 1972. *Critical Essays*. Trans. Richard Howard. Evanston: Northwestern University Press.

————. 1975. *Pleasure of the Text*. Trans. Richard Miller. New York: Noonday Press.

Beaulieu, David. 1984. Curly Hair and Big Feet: Physical Anthropology and the Implementation of Land Allotment on the White Earth Chippewa Reservation. *American Indian Quarterly* 8, no. 4 (Fall): 281–314.

Bell, Betty Louise. 1994. Linda Hogan's Lessons in Making Do. *Studies in American Indian Literatures* 6, no. 3 (Fall): 3–5.

Bennett, William John. 1992. *The Devaluing of America: The Fight for Our Culture and Our Children*. New York: Summit Books.

Bevis, William. 1987. Native American Novels: Homing In. In *Recovering the Word: Essays on Native America Literature*, ed. Brian Swann and Arnold Krupat, 580–620. Berkeley: University of California Press.

Bhabha, Homi K. 1990. *Nation and Narration*. Routledge: London and New York.

Blaeser, Kimberly M. 1989. Momaday's Work in Motion. In *Narrative Chance: Postmodern Discourse on Native American Literatures*, ed. Gerald Vizenor, 39–54. Albuquerque: University of New Mexico Press.

————. 1996. *Gerald Vizenor: Writing in the Oral Tradition*. Norman: University of Oklahoma Press.

Blair, Elisabeth. 1995. Text as Trickster: Postmodern Language Games in Gerald Vizenor's *Bearheart*. *MELUS: The Journal of the Society for the Study of the Multi-Ethnic Literature of the United States* 20, no. 4 (Winter): 75–90.

Broderick, Therese. 1909. *The Brand: A Tale of the Flathead Reservation*. Seattle: Alice Harriman Co.

Brown, Alanna Kathleen. 1988. Mourning Dove's Voice in *Cogewea*. *Wicazo Sa Review* 4, no. 2 (Fall): 2–15.

————. 1993. Through the Glass Darkly: The Editorialized Mourning Dove. In *New Voices in Native American Criticism*, ed. Arnold Krupat, 274–90. Washington, D.C.: Smithsonian.

Buller, Galen. 1980. New Interpretations of Native American Literature: A Survival Technique. *American Indian Culture and Research Journal* 4, no. 2: 165–77.

Clifford, James. 1988. *Predicament of Culture: Twentieth-Century Ethnography, Literature, and Art*. Cambridge, Mass.: Harvard University Press.

Cohn, Dorrit. 1978. *Transparent Minds: Narrating Modes for Presenting Consciousness in Fiction*. Princeton, N.J.: Princeton University Press.

Coleman, Elizabeth Burns. 2001. Aboriginal Painting: Identity and Authenticity. *Journal of Aesthetics and Art Criticism* 59, no. 4 (Fall): 385–402.

Coskan-Johnson, Gale P. 2006. What Writer Would Not Be an Indian for a While? Charles Alexander Eastman, Critical Memory, and Audience. *Studies in American Indian Literatures* 18, no. 2: 105–31.

Culler, Jonathan. 1982. *On Deconstruction: Theory and Criticism after Structuralism*. Ithaca, N.Y.: Cornell University Press.

Deloria, Vine. 1969. *Custer Died for Your Sins*. London: Macmillan Company.

Deloria, Vine, Jr., and Clifford M. Lytle. 1984. *The Nations Within: The Past and Future of American Indian Sovereignty*. New York: Pantheon Books.

Eastman, Charles A. 1916. *From the Deep Woods to Civilization*. Lincoln and London: University of Nebraska Press.

Eliot, T. S. 1971. *The Complete Poems and Plays: 1909–1950*. San Diego, New York, and London: Harcourt Brace Jovanovich.

Erdrich, Louise. 1985. Where I Ought To Be. *New York Times Book Review* 28 (July): 1, 23–24.

———. 1986. *The Beet Queen*. New York: Holt.

———. 1993. *Love Medicine*. New and expanded version. New York: Harper Perennial.

Fanon, Frantz. [1952] 1967. *Black Skin, White Masks*, Trans. Charles Lam Markmann. New York: Grove Press.

———. [1961] 1991. *Les damnés de la terre*. Preface by Jean-Paul Sartre. Paris: Gallimard. Repr. Paris: François Maspero.

———. 1963. *The Wretched of the Earth*. Preface by Jean-Paul Sartre. Trans. Constance Farrington. New York: Grove Press.

Fine-Dare, Kathleen. 2002. *Grave Injustice: The American Indian Repatriation Movement and NAGPRA*. Lincoln: University of Nebraska Press.

Fisher, Dexter. 1981. Introduction to *Cogewea, the Half-Blood: A Depiction of the Great Montana Cattle Range*, by Mourning Dove. Lincoln: University of Nebraska Press.

Fitzgerald, Frances. 1981. *Cities on a Hill: A Journey through Contemporary American Cultures*. New York: Simon and Schuster.

Forbes, Jack. 1987. Colonialism and Native American Literature: Analysis. *Wicazo Sa Review* 3, no. 2 (Fall): 17–23.

Gates, Henry Louis, Jr. 1988. *The Signifying Monkey: A Theory of Afro-American Literary Criticism.* New York: Oxford University Press.

Gleason, William. 1987. "Her Laugh an Ace": The Function of Humor in Louise Erdrich's *Love Medicine. American Culture and Research Journal* 11, no 3: 51–73.

Greenblatt, Stephen. 1991. *Marvelous Possessions: The Wonder of the New World.* Chicago: University of Chicago Press.

Harlow, Barbara. 1987. *Resistance Literature.* New York: Methuen.

Hirsch, E. D., Jr. 1988. *Cultural Literacy: What Every American Needs to Know.* New York: Vintage Books.

Hochbruck, Wolfgang. 1992. Breaking Away: The Novels of Gerald Vizenor. *World Literature Today* 66 (Spring): 274–78.

Hogan, Linda. 1990. *Mean Spirit.* New York: Ivy Books.

Holler, Clyde. 1984. Black Elk's Relationship to Christianity. *American Indian Quarterly* 8, no. 1: 37.

Holt, Debra C. 1991. Transformation and Continuance: Native American Tradition in the Novels of Louise Erdrich. In *Entering the 90s: The North American Experience: Proceedings from the Native American Studies Conference at Lake Superior University, October 27–28, 1987,* ed. Thomas E. Schirer, 49–56. Sault Ste. Marie, Mich.: Lake Superior State University.

Huhndorf, Shari M. 2001. *Going Native: Indians in the American Cultural Imagination.* Ithaca, N.Y.: Cornell University Press.

Hutcheon, Linda. 1989. *The Politics of Postmodernism.* London and New York: Routledge.

Indyk, Ivor. 1992. Assimilation or Appropriation: Uses of European Literary Forms in Black Australian Writing. *Australian Literary Studies* 15, no. 4 (October): 249–60.

Jung, C. G. [1956] 1972. On the Psychology of the Trickster Figure. Trans. R. F. C. Hull. In *The Trickster: A Study in American Indian Mythology,* by Paul Radin. New York: Schocken Books.

Keady, Maureen. 1985. Walking Backwards into the Fourth World: Survival of the Fittest in *Bearheart. American Indian Quarterly* 9: 61–75.

Knudsen, Eva Rask. 1992. Fringe Finds Focus: Developments and Strategies in Aboriginal Writing in English. *Australian Literary Studies* 15, no. 2: 32–44.

Krupat, Arnold. 1989. *The Voice in the Margins: Native American Literature and the Canon.* Berkeley: University of California Press.

Lindholm, Charles. 2002. Authenticity, Anthropology, and the Sacred. *Anthropological Quarterly* 75, no. 2 (Spring): 331–38.

Lowenthal, David. 1999. Authenticity: Rock of Faith or Quicksand Quagmire? *Conservation: The Getty Conservation Institute Newsletter* 14, no. 3: 5–8.

Lyons, Gene. 1985. In Indian Country: Review of *Love Medicine*, by Louise Erdrich. *Newsweek* 11 (February): 70–71.

Magdaleno, Jana Sequoya. 2000. How! Is an Indian: A Contest of Stories. In *Postcolonial Theory and the United States: Race, Ethnicity, and Literature,* ed. Amritjit Singh and Peter Schmidt, 279–99. Jackson: University Press of Mississippi.

Mattina, Anthony. 1987. North American Indian Mythography: Editing Texts for the Printed Page. In *Recovering the Word: Essays on Native American Literature,* ed. Brian Swann and Arnold Krupat, 129–48. Berkeley: University of California Press.

McHale, Brian. 1987. *Postmodernist Fiction.* New York and London: Menthuen.

McKenzie, James. 1986. Lipsha's Good Road Home: The Revival of Chippewa Culture in *Love Medicine. American Indian Culture and Research Journal* 10, no. 3: 53–63.

Mihesuah, Devon. 2000. *Repatriation Reader: Who Owns American Indian Remains?* Lincoln: University of Nebraska Press.

Mitchell, David. 1991. A Bridge to the Past: Cultural Hegemony and the Native American Past in Louise Erdrich's *Love Medicine.* In *Entering the 90s: The North American Experience: Proceedings from the Native American Studies Conference at Lake Superior University, October 16–17, 1987,* ed. Thomas E. Schirer, 162–70. Sault Ste. Marie, Mich.: Lake Superior University Press.

Momaday, N. Scott. 1968. *House Made of Dawn.* New York: Harper and Row.

———. 1969. *The Way to Rainy Mountain.* Illustrated by Al Momaday. Albuquerque: University of New Mexico Press.

———. 1981. The Man Made of Words. In *The Remembered Earth: An Anthology of Contemporary American Indian Literature,* ed. Geary Hobson, 162–73. Albuquerque: University of New Mexico Press.

Mourning Dove. 1981. *Cogewea, The Half Blood: A Depiction of the Great Montana Cattle Range.* Lincoln: University of Nebraska Press. 1927; Boston: Four Seas, Co.

———. 1990. *Coyote Stories*. Lincoln: University of Nebraska Press. Ed. Heister Dean Guie. 1933; Caldwell, Idaho: Caxton Printers, Ltd.

Murray, David. 1991. *Forked Tongues: Speech, Writing, and Representation in North American Indian Texts*. Bloomington and Indianapolis: Indiana University Press.

Narogin, Mudrooroo. 1990. *Writing from the Fringe: A Study of Modern Aboriginal Literature*. South Yarra/Melbourne: Hyland House.

Neihardt, John G. [1932] 1988. Black Elk Speaks: Being the Life Story of a Holy Man of the Oglala Sioux. Ed. John G. Neihardt (Flaming Rainbow). Intro. Vine Deloria Jr. Lincoln: University of Nebraska Press.

O'Connell, Barry. 1992. *On Our Own Ground: The Complete Writings of William Apess, a Pequot*. Ed. and intro. Barry O'Connell. Amherst: University of Massachusetts Press.

O'Sullivan, John. 1845. Annexation. *United States Magazine and Democratic Review* 17 (July): 5–10.

Ortiz, Simon J. 1981. Towards a National Indian Literature: Cultural Authenticity in Nationalism. *MELUS: The Journal of the Society for the Study of the Multi-Ethnic Literature of the United States* 8, no. 2 (Summer): 7–12.

Owens, Louis. 1990. Afterword to *Bearheart: The Heirship Chronicles*, by Gerald Vizenor. Minneapolis, University of Minnesota Press.

———. 1992. *Other Destinies: Understanding the American Indian Novel*. Norman: University of Oklahoma Press.

Pasquaretta, Paul. 1996. Sacred Chance: Gambling and the Contemporary Native American Novel. *MELUS: The Journal of the Society for the Study of the Multi-Ethnic Literature of the United States* 21, no. 2 (Summer): 21–33.

Peres, Phyllis. 1997. *Transculturation and Resistance in Lusophone African Narrative*. Gainesville: University of Florida Press.

Peterson, Erik. 1992. An Indian, An American: Ethnicity, Assimilation and Balance in Charles Eastman's *From the Deep Woods to Civilization*. Studies in American Indian Literatures 4, no 3: (Summer/Fall) 145–160.

Pevar, Stephen L. 1992. *The Rights of Indians and Tribes: The Basic ACLU Guide to Indian and Tribal Rights*. Carbondale and Edwardsville: Southern Illinois University Press.

Pittman, Barbara L. 1995. Cross-Cultural Reading and Generic Transformation: The Chronotope of the Road in Erdrich's *Love Medicine*. *American Literature: A Journal of Literary History, Criticism, and Bibliography* 67, no. 4: 777–92.

Pratt, Mary Louise. 1992. *Imperial Eyes: Travel Writing and Transculturation*. New York: Routledge.

Radin, Paul. [1956] 1972. *The Trickster: A Study in American Indian Mythology*. Commentaries by Karl Kerényi and C. G. Jung. Intro. Stanley Diamond. New York: Schocken Books.

Ram, Kalpana. 2000. Listening to the Call of Dance: Rethinking Authenticity 'Essentialism.' *Australian Journal of Anthropology* 11, no. 3: 358–64.

Rigel-Cellard, Bernadette. 1997. Doubling in Gerald Vizenor's *Bearheart*: The Pilgrimage Strategy or Bunyan Revisited. *Studies in American Indian Literatures* 9, no. 1 (Spring): 93–114.

Ruoff, A. Lavonne Brown. 1985. Gerald Vizenor: Compassionate Trickster. *American Indian Quarterly* 73: 67–73.

———. 1990. *American Indian Literatures: An Introduction, Bibliographic Review, and Selected Bibliography*. New York: Modern Language Association of America.

Salzer, Maureen. 1995. Ray Young Bear's Cantaloupe Terrorist: Storytelling as a Site of Resistance. *American Indian Quarterly* 19, no. 3: 301–18.

Sarvé-Gorham, Kristan. 1995. Power Lines: The Motif of Twins and the Medicine Women of *Tracks* and *Love Medicine*. *Bucknell Review* 39, no. 1: 167–90.

Schneider, Lissa. 1992. *Love Medicine*: A Metaphor for Forgiveness. *Studies in American Indian Literatures* 4, no 2 (Spring): 15–27.

Schultz, Lydia. 1993. Fragments and Ojibwe Stories: Narrative Strategies in Louise Erdrich's *Love Medicine*. In *Emerging Voices: Readings in the American Experience*, ed. Janet Madden and Sara M. Blake. Fort Worth, Tex.: Harcourt, Brace, Javanovich.

Sheffield, Gail K. 1997. *The Arbitrary Indian: The Indian Arts and Crafts Act of 1990*. Norman: University of Oklahoma Press.

Shiner, Larry. 1994. "Primitive Fakes," "Tourist Art," and the Ideology of Authenticity. *Journal of Aesthetics and Art Criticism* 52, no. 2 (Spring): 225–32.

Silberman, Robert. 1989. Opening the Text: *Love Medicine* and the Return of the Native American Woman. In *Narrative Chance: Postmodern Discourse on Native American Literatures*, ed. Gerald Vizenor, 101–20. Albuquerque: University of New Mexico Press.

Silko, Leslie Marmon. 1977. *Ceremony*. New York: Penguin Books.

———. 1981a. *Storyteller*. New York: Seaver Books.

———. 1981b. Language and Literature from a Pueblo Indian Perspective. In *English*

Literature: Opening Up the Canon, ed. Leslie A. Fiedler and Houston A. Baker Jr., 54–72. Baltimore: Johns Hopkins University Press.

———. 1986a. Landscape, History, and the Pueblo Imagination. *Antaeus* 51: 83–94.

———. 1986b. Review of *The Beet Queen*, by Louise Erdrich. *Studies in American Indian Literatures* 10: 177–84. Repr. 1986. Here's an Odd Artifact for the Fairy-Tale Shelf. *Impact/ Albuquerque Journal Magazine* (October 7): 10–11.

Sollers, Werner. 1996. Comments. In *Cultural Difference and the Literary Text: Pluralism and the Limits of Authenticity in North American Literatures*, ed. Winfried Siemerling and Katrin Schwenk, 154–55. Iowa City: University of Iowa Press.

Somers, Margaret R., and Gloria D. Gibson. 1994. Reclaiming the Epistemological "Other": Narrative and Social Constitution of Identity. In *Social Theory and the Politics of Identity*, ed. Craig Calhoun, 37–99. Cambridge, Mass.: Blackwell.

Spivak, Gayatri Chakravorty. 1993. Interviewed by Sara Danius and Stefan Jonsson. *boundary 2* 20, no. 2: 24, 27.

Tedlock, Dennis. 1978. *Finding the Center: Narrative Poetry of the Zuni Indians*. Lincoln: University of Nebraska Press.

Tompkins, Jane. 1989. *Sensational Designs: The Cultural Work of American Fiction, 1790–1860*. New York: Oxford University Press.

Towery, Margie. 1992. Continuity and Connection: Characters in Louise Erdrich's Fiction. *American Indian Culture and Research Journal* 16, no. 4: 99–122.

Treuer, David. 2002. Reading Culture. *Studies in American Indian Literatures* 14, no. 1 (Spring): 51–64.

Turney, Laura. 1999. Ceci n'est pas Jimmie Durham. *Critique of Anthropology* 19, no. 4 (December): 423–42.

Tyler, Stephen A. 1987. *The Unspeakable: Discourse, Dialogue, and Rhetoric in the Postmodern World*. Madison: University of Wisconsin Press.

Underhill, Ruth Murray. [1936] 1985. *Papago Woman*. Prospect Heights, Ill.: Waveland Press, Inc. 1979; New York: Holt, Rinehart and Winston.

Velie, Alan. 1989. The Trickster Novel. In *Narrative Chance: Postmodern Discourse on Native American Literatures*, ed. Gerald Vizenor, 121–39. Albuquerque: University of New Mexico Press.

Vizenor, Gerald. 1970. *anishinabe adisokan: Tales of the People*. Ed. Gerald Vizenor, with Anishinabe words. Minneapolis: Nodin Press.

———. 1981. *Earthdivers: Tribal Narratives on Mixed Descent*. Illustrations by Jaune Quick-to-See Smith. Minneapolis: University of Minnesota Press.

———. 1984. *The People Named the Chippewa: Narrative Histories.* Minneapolis: University of Minnesota Press.

———. 1989. Trickster Discourse: Comic Holotropes and Language Games. In *Narrative Chance: Postmodern Discourse on Native American Indian Literatures,* ed. Gerald Vizenor, 187–211. Albuquerque: University of New Mexico Press.

———. 1990. *Bearheart: The Heirship Chronicles.* Minneapolis: University of Minnesota Press. Orig. pub. 1978 as *Darkness in Saint Louis Bearheart.* St. Paul, Minn.: Truck Press.

Vizenor, Gerald Robert, and A. Robert Lee. 1999. *Postindian Conversations.* Lincoln: University of Nebraska Press.

Walsh, Dennis M., and Ann Braley. 1994. The Indianness of Louise Erdrich's *The Beet Queen*: Latency as Presence. *American Indian Culture and Research Journal* 18, no. 3: 1–17.

Warrior, Robert Allen. 1995a. Review of *The Deaths of Sybil Bolton,* by Dennis McAuliffe. *Wicazo Sa Review* 11, no. 1 (Spring): 52–55.

Wilson, James. 1999. *The Earth Shall Weep: A History of Native America.* New York: Atlantic Monthly Press.

Wilson, Terry P. 1985. *The Underground Reservation: Osage Oil.* Lincoln: University of Nebraska Press.

Womack, Craig. 1997. Review of *Gerald Vizenor: Writing in the Oral Tradition,* by Kimberly M. Blaeser. *Studies in American Indian Literatures,* series 2, vol. 9, no. 4 (Winter): 97–100.

Wong, Hertha Dawn. 1992. *Sending My Heart Back across the Years: Tradition and Innovation in Native American Autobiography.* New York: Oxford University Press.

———. 1995. Louise Erdrich's *Love Medicine*: Narrative Communities and the Short Story Sequence. In *Modern American Short Story Sequences: Composite Fictions and Fictive Communities,* ed. Gerald J. Kennedy, 170–93. Cambridge: Cambridge University Press.

Young Bear, Ray A. 1992a. *Black Eagle Child: The Facepaint Narratives.* Foreword by Albert E. Stone. Iowa City: University of Iowa Press.

———. 1992b. Staying Afloat in a Chaotic World: A Conversation with Ray Young Bear. Interviewed by Michael Wilson and David Moore. *Akwe:kon Journal* 9, no. 4 (Winter): 22–26.

———. 1996. *Remnants of the First Earth.* New York: Grove.

Index

F

Fanon, Frantz: *Black Skins, White Masks,*
   xix; *The Wretched of the Earth,* xviii–
   xxii, 43, 61, 131–34
Fine-Dare, Kathleen, 166 (n. 1)
Fisher, Dexter, 63, 73, 83
Fitzgerald, Frances, 23, 165 (n. 1)
Fogarty, Lionel, xvii, 163 (n. 4)
Forbes, Jack, 22, 30–32
frontier, 60, 152

G

Gates, Henry Louis, Jr., 90, 164 (n. 2)
General Allotment Act, xxiii, 32, 153; in
   Love Medicine, 114; in Tracks, 129
Gibson, Gloria D., 40–41
Gleason, William, 170 (n. 6)
Greenblatt, Stephen, 1–2

H

half-blood. *See* mixed blood
Harlow, Barbara, xv–xvi
Hirsch, E. D., Jr., 169 (n. 11)
Hochbruck, Wolfgang, 168 (n. 3)
Hogan, Linda, 56–59
Holler, Clyde, 31
Holt, Debra C., 125–26
Holy Bible, 57
Hopi, 45, 47, 93, 102, 104
Huhndorf, Shari M., 37
Hutcheon, Linda, 99

I

Indian Arts and Crafts Act, 25, 166 (n. 4)

Indian Reorganization Act of 1934, xxiii,
   152, 153
Indyk, Ivor, 163 (n. 3)

J

Jenkins, Leigh, 45
Johnson, Elias, ix
Johnston, Basil, 167 (n.3)
Jung, C. G., 89–92

K

Keady, Maureen, 97–98, 168 (n. 5)
Knudsen, Eva Rask, 163–64 (n. 4)
Krupat, Arnold, 6, 13–14, 16–18

L

Lindholm, Charles, 23–24, 39
Lowenthal, David, 165 (n. 2)
Lyons, Gene, 123
Lytle, Clifford M., xxi, 12, 17, 19, 152

M

Magdaleno, Jana Sequoya, xiii–xiv, 22,
   32–34, 36, 44–45, 47–48
Manifest Destiny, xii, xxi, 92–93, 95,
   108–9, 152
mascots and logos, xxi, 31, 33, 51, 161
master narrative. *See* metanarrative
Matthews, John Joseph, xi, 157
Mattina, Anthony, 164 (n. 3)
McHale, Brian, 164 (n. 1)
McKenzie, James, 118
McNickle, D'Arcy, 157
McWhorter, Lucullus, xiv, 62–64, 70,